TRANSFORMING ORGANISATIONAL CULTURE THROUGH COACHING

TRANSFORMING ORGANISATIONAL CULTURE THROUGH COACHING

Dr. Susanne Knowles

Copyright © 2020 by Dr. Susanne Knowles.

Library of Congress Control Number:	2020900631
ISBN: Hardcover	978-1-7960-0931-6
Softcover	978-1-7960-0930-9
eBook	978-1-7960-0929-3

All rights reserved. No part of this book may be reproduced or transmitted in any form or by any means, electronic or mechanical, including photocopying, recording, or by any information storage and retrieval system, without permission in writing from the copyright owner.

Any people depicted in stock imagery provided by Getty Images are models, and such images are being used for illustrative purposes only.
Certain stock imagery © Getty Images.

Print information available on the last page.

Rev. date: 10/27/2020

To order additional copies of this book, contact:
Xlibris
AU TFN: 1 800 844 927 (Toll Free inside Australia)
AU Local: 0283 108 187 (+61 2 8310 8187 from outside Australia)
www.Xlibris.com.au
Orders@Xlibris.com.au
789234

CONTENTS

Acknowledgements..xv
Introduction..xvii

CHAPTER 1   FROM THE BEGINNING 1

   1.1 Introduction..1
   1.2 What is Coaching? 2
   1.3 Benefits of Coaching 4
   1.4 Misconceptions of Coaching 5
   1.5 Contemporary Views of Coaching 6
   1.6 Research Study 10
   1.7 Summary of findings 11
   1.8 Structure of the Chapters 14

CHAPTER 2   COACHING AND COACHING
                    CULTURE RESEARCH 15

   2.1 Research on Coaching 15
   2.2 Difference between Coaching and Mentoring 17
   2.3 Types of Coaching..19
   2.4 Theoretical Basis for Coaching 22
   2.5 Coaching Practice...25
   2.6 Coaching Purpose 26
   2.7 Organisational Culture 27
   2.8 Coaching Culture..30

CHAPTER 3 STAGE 1 COACHING-AS-INTERVENTION 33

3.1 Utilitarian Conceptualisation 34
   3.1.1 Coaching Is a Skill 35
   3.1.2 Coaching Is a Tool 36
   3.1.3 Coaching Achieves an Immediate Outcome 37
   3.1.4 Coaching Is a One-Off Investment 37

3.2 Instrumental Motivation 38
   3.2.1 'Fix' a Problem 39
   3.2.2 Remediate an Underperformer 39
   3.2.3 Comply with Legislation 40

3.3 Individual Drivers 41
   3.3.1 Line Managers Arrange for Coaching to be Conducted 41
   3.3.2 Coaching Is Positioned with the Line Management Structure 43

3.4 Outsourced Delivery 43
   3.4.1 Coaching Is Outsourced to External 'Expert' Coaches 44
   3.4.2 Coaching Is Expensive 45

3.5 Summary of Stage 1—Coaching-as-Intervention 46
3.6 Case Studies: Stage 1—Coaching-as-Intervention 47

CHAPTER 4 STAGE 2 COACHING-AS-HR-FUNCTION 57

4.1 Pedagogical Conceptualisation 58
   4.1.1 HR Professionals Are Trained in Coaching Skills or as qualified Coaches and Experience Being Coached 59
   4.1.2 HR Professionals Develop In-House Coach-Training Curriculum 60
   4.1.3 Coaching Is a Short-Term Investment 61

4.2 Developmental Motivation 62
   4.2.1 Change Mindset and Behaviour 63
   4.2.2 Improve Individual Performance 66

  4.2.3 Support Career Progression 67
 4.3 Functional Drivers 70
  4.3.1 Human Resources 71
  4.3.2 Positioned within HR 72
 4.4 Targeted Delivery 77
  4.4.1 Leader-as-Coach Training Program 77
  4.4.2 HR Appoints Coaching Panels 80
 4.5 Summary of Stage 2—Coaching-as-HR-Function 81
 4.6 Case Studies: Stage 2—Coaching-as-HR-Function 82

CHAPTER 5 STAGE 3 COACHING-AS-LEADER-CAPABILITY 87

 5.1 Practice Conceptualisation 88
  5.1.1 Coaching Is a Core Capability of Leaders 88
  5.1.2 Coaching Is Embedded within a Capability Development Framework 91
  5.1.3 Coaching Is a Medium-Term Investment 93
 5.2 Performance Motivation 94
  5.2.1 Improve Team and Business Performance 95
  5.2.2 Increase Team Engagement 98
  5.2.3 Retain Talent 100
 5.3 Business Drivers 103
  5.3.1 Leaders Drive Business Performance as an Expectation of Their Role 103
  5.3.2 Coaching Is Positioned within Sales and Services Functions 105
 5.4 Internalised Delivery 107
  5.4.1 Leaders Deliver Coaching to Their Team and Team Members 107
  5.4.2 Specialist Coaches "Coach to Revenue" 112
  5.4.3 Internal Coaches and Coaching Teams Deliver Behavioural and Performance Coaching 113
 5.5 Summary of Stage 3—Coaching-as-Leader-Capability 115
 5.6 Case Studies: Stage 3—Coaching-as-Leader-Capability 116

CHAPTER 6   STAGE 4 COACHING-AS-CULTURE 121

- 6.1 Organic Conceptualisation 122
  - 6.1.1 Coaching Is Part of the DNA and Fabric of the Organisation 123
  - 6.1.2 Coaching Provides a Platform for Cultural Change 124
  - 6.1.3 Coaching Is a Long-Term Investment 126
- 6.2 Transformational Motivation 127
  - 6.2.1 Coaching Promotes Personal Transformation 128
  - 6.2.2 Coaching Results in Productivity Increases for the Organisation 130
  - 6.2.3 Coaching Achieves Competitive Advantage for the Organisation 131
- 6.3 Top-Down Drivers 134
  - 6.3.1 CEO and Senior Executives Drive the Coaching Agenda 135
  - 6.3.2 CEO and Senior Executives Make Coaching a Strategic Priority 140
- 6.4 Integrated Delivery 145
  - 6.4.1 Coaching Is Applied to All Business Processes and Systems 146
  - 6.4.2 All Business Transactions Are Analysed through a Coaching Lens 146
  - 6.4.3 Coaching Is Conducted in All Business Units 147
  - 6.4.4 Coaching Is Extended to All Business Relationships and Transactions 148
- 6.5 Summary of Stage 4—Coaching-as-Culture 149
- 6.6. Case Studies: Stage 4—Coaching-as-Culture 152

CHAPTER 7   TRANSITIONS BETWEEN STAGES 159

- 7.1 Foundations Underlying a Coaching Culture 159
- 7.2 Transitions between Stages 160

CHAPTER 8 TRANSITION FROM STAGE 1 TO STAGE 2 ...165

- 8.1 Learn (Education)—Mindset Shift 165
  - 8.1.1 HR Professionals Are Formally Trained as Coaches 166
  - 8.1.2 HR Develops In-House Coaching Curriculum 166
- 8.2 Grow (Psychology)—Cognitive Restructuring 167
  - 8.2.1 HR Professionals Experience Being Coached 167
- 8.3 Lead (Management)—Acquisition of Leader Competencies 168
  - 8.3.1 Coaching Positioned within HR 168
  - 8.3.2 HR Develops the Infrastructure for Coaching 169
  - 8.3.3 HR Establishes the Support for Coaching 170
  - 8.3.4 HR Establishes Coaching Panels 171

CHAPTER 9 TRANSITION FROM STAGE 2 TO STAGE 3 ...173

- 9.1 Learn (Education)—Malleable Perspective 173
  - 9.1.1 Coaching Is a Core Capability of Leaders and Is Embedded in a Leadership Development Framework 173
  - 9.1.2 Managers Are Trained in Coaching Skills to Become Leaders 174
  - 9.1.3 Coaching Is Embedded into All Leadership and Executive Development Programs 175
- 9.2 Grow (Psychology)—Social Restructuring 175
  - 9.2.1 Leaders Experience Being Coached 175
  - 9.2.2 A Coaching Leadership Style Replaces Command-and-Control 176
  - 9.2.3 Any Unwillingness of Leaders to Coach Is Addressed 177
- 9.3 Lead (Management)—Motivation and Performance Improvement 178
  - 9.3.1 Coaching Is Positioned within Business Units 178
  - 9.3.2 Leaders Coach their Direct Reports and Others in the Organisation 179
  - 9.3.3 Leaders Create a Safe Environment in Which to Coach 180

9.3.4 Regular Feedback Coaching Sessions Replace the Annual Performance Review...............................181
9.3.5 Specialist Coaches Are Trained to Coach within Business Units..181
9.3.6 Internal Coaches Are Appointed to Work within Business Units..182
9.3.7 An Internal Coaching Team Is Established to Work across Business Units 183

CHAPTER 10 TRANSITION FROM STAGE 3 TO STAGE 4 ...185

10.1 Learn (Education)—Learning, Growth, and Development..187
    10.1.1 CEO and Senior Executives Are Formally Trained as Coaches...187
    10.1.2 CEO and Senior Executives Have Absolute Clarity about What Coaching Is and What It Is Not 187
    10.1.3 CEO and Senior Executives Model Buy-In, Engagement, and Sponsorship for Coaching 188

10.2 Grow (Psychology)—Self-Regulation and Emotional Intelligence 189
    10.2.1 CEO and Senior Executives Experience Being Coached..189
    10.2.2 CEO and Senior Executives Adopt a Growth Mindset..190
    10.2.3 CEO and Senior Executives Believe in the Value and Potential of All Employees and Identify Opportunities to Unleash That Potential....191

10.3 Lead (Management)—Business and Relationship Improvements 193
    10.3.1 Coaching Is Positioned at the Organisational Level as a Strategic Priority..193
    10.3.2 CEO and Senior Executives Align Coaching with Organisational Vision, Values, and Behaviours 194
    10.3.3 CEO and Senior Executives Define the Organisational and Business Goals from Coaching..194

  10.3.4 A Senior Executive Is Appointed as a
    Champion for Coaching 197
  10.3.5 A Communication Strategy Is Developed to
    Introduce and Sustain Coaching Practice 197
  10.3.6 CEO and Senior Executives Analyse Every
    Aspect of the Organisation through a Coaching
    Lens 198
  10.3.7 Organisational Levers to Maximise the
    Impact of Coaching Are Identified 199
  10.3.8 Coaching Is Applied more Broadly across
    the Organisation 199
  10.3.9 Coaching Relationships Are Extended to
    External Customers and Suppliers 202

CHAPTER 11 TO THE END 205

 11.1 Insights from the Research Findings 205
 11.2 Implications of This Research 210
  11.2.1 CEO and Senior Executives 210
  11.2.2 HR Professionals 211
  11.2.3 Organisational Leaders 212

Appendix 1: Summary of the Psychological and Educational
  Evidence for Coaching 213
References 221
Index 245
About the Author 249

TABLES

Table 2.1: The Evidence for Coaching 24
Table 6.1: Key Elements of the Four Stages in the
    Development of a Coaching Culture 151
Table 7.1: Strategies and Mechanisms to Develop and Embed
    a Coaching Culture 164

FIGURES

Figure 3.1: Overview of the Four Stages and their Defining Characteristics 33
Figure 3.2: Coaching-as-Intervention Stage 34
Figure 3.3: Coaching is a Skill or Tool 36
Figure 3.3: Coaching-is used to 'fix' a problem 39
Figure 4.1: Coaching-as-HR-Function Stage 58
Figure 4.2: Coaching is a training and learning experience 59
Figure 4.3: Coaching changes individual behaviour 62
Figure 4.4: Human Resources build the infrastructure for coaching ... 71
Figure 4.5: Human Resources train managers and talented individuals 77
Figure 5.1: Coaching-as-Leader-Capability Stage 87
Figure 5.2: Coaching is a core capability of leaders 88
Figure 5.3: Coaching is used to improve team and business performance 94
Figure 5.4: Business Unit leaders drive coaching to increase performance 103
Figure 6.1: Coaching-as-Culture Stage 122
Figure 6.2: Coaching is a long-term investment 123
Figure 6.3: Coaching is used to bring about personal and organisational transformation 128
Figure 6.4: CEO and senior executives drive coaching through the organisation 134
Figure 6.5: Coaching is applied to all business processes and systems 145

Figure 7.1: Foundations of Coaching Culture Development 160
Figure 7.2: Three Transitions between the Four Stages 161
Figure 10.1: 8 Steps to Transformational Cultural Change
     through Coaching 186

ACKNOWLEDGEMENTS

My gratitude and thanks go to my team at the Australian Institute of Professional Coaches during the development of this book.

Particular thanks go to Joel Hudson, who stewarded the team throughout this important time, Meryl Garcia for her graphic design of the internal images, and Jessica Harkins for her design of the book cover.

My thanks also go to Glenda Waring, Marty Doyle, and Suzanne O'Shea for their editorial services and valuable feedback on the text.

Special thanks go to my university supervisors, Professor Polly Parker and Associate Professor April Wright from the University of Queensland Business School, for their invaluable assistance during my research study and development of its findings.

INTRODUCTION

This book has been designed for organisational leaders and HR professionals who are most usually entrusted with the responsibility for developing a coaching culture in their organisation. It is a step-by-step guide to how coaching transforms individuals and teams, leading to a complete transformation of the organisation's culture. The aim of the book is to inform, persuade, and influence leaders to better understand coaching and how it can be used to benefit all employees in the organisation, not just a few.

Developing a coaching culture is a journey over four stages and many years. It requires the dedication and commitment of a senior executive team to make coaching a strategic priority to which recurrent funding is allocated. Individuals who have experienced being coached are in the best position to appreciate how revelationary coaching can be and understand how it can be used as a lens through which to analyse every business transaction to leverage increased productivity and competitive advantage. When a coaching culture has been achieved, coaching becomes part of the DNA and fabric of the organisation and coaching occurs naturally on a daily basis.

CHAPTER 1
FROM THE BEGINNING

1.1 Introduction

Organisations continue to look for ways to increase the profitability of their business and gain competitive advantage in the marketplace. Having downsized, rightsized, and exploited their physical assets, they turn to maximising the returns from their human assets. They endeavour to increase the capability of their leaders to improve the performance of their staff and retain valuable talent. A particularly effective developmental tool to improve employee engagement, motivation, and performance is *coaching*.

The term *coach* originated in Hungary in the 1800s. At that time, a coach was a horse-drawn carriage that took very important people from their present location to where they wanted to go. Over the years, the service expanded throughout Europe, and the Hungarian word *kocs* was translated into the French word *coach*. From there, it spread across the channel to England where, in the early 1900s, a *coach* was reported to be a tutor of scholars in Oxford and Cambridge. The term *coach* migrated into the sporting arena in the early 1950s and became entrenched in the sporting culture where it remains today.

Coaching in organisations is a relatively new phenomenon which has evolved over the past thirty years from a 'life coaching' philosophy and practice. Initially, coaching was not viewed favourably by organisational leaders as it had no reputable evidence-based foundation even though professional associations such as the European Mentoring and Coaching Council (EMCC), the Chartered Institute of Personnel and Development (CIPD) and the International Coaching Federation (ICF) had been established in the northern hemisphere in the 1990s. These professional organisations set the standards for ethical, legal, and competent coaching practice worldwide. They began to conduct their own research into the concept of coaching and how it can benefit individuals and organisations. This push by practitioners resulted in increasing interest in coaching from academics and the growth in empirical evidence for coaching from the early 2000s onwards.

1.2 What is Coaching?

Coaching is a particularly effective way of helping individuals solve their own problems and achieve their goals more quickly than they would have if they were to attempt to achieve these alone. As a relational process, coaching supports the coachee's attempts to change. Pure coaching (as defined by the ICF) is coachee-led, focused on the coachee's agenda, with no predetermined outcomes or expectations of how the coaching will unfold. As a reflective practice, coaching allows non-clinical coachees the time to consider their situation and resolve the problems they currently face. Tacit understandings are surfaced to a level of conscious awareness which allows them to identify who they really are and want to be. They acknowledge the part they have played in creating their situation, and the part they will play in resolving it. The coaching that occurs is a facilitative process focused on achieving present and future goals that promote the coachee's well-being and happiness. Together, coach and coachee design actions to improve existing skills, competence, and performance and embrace personal growth and development. The coach does not provide answers or solutions to issues raised by the coachee but instead assumes that the coachee, with their help, will gain the necessary insights to solve their own problems. The coachee is responsible for taking action; however, there is joint accountability for achieving results and revisiting the desired goals as necessary throughout the process. Before coachees can change their behaviour, they often need to let go of limiting beliefs and change their *mindset* so that they can achieve a different outcome.

The definition of coaching proposed by the International Coach Federation (ICF) highlights the quintessential nature of coaching:

> *Partnering with clients in a thought-provoking and creative process that inspires them to maximize their personal and professional potential, which is particularly important in today's uncertain and complex environment. Coaches honour the client as the expert in their life and work and believe every client is creative.* (www.coachfederation.org)

This definition characterises *pure coaching*, that is, coaching which is content-free, client-led, with no predetermined outcomes. In contrast, coaching by leaders of their direct reports usually has an agenda which is leader-led, with predetermined business outcomes for how an individual should behave or what they need to do to improve their performance - *performance coaching*. Because coaching in organisations can be a combination of both *pure* and *performance* coaching, the definition that I used as a starting point for this research—the definition that underlies my coaching philosophy and executive coaching experience in organisations—is the one that I developed for the Australian Institute of Professional Coaches:

Coaching is the process of working with individuals to help them achieve their life goals and create a more positive future. This involves facilitating self-awareness of issues and problems concerning them in their work and/or personal life, or goals to be achieved. It is a supportive and encouraging process that utilises clients' existing knowledge and strengths to help them understand their current situation, broaden their horizon, be open to other possibilities and lead them towards effective, often creative, solutions to their problems. (www.professionalcoachtraining.com.au)

1.3 Benefits of Coaching

Research has shown that organisations which embrace a coaching culture benefit in three major ways: higher employee engagement (60 per cent of employees rated as highly engaged compared with 48 per cent of all other organisations), higher revenue growth (63 per cent of organisations report being above their industry peer group in 2014 revenue compared with 45 per cent of all other organisations), and higher engagement levels for high potentials with access to external coaches or leaders as coaches (as reported by 60 per cent of organisations) (International Coach Federation, 2015a). Employees who are coached tend to stay longer in the organisation because of their belief that they are valued and that the organisation wants to support their development and career progression. Within European and North American organisations, coaching has become an accepted practice and a billion-dollar industry (International Coach Federation, 2014b). However, within many organisations, coaching is still not well known and accepted as a valid organisational practice (International Coach Federation, 2015b).

There are significant benefits for individuals who are coached. They gain in self-awareness and insight, change their behaviour to be more consistent with organisational values and expectations, improve in the performance of their role, and communicate better with others to form strong relationships within and external to the organisation. In addition, leaders develop their leadership capability and ability to influence key stakeholders to meet business needs. Team coaching improves team cohesion, increases cooperation and collaboration, reduces conflict, and raises team morale. Issues can be addressed as they occur, negating the need to take the matter further and cause loss of staff motivation and engagement. The organisation benefits from increased productivity as the team forges to higher performance levels, resulting in an improved market position and competitive advantage.

1.4 Misconceptions of Coaching

Common misconceptions of organisational coaching as it has emerged from community-based, life coaching beginnings are that coaching is 'weird' and 'fluffy' with no solid underpinnings for professional practice. However, if one extrapolates from a sports-coaching perspective, coaching is definitely not 'weird' or 'fluffy'. It is calculated, measured, and controlled. It is a team-oriented strategy to achieve a targeted, performance-based outcome. Sports coaches are on the field with their team every day, motivating their players to succeed. The notion of leaders in the workplace using coaching to motivate their employees towards improved performance was initially foreign to organisations. However over time, many organisational leaders who are also sports coaches have begun using the sporting analogy within their business teams to motivate employees to succeed. This has, in part, caused the benefits of coaching to migrate into organisations.

Coaching was also once viewed as a 'fringe' activity conducted by those without formal qualifications in human behaviour or psychology. Coaches were considered to be practicing in areas beyond their expertise. This perception was, and still is, accurate to some extent because coaching is an unregulated industry in which anyone can participate. However, as international coaching associations were formed and developed coaching standards, private coach-training companies were also established to train individuals as coaches to these standards. Most of the private coach-training companies and organisations (including some universities) adhere to the self-regulated industry standards that have been developed to guide practitioner coaching, which brings greater rigour to the coaching practice that is conducted in organisations and increases confidence in its veracity and effectiveness as a valid developmental tool. Research into individual differences, motivation, and organisational behaviour over the past seventy years has informed the evolving coach-training and coaching practice. In recent years, the benefits of coaching have been more rigorously researched, including how coaching may be applied to leadership practice in organisations.

Those who view coaching as a 'waste of time' have typically had negative experiences of coaching in the past and not regarded coaching highly. They may have been misled or misinformed as to what coaching is and how it could help them and, consequently, may have found that coaching didn't meet their expectations or needs. The disappointed individual may not have been coached by a professional coach and found the experience less than fulfilling. As a result, they may have become suspicious of coaching and sceptical of any value that coaching can offer. Unfortunately, individuals whose needs have not been met do what any customer does—they tell their friends about the bad experience—and as we know, word of mouth spreads, and negative publicity has a way of being transmitted quickly through the peer group and colleagues.

1.5 Contemporary Views of Coaching

Coaching was initially introduced into the organisational arena as a remedial exercise—a 'last resort' effort to reorient employees who were underperforming. Underperformers thought that being sent to coaching was shameful, and it was particularly stressful since the individual knew that if they didn't improve their performance, they would be fired. Managers under the old-school *command-and-control* style of management considered employees who were sent to coaching to be weak, a view which is still firmly entrenched in some organisations today. An executive coach who has been coaching since the early 1990s tells the story of how this view started to change: *"When I first started coaching, I remember working with [a coaching guru] on the coaching standards and we had to make a point of differentiation between remedial coaching and development coaching and you wouldn't even hear that language any more today would you*—remedial coaching? *And yet it was the dominant form in, probably 2008 or somewhere like that, or 2009.'* He went on to note that *'nobody gets badged* remedial *anymore."*

These days, employees are more discerning about the organisations they work for. Hence, when there is a misalignment between personal and organisational values, purpose, and direction, the individual being coached for remedial purposes may choose to leave the organisation voluntarily rather than be exited involuntarily from their position. An executive coach estimates that about 30 per cent of coaching engagements result in the coachee leaving the organisation not because they've been 'given the push' but because, through coaching, they have recognised a mismatch of their personal values with the organisation's values, and hence, they self-select out of the organisation.

Some sceptics of coaching view coaching as a fad, something that won't stand the test of time and will soon be replaced by the 'next best thing'. One reason for this view may be lack of knowledge about coaching. Another reason may be that most individuals don't like change, and as managers, they may be asked to do things differently. Some HR professionals may be scared of losing their job or, at least, their skills base if coaching moves into the leadership arena: What HR activities will leaders take over next? However, in those organisations that really believe in the benefits of coaching, have embraced coaching, and are establishing the beginnings of a coaching culture, coaching is definitely not a fad as one organisational leader explains:

> *"If it is a fad, then we're goners. If we're ever going to revert to the old* command-and-control, *no one responds—if they ever did. The hierarchies are disheartening. It's a dead hand—some of the disempowerment of the hierarchies*

and the bureaucratic nature of government—and this [coaching] is a glimmer of light."

As coaching becomes more accepted within organisations, it is conducted as an effective intervention for *developmental* purposes. Line managers may recommend that certain talented individuals who are included in the organisation's succession plan be coached. Thereafter, as the benefits of coaching spread, employees who aren't being coached may express discontent at what they see as an unfair situation, expecting to be coached as well. An executive coach tells the story of working with an individual for four months, and then one of her peers said, *"So if so-and-so is entitled to a coach, surely I can have one too?"*

From an organisational perspective, as HR professionals become better acquainted with coaching either from knowing someone who has been coached, being coached themselves, or undertaking formal coach-training from an external provider, they may feel compelled to check out coaching as possibly a highly valuable addition to their organisation's suite of development tools for leaders. An organisational leader explains this 'me too' perspective thus:

> *"I think somebody may have been exposed to coaching, and then they thought,* Hey, we probably need some of that here. *And this is probably not just in Australian companies. It's probably most companies, and much like other management fads or hot topics, they say,* Oh, we need to get that here . . . We need to get some coaching. We need to get some . . . whatever, *and they just push for a token sort of representation in that arena to say,* Oh yeah, we've hired a coach for these two people. We do that here. *And of course, there's always the 'copy-cat' syndrome that,* Well, everybody does it. We should do it too."

On the contrary, organisational leaders and HR professionals who are better informed about coaching may be concerned that their organisation is missing out on one of the latest, evidence-based, effective development tools available to leaders. From this valued perspective, as coaching enters their organisation, it takes on a completely different conception—as an intervention that is considered *prestigious* and sought after by discerning individuals who want to benefit from the insights and developmental opportunities that the coaching process enables. An organisational leader notes that ten years ago, individuals were adamant that they didn't need a coach, and consequently, coaching was often sugar-coated as mentoring to get individuals involved in personal conversations in a way that they understood. Nowadays, however, that view has changed:

> "*I think in the private sector, it is becoming* prestigious *to have a coach. It used to be a stigma. It used to be,* I don't need a coach. I don't need help. *A coach was seen as a psychologist. These days, it's my observation that they see it as,* Oh I'm having a coach. I must be on a fast track for a promotion. *So it's seen as a prestige status thing rather than an* I need help *thing.*"

In summary, these early conceptions of coaching have changed over the past decade as the coaching profession has matured and as individuals and organisations have gained more knowledge and understanding of what coaching is and how it can benefit individuals, teams, and organisations. Coaching has shaken off the *stigma* that it once had. Individuals who are coached now consider coaching to be a *prestigious* activity in which they are fortunate to engage. As the demand for coaching grows, organisations proudly display the fact that they coach as a *badge of honour.* Many executives expect that once they get to a certain level within the organisation, they'll be entitled to a coach even though they may not actually know what a coach can do for them or what they want out of the coaching experience. The coaching process identifies their individual coaching needs and assists them to reach their goals much sooner than expected, overcoming any barriers along the way.

1.6 Research Study

The research I conducted set out to identify the extent to which coaching is prevalent in Australian organisations and how these organisations are attempting to develop a coaching culture. Why is coaching being introduced? Is it a fad? Is it the 'next big, shiny thing'? Or is there some real purpose for introducing coaching as an organisational initiative? Semi-structured interviews were conducted with leaders whose titles included positions such as: Manager, People & Culture; Organisation Capability Manager; Human Resource Manager; Executive Sales Coach; General Manager, Sales Operations; Executive General Manager, People Services; Manager, Organisational Capability and Talent Management; Organisational Development Manager; Learning and Development Consultant. In addition, a number of executive coaches in private practice were interviewed to obtain a broader industry perspective from their knowledge of what's happening in the organisations to which they consult and coach. The interviews were conducted to discover what *coaching* and a *coaching culture* mean to participants and how a coaching culture can be developed to embed transformational cultural change into an organisation.

A qualitative, inductive research design was used to generate as wide a range of views as possible from the interviewees. Data analysis revealed findings in four key areas: (1) conceptions of coaching and how this understanding affects learning and growth in organisations, (2) the motivations and expectations that drive leaders to introduce coaching into their organisation, (3) the people who are the key drivers of coaching throughout the organisation, and (4) the various ways that coaching is delivered within organisations. Themes were combined into a process model of coaching culture development over four stages, and illustrative organisational examples revealed the strategies and mechanisms essential for organisations to learn, grow, and lead differently in order to transition between stages to achieve transformational cultural change.

The views of research participants provided a window into the workings and aspirations of organisations as leaders attempt to influence those in more senior decision-making positions to adopt what research has shown to be one of the most powerful ways of developing employees, growing an organisation's productivity and competitive advantage, and achieving transformational cultural change – establishing a coaching culture. Interviewees provided powerful stories of how individuals are coached, how they respond to being coached, and how leaders attempt to spread the news about how coaching can assist individuals and teams improve their performance.

1.7 Summary of findings

Findings from the research study indicate that, in a coaching culture, coaching is undertaken at all levels of the organisation for both individuals and teams. A leader passionate about coaching may emerge at any level of the organisation. However it is not until a champion for coaching is nominated at the senior executive team, and sufficient funds allocated to support the coaching initiative and build the coaching infrastructure, that the organisation commits to a journey to develop a coaching culture. Often, an external executive coach is engaged to assist the champion design the transformational cultural change program. A Coaching Culture Development Team may also formed to support the implementation of the cultural change plan.

As the coaching is cascaded down and across organisational levels, additional external coaches may be engaged to work with business unit leaders to customise the training of their leadership team in coaching skills. In addition, to ensure that the learnings are transferred back into the workplace, the experience of being coached is integrated as an essential component within the coaching skills training program. Thereafter, coaching becomes the predominant way of interacting with, and relating to, individuals within and without the business unit. The coaching philosophy and practices are applied to everyday relationships and business transactions. Leaders formally coach their direct reports and others including managers and team leaders who go on to coach their front-line staff. Peer coaching is introduced to ensure that all employees have access to informal coaching when needed. The coaching approach is extended to others external to the organisation resulting in improved customer engagement, longer-term customer loyalty and retention, and increased revenue in long-term, secure pipelines.

A coordinated approach to training in coaching skills and the delivery of coaching to individuals and teams is necessary to ensure 'blanket' coverage across the organisation. A fragmented approach has no long-term benefits. The coaching commences. The individual or team improves. The coaching concludes. Some change occurs. However, if the coaching is not sustained or internalised, individuals often return to previous habits, drawn back into expected behaviours by colleagues and/or the contextual environment or both. The benefits of coaching are lost. This type of coaching has typically been arranged by an organisational leader with little or no knowledge of, or skills in, coaching—someone who just wants a 'problem' to go away or a team to 'work better together'. However, when there is an organisational leader with a passion for coaching who knows or has personally experienced the benefits of coaching, the outcome is different. The piecemeal approach to coaching is replaced by a whole-of-organisation focus which starts to develop a coaching culture in *pockets* of the organisation. These *pockets* of coaching occur in areas of the business where there is a committed manager with the authority to make decisions and allocate resources, typically within revenue-generating sales and services functions. As *pockets* develop in all business units, a coaching culture starts to form. But organisational culture is not "*something that grows in the corner of an office*" as one of the interviewees flippantly suggested. Rather, it's "the way we do things around here" (Schein 1985) and is represented in the signs, symbols, artefacts, stories and toolkits (Giorgi, Lockwood, and Glynn 2015) that develop over the life of an organisation as it grows and evolves.

The main conclusions that I drew from the research, which may guide organisations wanting to develop a coaching culture, are as follows:

1. A coaching culture is more effectively developed from the top down by the CEO and senior executives of the organisation, although it can develop in *pockets* within the organisation where the business unit leader is passionate and committed and has the authority to expend to gain productivity improvements, increase staff engagement, and retain talent.
2. Cultural change takes investment. The organisation needs to be prepared to make a considerable financial investment and measure the return on investment (ROI) from the coaching programs that will operate until a coaching culture is developed and embedded. By this time all employees will be taking a coaching approach to internal and external relationships and business transactions on a daily basis. The return will be able to be measured in real dollar value, for example, by profitability, share price, and/or market share increases.
3. Cultural change takes time. To introduce and embed a coaching culture takes eighteen months minimum. To sustain it takes a coaching champion, ongoing training and development, and mindsets that believe in the potential of all individuals to grow and reach their potential.
4. The journey to develop a coaching culture is best guided by an external executive coach who has a broader industry perspective beyond that of the organisation's boundaries—someone who can expand and challenge organisational leaders' current thinking, mindset and outlook.
5. The organisation should be prepared to be disturbed by out-of-the-box distractors in terms of different processes, systems, and procedures—different 'ways we do things around here'. Leaders need to be prepared to examine every aspect of the business to identify where coaching can deliver maximum benefit. As coaching practice spreads throughout the organisation, it may create a tsunami of possibilities requiring small and, at times, large changes all creating maybe unexpected or unintended yet positive outcomes for individuals, teams, and organisations.

1.8 Structure of the Chapters

Findings from the research study revealed that, conceptually, leaders view coaching in four distinct ways: (1) as an intervention to fix a problem in individuals, (2) as an HR function to train leaders in coaching skills, (3) as an essential capability of leaders as they progress in their career, and (4) as a vehicle to bring about transformational cultural change. I labelled the four stages as Stage 1- *Coaching-as-Intervention* (Chapter 3), Stage 2 - *Coaching-as-HR-Function* (Chapter 4), Stage 3 - *Coaching-as-Leader-Capability* (Chapter 5) and Stage 4 - *Coaching-as-Culture* (Chapter 6). These four stages explain organisational leaders' *understanding* of what *coaching* and a *coaching culture* mean to them and their organisations, organisational leaders' *motivation* for engaging in coaching, the *key drivers* of coaching in their organisations, and the *delivery mechanisms* that are used by organisations to achieve transformational personal, business, and organisational change.

Chapters 2 details the research that underpins and provides the evidence for *coaching* and a *coaching culture*. Chapters 3-6 discuss the findings from the research in relation to each stage in turn. The process model and transition strategies and mechanisms based on the disciplines of education, psychology, and management are outlined in Chapter 7 and elaborated in Chapters 8–10. A blueprint for transformational cultural change through coaching is depicted in Figure 10.1. Insights and implications for CEOs and senior executives, HR professionals, and organisational leaders are outlined in Chapter 11.

CHAPTER 2

COACHING AND COACHING CULTURE RESEARCH

2.1 Research on Coaching

There is broad agreement within the research literature that coaching can help people improve their performance and achieve their goals. Coaching is a well-accepted business practice in Europe and the United States and an emerging growth industry elsewhere, including Australia. The incidence of coaching within organisations is expanding rapidly, becoming an extensive new field of practice and one of the fastest-growing interventions in the professional development of managers especially those in large organisations. In 2010, an estimated 16,000 coaches operated in the United States and 4,000 in the United Kingdom. By 2012, this number had grown to an estimated 47,500 professional coaches operating worldwide. Global revenues from coaching were estimated in 2013 to be US$1.5 billion, with Australia's share of this being just US$105 million. Throughout Europe, coaching associations have been established in countries such as Austria, France, Germany, Sweden, Switzerland, and Turkey, with several in the UK, the leading ones being the International Coach Federation (ICF) and the European Mentoring and Coaching Council (EMCC). Both the ICF and the EMCC share interests and concerns related to the state of coaching, specifically regarding the credentialing of coaches, quality assessment, continuing professional education, governance, and regulatory affairs.

In the UK, the Chartered Institute of Personnel and Development reported that 32 per cent of respondent organisations use coaching by line managers or peers and 12 per cent engage with external coaches (CIPD 2014); hence, over a third of organisations in the UK sample use coaching in some way. Furthermore, 46,800 people worldwide call themselves *executive coaches*, an increase of 75 per cent from 26,800 people ten years ago. Whilst the evidence clearly demonstrates the growth of coaching within the UK, European, and United States business communities over the past ten years, coaching is not well known or accepted as a valid organisational practice in many organisations.

Coaching was introduced into organisational settings in the 1950s as a master–apprentice relationship. In the 1970s, concepts from sports coaching became integrated into what was then called Human Resource Development (HRD). In 2004, the American Society for Training and Development (ASTD), in their 2004 Competency Framework, identified coaching as an area of expertise amongst workplace learning and performance specialists, a view that was reinforced in their 2013 revised version of the *ASTD Competency Model*. Within organisations, research has shown that coaching was originally viewed as an organisational development (OD) intervention or a special form of OD that helps organisational members clarify their goals, remove roadblocks and obstacles, and improve performance effectiveness. More recently, coaching has been incorporated within the Human Resource (HR) function as an important organisational activity, although in some organisations, coaching still sits within OD or the workforce development function.

Most references to coaching in the academic literature note the formal, dyadic nature of the coaching relationship. In the practitioner literature, coaching has been recognised as a practice strategy to help individuals develop and improve their capabilities to exceed prior levels of performance and go beyond their organisation's expectations. Coaching involves the use of a variety of techniques which enable coachees to learn new behaviours, communication and relationship skills through intensive feedback and role modelling. Using these techniques, coaches help individuals increase their self-awareness and insight, change their behaviour, and improve their performance.

The value of coaching is that it can be customised to meet both an individual's specific learning needs and organisational expectations; hence, it develops individual and team capabilities, leading to simultaneous improvements in the individual's work performance and team productivity. The benefits of coaching in an organisational setting most typically cited in the academic literature include performance improvement, behavioural change, leadership development, and talent management. Coaching has been described as "more than a set of skills; it is a rich, holistic approach for releasing the potential in people and in organisations" (Anderson and Anderson 2005: 127).

2.2 Difference between Coaching and Mentoring

No single, clear definition of coaching exists, or of when, how and by whom it can be delivered to benefit individuals, teams and organisations. A review of the relevant literature reveals the confusion for organisations wishing to offer coaching and for coaching recipients, with 37 definitions of coaching based on the audience and purpose for coaching including what and for whom it is for, what it involves, and the context in which it is applied (Bachkirova & Kauffman, 2009). These definitions highlight the essential ingredients of coaching and the coaching relationship as personal responsibility, dyadic relationship, achieving individual personal and professional goals, reflection and self-development, and behavioural change. Within organisations, a plethora of approaches claim to stimulate individual development and growth including coaching, mentoring, training, supervision and counselling. However these approaches create uncertainty in clients' minds as to the best approach to adopt. A composite definition of coaching as it is enacted within the HRM environment was provided by Hamlin et al. (2008):

> "[Coaching] is designed to improve existing skills, competence and performance, and to enhance ... personal effectiveness ... development or ... growth" (p. 295).

In many organisations and to many people's minds, the terms *coaching* and *mentoring* are used interchangeably. However, these two activities are not the same, nor are they related to other organisational activities such as training, supervision, and counselling. Whilst coaching and mentoring promote both personal and professional growth, mentoring usually involves an ongoing professional relationship between a junior and a more senior person within the same or possibly a different organisation in which the more senior person imparts wisdom and knowledge to the mentee. Mentors are role models, and the mentoring relationship is based on the sharing of professional experience to improve the mentee's personal and professional effectiveness as well as deepen understanding of their career prospects. The relationship is hierarchical and sometimes paternalistic. The mentor has extensive skills and experience to share with the mentee in what is typically a *telling* rather than an *asking* relationship.

Instead, coaching is a partnership between two people of equal status who, together, surface a solution from the coachee's subconscious to resolve a problem or achieve a specific goal. The coaching is conducted in a supportive and non-judgemental way, allowing a trusting relationship to form. Coaches bring essential skills of rapport building, active listening, and powerful questioning to the process. The coachee brings knowledge of their situation and needs. Coach and coachee work together to achieve an outcome that promotes the coachee's well-being and productivity. The coaching conversation is focused on expanding the coachee's awareness of self and others, encouraging insight and discovery, and taking action. Coaches assist coachees discover what they really want and need in life and work. Together, they explore the unexplored—the world of possibilities—during which process coachees discover their true self, what motivates them, and what causes them conflict and concern. Coaches work with coachees to envision their best possible future, then goal set and action plan with them to achieve their desired outcomes, revisiting the goals throughout the process.

In an organisational setting, individual coaching focuses on behavioural or performance issues which are causing concern for the manager and employee, such as communication and relationship difficulties, stress-related anxiety, and role clarity. At the team level, coaching may address issues relating to collaboration, cooperation, and conflict, which may be causing job dissatisfaction and low team morale. At the organisational level, coaching may be used to extend executives' leadership capability, improve their role performance, and identify opportunities for career progression.

2.3 Types of Coaching

Different types of coaching are conducted in organisations depending on the audience and purpose for coaching. These include executive, managerial, leadership, team, and peer coaching.

Executive coaching is a developmental process which is both personal and performance-related, delivered by an external executive coach who is engaged on an outsourced contract. Executive coaching improves the executive's ability to relate and communicate more effectively with colleagues, customers, and direct reports; perform as a strategic leader; and transform into peak performance. The coaching positively affects the executive's judgement, improves critical-thinking and decision-making skills, increases their social influence, and promotes a transformational leadership style. The confidential one-on-one relationship that is formed focuses on improving personal and professional effectiveness based on the coachee's expressed concerns and possibly also on the results of a 360-degree assessment of the executive's strengths, weaknesses, and organisational performance. As the coaching proceeds, the executive develops strategic leadership competencies, plans for the future growth of the business, and identifies ways to manage and lead transformational cultural change.

Managerial coaching is focused on enhancing the planning, organising, staffing, and controlling capability of line managers (Kotter 2001). Managers are coached to facilitate learning of work-related skills and abilities by providing knowledge or role-modelling desired behaviours to improve their performance. The coaching provides timely feedback to assist coachees better manage workplace challenges and difficult situations. Work goals are formulated, performance targets and expectations are clarified, and specific adjustments are made to job/role functions during this process. Managerial coaching is reported to be a more effective process for performance improvement than training programs alone. The mediating mechanisms between managerial coaching and work-related outcomes have been identified as *role clarity* and *satisfaction with work*. The benefit of managerial coaching is that it impacts on the coachee's ability to self-regulate their behaviour and performance, particularly their persistence to cope with and overcome challenging problems.

Leadership coaching is a developmental process in which leaders use a *coaching leadership style* to motivate and inspire their direct reports to greater levels of engagement with their work and team (Kotter 2001), thereby uplifting their work performance, and increasing job satisfaction, employee engagement, and retention. Leadership coaching may also be conducted by external leadership coaches who are engaged by the organisation to perform a specific task within a work group. Employees who are coached develop increased self-efficacy, motivation and engagement, and commitment to their role and the team. Leadership coaching enables greater involvement of employees in decision-making and empowers them to try new ideas and develop innovative processes and systems. Leadership coaching is the most common form of coaching in organisations today, and its prevalence continues to rise.

> In this book, the term *leader* is used to emphasise the importance of the 'people' aspect of the *manager's* role in an organisation. When *managers* adopt a *coaching leadership style*, they become *leaders* who enable and empower their direct reports to improved work performance and other personally related outcomes, resulting in more enthusiastic employees who use their initiative in the performance of their role. Hence, as organisations transition to develop a coaching culture, the term *manager* is replaced by *leader,* and a *coaching leadership style* becomes the prevalent style of interaction with their direct reports.

Team coaching is an emerging organisational practice which focuses on results and relationships, facilitating problem-solving and conflict management and coordinating the task-appropriate use of collective resources to achieve team targets. As teams are coached, they learn how to increase their collective capability to achieve a common goal, paying attention to individual performance as well as group collaboration to discover more effective ways to engage with each other and key stakeholders. Models of team coaching focus on how coaching can best serve the team, the specific times in the performance process when coaching is most likely to have its intended effect, and the conditions under which team-focused coaching promotes improved performance. Models of team coaching have been developed from theories of individual differences and human motivation, developmental theories of self-reflective behaviours and learning, and psychosocial theories of group dynamics, all of which support team coaching efforts at different stages in the life cycle of the team. Key to performance progression is the opportunity for teams to review their purpose and task objectives, reflect on the outcomes of work conducted to date, and identify any issues that the team or team members may have that need to be dealt with so they are not holding back peak performance.

Peer coaching is a recent addition to the traditional forms of coaching used in organisations. It is conducted one-on-one by one employee with another for their mutual support. The concept of peer coaching was originally introduced into the literature on pre-service education of teachers by Joyce and Showers (1980) who found an 80 per cent transfer rate of learnings from training programs into the workplace when a coaching component was added (as opposed to a 20 per cent transfer rate if coaching was not included). Within a management context, peer coaching has been defined as "a helping relationship that facilitates mutual learning and development to accomplish specific tasks or goals" (Parker et al. 2015: 231). The process of peer coaching is collaborative and supports the achievement of individual and team immediate and short-term goals. It has been described as an overlooked resource in the development of an employee's critical thinking, reasoning skills, and effective judgement. Peer coaching is a low-cost activity which has high impact and can be delivered on the spot as and when needed. Because peer coaching is a relational activity based on mutual trust and support, it can also serve to promote an individual's leadership and career aspirations.

2.4 Theoretical Basis for Coaching

The historical evidence for coaching as an effective intervention to promote personal insight, behavioural change, and performance improvement lies within two well-established disciplines—education and psychology—and management perspectives, as explained below.

(See Appendix 1: Summary of the Educational and Psychodynamic Evidence for Coaching.)

Within *education*, implicit person theory (Dweck 2012, 2014) proposes that people who believe their ability to be fixed will behave in ways different from people who believe that their ability to learn, perform, or change as a result of effort, persistence, and at times, assistance is malleable. Mindset theory has been variously applied in organisations but particularly in relation to an employee's ability to change and grow. Combined with principles of adult learning (Knowles 1980, 2004; Kolb 1984), these frameworks provide the basis for the development of adult and organisational learning strategies in the workplace.

Coaching practice is informed by an understanding of human behaviour from psychological approaches which are based on well-researched methods of modifying behaviour and motivating individuals to better meet their needs. Within *psychology*, coaching research has focused on the psychodynamics of the individual (Grant, Passmore, Peterson, and Freire 2013). The primary influences on personal effectiveness began from observations of human behaviour and behavioural manipulation to condition new responses (Skinner 1938). Cognitive therapeutic approaches then proposed that difficulties are caused by habits and associated thought patterns which can be rectified by focusing on goal-oriented behaviours (Locke and Latham 2002) so that coachees find their own solutions rather than blame external forces (Neenan 2008). Subsequently, solution-focused coaching was found to reduce negative affect, increase positive affect, and support goal attainment (Grant et al. 2012; Nagel 2008; Wakefield 2006), helping coachees build a greater depth of understanding and self-efficacy (Ives and Cox 2012; O'Connell, Palmer, and Williams 2013; Roeden, Maaskant, and Curfs 2012). Coaching has been found to be most effective when solution-focused coaching is combined with cognitive and rational–emotive behavioural approaches (Beck 1976; Ellis 1962).

Motivational and developmental *psychology* address issues that promote mental and emotional well-being, growth, and development (Maslow 1943, 1987; McClelland 1951). The coach uses humanistic psychology to identify the coachee's needs, drives, and expectations and ensure that they are realistic and attainable (Adler, Ansbacher, and Ansbacher 1956; Jung 1921; Rogers 1951). Positive psychology seeks ways in which the coachee can become authentically happy and achieve 'flow' in their life (Csikszentmihalyi 1990; Seligman 2011). Social psychology recognises the importance of the social environment as coachees attempt to conform with, and make sense of, their environment and adjust their behaviour to meet their needs (Bandura 1977; Bandura, Davidson, and Davidson 2003). Social psychologists encourage individuals to adopt new ways of relating to others and the external world to develop self-regulation and goal attainment, motivation and personality, and emotional competence (Allard-Poesi 1998; Bandura 2006; Bandura and Locke 2003; Dweck and Leggett 1988; Johan 1997; Mizokawa and Koyasu 2015). These different streams of psychology provide the theoretical underpinnings for coaching practice (see Table 2.1).

Theoretical Area	Key Elements of Investigation (see Appendix 1 for details)
Behavioural psychology	Classical versus operant conditioning, observation of human behaviour
Cognitive psychology	Cognitive-based therapy, rational–emotive behaviour therapy, goal setting, solution-focused coaching
Motivational psychology	Needs, drives, motivations, expectations, satisfaction
Developmental psychology	Experiential learning, prosocial development, brain malleability, growth and persistence
Personality psychology	Attitudes, preferences, traits
Humanistic psychology	Self-psychology, individuation, unconscious competence, person-centred therapy
Social psychology	Social learning, social conformity, cognitive dissonance, self-efficacy
Positive psychology	Authentic happiness, 'flow', learned helplessness, mindset

Table 2.1: The Evidence for Coaching

From a management perspective, research on coaching has traditionally been set within HR, psychology, and related fields. Organisational research has focused on the acquisition of coaching competencies to enhance leadership development (Goleman 1995), job satisfaction, motivation and work performance (Locke and Latham 2002), and interpersonal and team relationships (Avolio and Bass

2002). The considerable growth in coaching over the past decade and the identified benefits for individuals, teams, and organisations have legitimised coaching as a function of line managers as well as HR professionals to stimulate employee growth and development, and performance improvements. As the evidence for coaching has emerged from research in these discipline areas, it has become a pluralist practice to support individuals and teams find new and novel solutions to their problems and ways to achieve their goals.

2.5 Coaching Practice

Coaching has traditionally been delivered in organisations by external coaches who have been engaged by a line manager to fix an individual. More recently, the focus of coaching is on developmental and empowerment perspectives so that individuals can improve their own performance. From vague conceptions of coaching as "an activity, a function with specific outcomes or a process" (Grant 2004: 2), coaching is now a "facilitative process designed to improve existing skills, competence and performance and embrace personal effectiveness, personal development or personal growth" (Hamlin et al. 2008: 259). In an organisational setting, coaching practice has been described as a "goal-directed interaction between the coach and the coachee which reflects what leaders do when engaging with their direct reports to improve their performance" (Sue-Chan et al. 2012: 810). As coaching has become an accepted leadership practice, the need to build the internal coaching capability of, in particular, front-line supervisors and managers has been recognised as these are the leaders who are increasingly being charged with additional responsibility for a range of HR management and development functions, including coaching their employees.

2.6 Coaching Purpose

There are many purposes for delivering coaching in organisations, including performance improvement, behavioural change, and talent management. One-on-one coaching sessions help employees improve their performance, develop personally and professionally, and progress in their career. Coaching assists employees gain greater clarity on what is expected of them in their role, provides immediate feedback to improve communication and interpersonal skills, and develops new strategies to resolve conflict in the workplace. In some organisations, coaching is emerging as an important vehicle to enhance the performance of all team members to produce peak performance. When employees are coached, feedback on work performance is given in a timely and supportive rather than punitive manner, the underlying belief being that all employees are capable of additional growth and development when they are provided with personalised, constructive feedback on their performance. The assumption of leaders is that employees want to utilise their strengths and initiative in a way that is meaningful and purposive and which supports the strategic direction of the organisation.

When coaching is used as a talent management strategy, it assists in the identification of high-potential individuals whose strengths and abilities contribute to the achievement of both short- and long-term benefits for the organisation as they progress into other positions or accept other developmental opportunities within the organisation. Talent management has been identified as one of the main strategies used by organisations to grow the human capital of the business, thereby securing competitive advantage for the firm. Research has shown that the coaching of talented individuals is an essential component of the succession planning process (Brant, Dooley, & Iman, 2008). Global talent management has been increasingly explored in the cross-cultural literature, especially in relation to the management of expatriates, the search for global leadership talent, organisational success, and organisational reputation (Kim & McLean, 2012).

The need for organisations to be flexible in a global environment has highlighted the importance of two key factors: adaptive leadership and organisational culture. Leadership models which include a coaching component show how, by the use of specific coaching processes and sense-making techniques, coaching can assist in decision-making, leading to a different form of personal leadership and corporate citizenship behaviour (McLaughlin and Cox 2015). Leadership is an important element in developing a coaching culture, although an understanding of the dynamics and nuances of how leaders and leadership shape coaching culture is not well known.

2.7 Organisational Culture

Research into organisational culture came into prominence in the 1990s when Edgar Schein, one of the most influential leaders of his time, described culture as "what a group learns over a period of time as that group solves its problems of survival in an external environment and its problems of internal integration. Such learning is simultaneously a behavioural, cognitive and an emotional process" (Schein 1990: 111). The term *culture* has been used to indicate how *values* guide and constrain people in organisations (Schein 1985) and how individuals weave stories to obtain resources (Lounsbury and Glynn 2001) or discriminately use tools to meet personal needs and interests (McPherson and Sauder 2013; Weber 2005).

Schein identified three fundamental levels at which culture manifests itself: observable artefacts, values, and basic underlying assumptions. *Artefacts* are the external representations of what an organisation holds dear. *Values* are represented by the behavioural norms that develop within an organisation. Underlying *assumptions* are uncovered by a process of enquiry that brings them to the surface to create mutual understanding. The process of questioning and reflective listening is the basis for the development of cultural norms within an organisation in relation to values and appropriate behaviours. Creating a common language and shared understanding enables the space for trust, friendship, and inclusion to evolve and grow. Questioning, reflective listening, and developing a common language and shared understanding are some of the basic processes that coaches use in their coaching practice.

Giorgi et al. (2015) reviewed the organisational culture research over the past thirty years as the concept has incorporated educational and developmental perspectives, psychological and social constructs, and management and leadership research findings. They identified five dominant models of culture: culture as *values, stories, frames, categories,* and *toolkits*. When related to coaching, the *culture as values* model represents the shared understanding of what coaching is about and the philosophy that underpins the coaching process. The *culture as stories* model represents the narrative and conversations that transact between coach and coachee as the coaching unfolds. The *culture as frames* model represents the coaching interventions that assist coachees reframe their view of the world by identifying limiting beliefs and unblocking barriers to their efforts to move forward. Within an organisational context, the *frames* relate to capability or leadership development frameworks that guide organisational activity and career progression. The *culture as categories* model allows the coachee to make sense of their situation and focus on how to take action. The *culture as toolkits* model provides the coach with the skills to coach non-judgementally and professionally, remaining centred on the coachee and the coachee's agenda and guiding the coachee to take action.

Of these five dominant models, the *culture as toolkits* model most aptly represents the practice used in organisations to develop a *coaching culture* since it is the one most usually associated with coordinating and taking action, helping people reach agreements and promoting change (Gormley and van Nieuwerburgh 2014). To Giorgi et. al. (2015), culture explains "the differences in outcomes that result not only from differences in individual behaviours and organisational practices but also from the culture of the organisation". They propose that "culture should remain a code of many colors that envelops different theoretical perspectives" (Giorgi et. al. 2015: 3).

In addition, they identified that *repertoires of actions* are the resources (or *toolkits*) that actors use to make meaning of their work (Hannerz 1969). The *culture as toolkits* model explains how actors use cultural repertoires in practice, that is, the various skills, knowledge, and resources that employees can draw upon to solve everyday problems (Swidler 1986). Repertoires of action bring together habits, styles, skills, and symbols (Giorgi et al. 2015) and operationalise the mental models, strategies, and actions they work from (e.g. how to manage their workload, how to be a good leader, and how to coach). These repertoires are backed up by skills, habits, and styles that are translatable into practice. Repertoires of action have been related to constructs such as cultural repertoires, cultural capital, and theories of coaching practice. Developing *coaching competencies* in order to coach others to peak performance is an essential component of a leader's behavioural repertoire. However, it cannot be assumed that leaders know how to coach; rather, they may need to be trained in coaching skills to guide and facilitate self-reflection and learning.

The use of cultural toolkits has been empirically verified in studies including justifying different life events, conferring worth to social standing, drawing social boundaries, and establishing identities. Employees use personal cultural resources and sociocultural values within their *toolkit* to make sense of specific work situations and events. Shared toolkits have been empirically associated with the coordination of team efforts in product innovation, evaluation of products at the field level, and work practices in organisations. Thus, the *culture as toolkits* model suggests that introducing a coaching culture into an organisation consists of sharing the values associated with coaching together with the cultural norms associated with coaching, for example, coaching language, philosophy and ethics, as well as the skills and knowledge required to enable leaders to coach confidently and consistently, that is, training them in how to coach as they develop their coaching skills and coaching toolkit.

The concept of organisational culture has been extended over the years to include understandings of more nuanced subcultures, for example, safety culture, service culture, sales culture. According to Antonsen (2009), the development of separate cultures has to do with creating the principles and processes necessary for that particular aspect of organisational culture to thrive, suggesting that separate cultures are a subset of the overarching organisational culture. When attention is paid to the particular principles and processes associated with that aspect of organisational culture in a coordinated fashion, that particular subset of the culture grows. Antonsen's (2009) model highlights the interplay between structural aspects of the organisation and the interactions between individuals who have a significant effect on the growth and development of shared language and cultural norms in relation to that aspect of culture. For example, a safety culture emerges from an organisational culture that has its own particular rules and regulations regarding how employees keep themselves and fellow employees safe in a workplace.

The majority of research into a safety culture has been based on a functionalist approach into how people think—their attitudes, beliefs, and perceptions—based on a belief that culture can be managed and changed (Caldwell 2018). Caldwell constructed an implementation *toolkit* that provides a practical guide for assessing, monitoring, and improving the leadership aspects of organisational culture in relation to safety. Studies from *safety culture* research demonstrate that a particular approach can be taken to investigating a nuanced aspect of an organisation's culture. This research study adopted the lens of *coaching* and a *coaching culture* rather than *safety* to investigate organisational activities. It investigated how coaching is defined, how cultural norms for coaching are developed, and how a coaching culture is operationalised within organisations. This research is important because as Smircich (1985) notes in Alvesson (2002), organisations are comprised of various systems of shared meanings which allow employees to readily interact in a continuous, organised way without the confusion of having to reinterpret meaning.

2.8 Coaching Culture

Like *coaching*, there is no shared understanding or definition of, or theoretical basis in the academic literature for, what constitutes a *coaching culture* (Gormley and van Nieuwerburgh 2014). Instead, there are several definitions which highlight the different components of a coaching culture as experienced by individuals in organisations. A *coaching culture* has been described as one in which "people coach each other all the time as a natural part of meetings, reviews and one-to-one discussions of all kinds" (Hardingham, Brearley, Moorhouse, and Venter 2005: 184), suggesting that frequent coaching can strengthen collaborative, supportive relationships and the sharing of constructive feedback. A coaching culture has also been described as existing when "coaching behaviour motivates people, increases job satisfaction and morale, and strengthens bonds between individuals" (Hart 2005: 7), suggesting a *developmental* component to a coaching culture. There is "a commitment to grow the organisation [alongside a parallel] commitment to grow the people in the organisation" (Clutterbuck and Megginson 2006: 19), suggesting a *business* component to a coaching culture. Coaching has also been described as "a key aspect of how the leaders, managers and staff engage and develop all their people and engage their stakeholders in ways that create increased individual, team and organisational *performance* and *shared value* for all stakeholders" (Hawkins 2012: 21). A coaching culture is also said to exist when "groups of people embrace coaching as a way of making *holistic improvements* to individuals within their organisations through formal and informal coaching interactions" (Gormley and van Nieuwerburgh 2014: 92). Coaching cultures have been found to promote *organisational learning* and *adaptability to change* and encourage *collaborative learning*. Developing the coaching competencies of organisational leaders results in benefits to individuals in terms of increased motivation, happiness, and job satisfaction; benefits to teams in terms of improved team communication, cooperation, knowledge sharing, and performance; and benefits to organisations in terms of reduced staff turnover and increased profitability from elevated performance.

A coaching culture in which everybody coaches everybody else aligns with what Kegan, Lahey, Fleming, Miller, and Markus (2014) call a *deliberately developmental organisation* (DDO). In a DDO, employees receive continuous development in the course of a day's work not by the traditional training methodology but by virtue of the coaching conversations they have with others to accelerate their growth. Conversations are deeply aligned with the individual's motivation to grow. As a result, "an organisational culture which supports people's ongoing development is woven into the daily fabric of working life, visible in the company's regular operations, day-to-day routines and conversations" (Kegan et al. 2014: 2). The DDO approach is about integrating deeper forms of personal learning into every aspect of individual and organisational interactions which, at a cultural level, is about making visible every day the procedural activities that demonstrate a total commitment to employees' learning and development.

CHAPTER 3

STAGE 1
COACHING-AS-INTERVENTION

The findings of the research study revealed four stages in the development of a coaching culture, labelled *Coaching-as-Intervention, Coaching-as-HR-Function, Coaching-as-Leader-Capability* and *Coaching-as-Culture*. Each stage is characterised by the understanding that organisational leaders have of coaching, their motivation for coaching, the key drivers of coaching, and how coaching is delivered throughout the organisation (see Figure 3.1). Each of these stages and the four characterisations is explained in Chapters 3 – 6.

Four stages in the development of a Coaching Culture	Stage 1 Coaching-as-Intervention	Stage 2 Coaching-as-HR-Function	Stage 3 Coaching-as-Leader-Capability	Stage 4 Coaching-as-Culture
Understanding of coaching	Skill / Tool, immediate investment	Learning experience, short-term investment	Capability / framework, medium-term investment	DNA and fabric of the organisation, long-term investment
Motivation for coaching	'Fix' a problem, remediate, comply	Individual behaviour & performance, career progression	Team performance, engagement and talent	Personal and organisational transformation
Driver of coaching	Line manager	HR professional	Business unit leader	CEO and senior executives
Delivery of coaching	Individual focus	Leader & talented individual focus	Team & team member focus	Everyone in the organisation

Figure 3.1: Overview of the Four Stages and their Defining Characteristics

The first stage in the development of a coaching culture is labelled *Coaching-as-Intervention*. During this stage, line managers arrange for individuals who are behaving inappropriately or not performing to role expectations to be coached. This first stage is characterised by a *utilitarian conceptualisation* of coaching as a skill set or tool, an *instrumental motivation* for coaching to remediate an underperformer, an intervention driven by *line managers* within a line management structure delivered by an *outsourced* external coach.

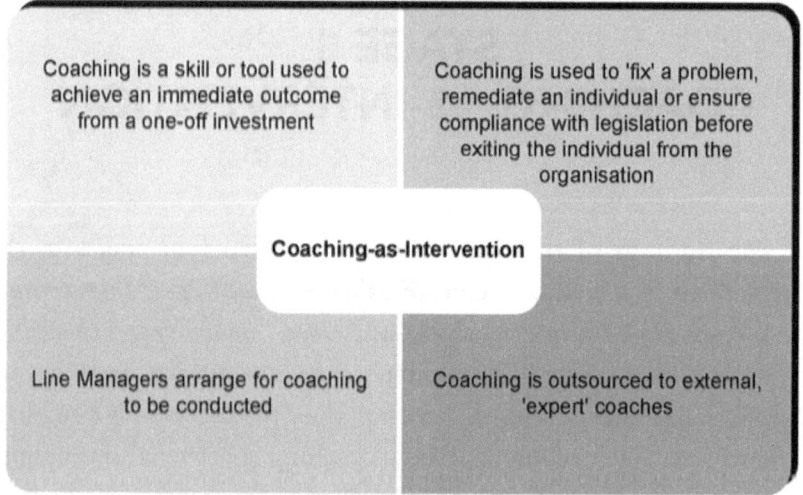

Figure 3.2: Coaching-as-Intervention Stage

3.1 Utilitarian Conceptualisation

In the *Coaching-as-Intervention* stage, coaching is a skill set or tool that is used to fix a problem or issue, driven by a line manager who has first-hand knowledge of the individual and the circumstances surrounding the presenting concern, and a one-off investment to achieve an immediate result.

3.1.1 Coaching Is a Skill

Coaching, in this first stage, is understood by managers as a skill set in the hands of experts. *"It's not my role to coach"* is their predominant view. The focus of coaching is on assisting the individual to behave more appropriately in the workplace and/or enhance their ability to improve their performance. The coach explores ways that the coachee can develop better interpersonal and relationship skills to interact more effectively with their manager and others in the team.

Improved interpersonal skills start with better listening skills. Most people only listen to half of what the other person is saying before they begin to develop a response; consequently, they don't hear the rest. They may interrupt the person before they are finished speaking because they think they know what the other person is going to say. Coaches listen to what their coachees are saying without interruption so that they understand the situation and circumstances completely before summarising to show the coachee that they are 'on the same wavelength'. They reflect what the coachee has said, the context in which the issue arose, and the feelings behind the issue. The coach assists the coachee to develop self-awareness and insight about what they need to do to bring about the desired behavioural change or performance improvement. Organisational leaders who want to optimise the opportunities for individuals in their team know that the coaching skill set is critical to their success.

> *It's the engine room, I think, this skill set—the engine room of actually unleashing that discretionary effort and engagement.*

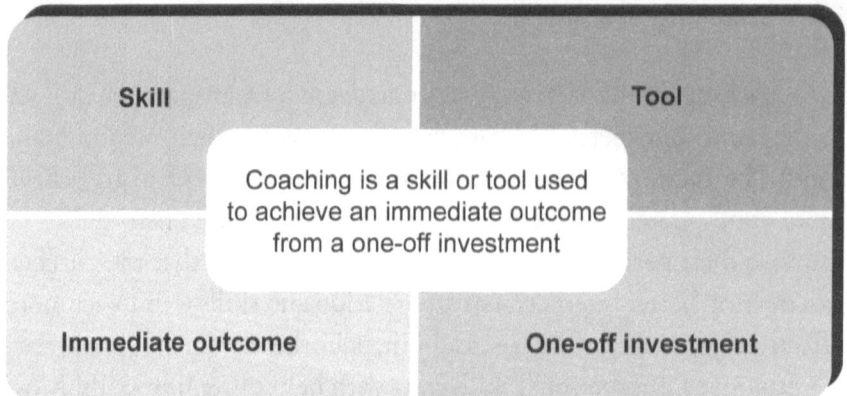

Figure 3.3: Coaching is a Skill or Tool

3.1.2 Coaching Is a Tool

When managers view coaching as a tool, the focus is on how coaching can be used to achieve a particular result, for example, to transfer learning from training programs into real-work application, innovate on a specific action or procedure, or re-engineer a tried and proven system or process. Some leaders who are trained in the use of proprietary software to identify business opportunities use coaching as a tool to show team members how to better interact with customers to win a greater number of sales. Coaching becomes a 'how to' tool within the leader's toolkit which allows them to have more open and robust conversations with colleagues and external stakeholders, thereby building stronger and deeper relationships with customers. When coaching is viewed as a tool that enables engagement and improved performance, the perception of coaching as 'weird' and 'fluffy', a 'fringe' activity, and a 'waste of time' is replaced by an appreciation of the ways that coaching can be used to benefit individuals and improve performance outcomes.

> *Primarily it's about giving them the tools and helping them to set their own goals and direction and keeping them, sort of, motivated and engaged to achieve those goals.*

3.1.3 Coaching Achieves an Immediate Outcome

In this first stage, coaching is seen as an immediate fix to resolve a problem or issue. Managers may have tried to fix the issue themselves but have been unsuccessful, and now they're at their wits' end. Hence, referral to an external coach is seen as the answer because, in this early stage of developing a coaching culture, coaching is viewed as a task-focused activity to achieve a particular outcome. Coaches help individuals break down the problem or issue into smaller chunks against which actions can be assigned to better manage the situation and achieve the desired outcome. In every job, there are a multitude of tasks to be completed, and whilst the individual may have both the motivation and the skill to complete some of those tasks, they don't necessarily have the motivation and skill to complete all the tasks. This is where a coaching conversation can fill the gap. However, in this early stage, managers may not understand how and why coaching should be considered as an intervention. They just want the problem to be fixed—immediately! They see coaching as, "*That's not my job. I'm not a coach. That's why I sent you to coaching.*" It's only in the last decade or so that coaching has started to become accepted as a valid development tool in organisations, often associated with its earliest use as a sports-related intervention:

> *I've been a rugby coach at the highest level, first grade. I can't play the game for my players. What I have to do is equip my team or individuals within a team . . . with the necessary skills, attributes, and standards of proficiency in terms of the profession that they had chosen.*

3.1.4 Coaching Is a One-Off Investment

When coaching is viewed as an investment to solve a problem or issue, it has been likened to a *fast-burn fire* which brings about an immediate outcome. The fire is lit, burns quickly, turns around the situation, and can be put out just as quickly. In an organisational context, coaching at this early stage brings about quick changes in an individual's behaviour or performance. Like a fire, individuals who are coached are expected to need coaching only once and learn from it. It is a one-off investment to achieve a particular outcome. Using the sporting analogy, individuals who are coached are offered insights that are outside of their own head and physical experience because, when 'in play', they are totally 'in the moment' and there's no time to self-reflect. However, from their new awareness as a result of being coached, they can make the changes they need to make almost immediately to save their job or career. Alternatively, they may decide to exit the organisation. The outcomes of the *fast-burn fire* approach to coaching are obvious both on the sporting field and in an organisational context.

Overall, when an organisation is in the first stage of developing a coaching culture, coaching is conceptualised as a skill set or tool of professional external coaches. An immediate outcome is required from the coaching.

3.2 Instrumental Motivation

In this first stage, managers who arrange for their difficult or problem person to be coached use coaching as an instrument to fix the individual and resolve the situation. The issue often relates to someone who is underperforming because of their behaviour, and their underperformance may also be affecting the team's performance, for example, because of conflict in the workplace. The individual is sent to coaching for *remedial* purposes related to their underperformance, but sometimes, it's just a 'box ticking' exercise so that the manager can say they have complied with the requirements of the organisation's performance management system or with legislative requirements before exiting the individual from the business.

3.2.1 'Fix' a Problem

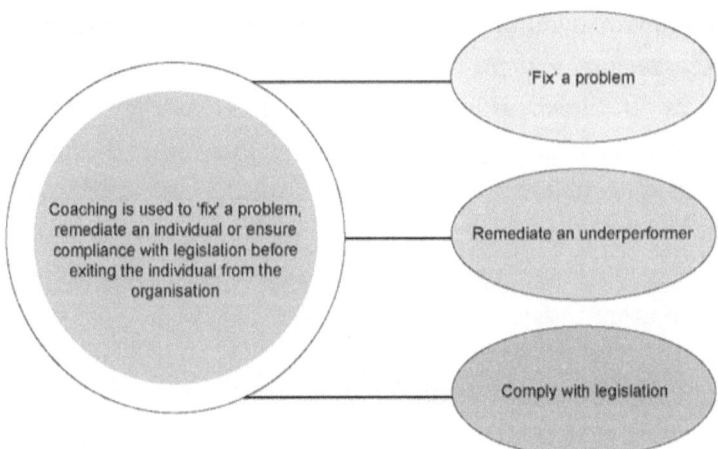

Figure 3.3: Coaching-is used to 'fix' a problem

In this first stage, an individual who is 'sent to coaching' approaches it with trepidation, knowing that, as an underperformer or badly behaved individual, this may be their last chance to redeem themselves or be exited from the organisation. For this reason, when coaching is used as an instrument to address poor performance or bad behaviour, there is often a *stigma* attached to being sent to coaching. External coaches typically refuse to fix an individual who has been 'sent to coaching', but they may undertake remedial coaching if the individual is considered to have the potential to improve.

3.2.2 Remediate an Underperformer

The role of a coach is not to fix an individual; it is to assist the individual identify barriers or constraints to their performance or behaviour and find ways to resolve these roadblocks. The individual may be performing well in a number of areas, but they're 'not firing on all cylinders'. In this instance, an external coach works with the coachee to identify the issues holding back their performance or affecting their behaviour and help them address these issues step by step until the situation is resolved. Unfortunately, this instrumental motivation for coaching does not take into account other factors that may be impacting on the individual's ability to perform, for example, the organisational context, systems, and processes; interpersonal relationships; or team dynamics. If the organisation is to progress to the next stage in developing a coaching culture, all these factors must be unpacked by the coach as possible areas of concern to assist the individual gain clarity in relation to their situation and how to resolve it. Fortunately, the view of coaching as a 'fix it' instrument of change is becoming less prevalent in organisations today.

> *When I first started coaching it was more seen for remedial. It wasn't a development focus. It was much more,* There's something wrong. Can you fix this person? *Nowadays, it's seen as almost like exercise. It's a fundamental part of professional development.*

3.2.3 Comply with Legislation

In this early stage of developing a coaching culture, many organisations use coaching as a 'box-ticking exercise' so that they can say, "*We do coaching*". In such circumstances, there's no real meaning behind the coaching because individuals aren't being held to account for their behaviours. Some line managers may be invested in seeing employees improve; others may simply be 'going through the motions' to comply with legislative requirements before 'letting go' an employee. For example, an executive coach tells the story of meeting with a partner in one of the major legal firms who told him that they use coaching as a 'last resort' to prove that they've done the 'right thing' before they exit someone from the business. As organisations progress in their understanding of coaching and how it can benefit them when they have the capability to conduct the 'tough discussions' with their direct reports rather than avoiding them, the *instrumental* motivation for coaching may change to *developmental*, which is the next stage in the development of a coaching culture.

Overall, when an organisation is in the first stage of developing a coaching culture, the motivation of coaching is *instrumental*. Individuals are coached to fix a problem that the line manager has been unable to resolve. Alternatively, the motivation for coaching may be to comply with legislative requirements.

3.3 Individual Drivers

The key drivers of coaching in this first stage of developing a coaching culture are managers positioned within the line management structure. They identify an individual who is underperforming and send them for coaching; alternatively, they may simply flick the problem to another manager. In certain circumstances, managers may give up on their ability to resolve the problem, unable to cope with the situation or fearful of an employee backlash, that is, employee claims of being bullied or harassed by the manager. Both the manager and the problem individual may become increasingly stressed as time goes by if the situation is not resolved quickly.

> *You've got people who are entrenched in a certain culture who don't speak to their staff whom, to manage someone, they'll just flick them over to another team.*

3.3.1 Line Managers Arrange for Coaching to be Conducted

Problems with underperformers are recognised at the line management level by managers of individuals who are underperforming, not pulling their weight, causing disruption within the team, or behaving rudely or aggressively. Consequently, team morale may slip, and there may be strained relationships or conflict within the team. The line manager wants the individual's performance or behaviour to improve so that they can become a fully functioning member of the team again and so that good working relationships can be restored within the team. In this early stage, line managers believe that an external coach is the best, and possibly the only, person who can deal with the individual and the situation. This view may have been formed after the line manager had a conversation with an external coach which triggered some insight or perspective around the challenge, resulting in the line manager thinking differently or realising that they may not be the best person to deliver the coaching because they're too close to the individual in their team. If the individual needs to make drastic changes in the way they perform or behave, this may require a completely new set of behaviours—a different style of engaging with people—and completely new outcomes to be achieved through coaching within a very short time.

    The line manager may have already tried to resolve the situation by using the organisation's performance management policies and procedures but without success, or their efforts may have been thwarted by legislative impediments, for example, in a unionised environment in which "*the legislation is so rigorous around getting rid of someone as such that you've got to go through a lot of hurdles to do that.*" Increasingly, employees may claim harassment or bullying by a line manager who tries to have them change their behaviour or performance as the following story illustrates:

> *So when it's a difficult person . . . what could happen is that person could turn around and say,* I'm being bullied, you know, Blah blah blah. *And so managers are running scared, and they don't manage. And I'm not saying that this is rife, but there is an element of this that has existed, and they're just flicking the problem over to someone else 'cause they don't want to manage the problem themself.*

3.3.2 Coaching Is Positioned with the Line Management Structure

In this first stage of developing a coaching culture, employees are sent to coaching by managers who just don't see that they have had any part to play in bringing about the situation and definitely have no intention of remediating it. They don't see that they are part of the system which created the problem. They see the individual's performance as separate from their own, and sending an individual to coaching is the only part that they have to play in making things right. Line managers who behave in this way leave the responsibility to fix the problem to an external coach when, in fact, it may be the manager who also needs coaching. Managers may know that coaching is a good thing because the research says that it is, but they don't want to coach or be coached. They tell themselves that they don't need coaching but that others do. Transferring their responsibility to fix an individual to an external coach is a completely different approach to that of leaders in more advanced stages of developing a coaching culture in which leaders want to learn how to coach and consider coaching to be a core capability that they require as a leader.

Overall, when an organisation is in the first stage of developing a coaching culture, line managers are the drivers of coaching. They send individuals to coaching and do not see themselves as in any way responsible for the situation even though they are part of the system that created the problem. They arrange for coaching to be conducted by an external coach to resolve the situation or for the individual to leave the organisation.

3.4 Outsourced Delivery

In this first stage of developing a coaching culture, coaching is outsourced to external or executive coaches who have the requisite skills to work with individuals to

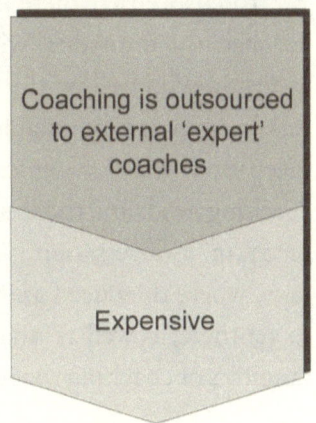

achieve the outcomes that the line manager desires. However, engaging an external coach to conduct a number of coaching sessions with an underperforming individual can be expensive, particularly if the individual decides to leave the organisation during or after the coaching, in which case the ROI to the organisation has not been realised.

3.4.1 Coaching Is Outsourced to External 'Expert' Coaches

Managers do not usually have the motivation or the skills to undertake individual coaching unless they have been formally trained as a coach. When an external coach is to be engaged to coach a problem individual, the manager approaches HR, who sets up an initial meeting for them with a coach, and together they establish the basis on which the coaching will be conducted. The coach gains information from the line manager about the context, purpose, and desired outcomes of the coaching program. Are they realistic? How will personal issues be handled if they arise? What are the ethical principles around coaching, confidentiality, accountability, and trust? The external coach also wants to obtain a clear understanding from the line manager as to the outcomes that are expected. Dates for triangulation meetings are agreed at suitable intervals. Afterwards and before the coaching commences, the coach will usually informally contract with the problem individual in addition to the formal contract they have with the organisation to make sure they are both on the same page before coaching commences.

To ensure that there is a chemistry match between the coach and coachee, the individual will usually meet with more than one coach to ascertain who will be the best fit for them so that a trusting coaching relationship can be established. Once the coach is selected, an initial 'deep-dive' goal-setting session is conducted to identify the individual's coaching needs and the specific goals to be achieved through the coaching program. Conversation is around determining where the individual is now, where they need and want to be, what key milestones are needed to get there, as well as what timelines and measures of success are—the tangibles of coaching that can be reported against as necessary. The next step is to gather information from a psychometric or similar assessment instrument to provide the individual with a reality check on how they and their behaviours, communication, relationship, and leadership styles are viewed by others around them, including any direct reports. There are a number of commercially available 360-degree instruments in the marketplace that the coach can use to obtain a behavioural profile on the individual before coaching commences. Alternatively, the organisation may have a preferred instrument that they use.

Then the coaching begins. Results from the 360-degree assessment are fed back to the individual as the coach guides the coachee towards self-awareness and insight, leading to behavioural and performance change. A close one-on-one coaching relationship is formed as the coach gets to know the individual and understand their coaching needs. Over four to six sessions to start with, although at times it may take up to sixteen sessions to shift mindsets and consciousness, the coaching conversations elicit the individual's concerns, hopes, and dreams before learning goals are identified and a personal development plan created with follow-up actions over time. At the end of the coaching program, a meeting of all parties determines if the coaching has been successful and if there is a need or desire to continue. A post-360-degree assessment is conducted to assess the effects of the coaching over the previous period of, say, six- to twelve-months.

3.4.2 Coaching Is Expensive

Delivering coaching to individuals can be expensive especially when many coaching sessions are conducted or many individuals are to be coached. The cost of the coaching comes out of the line manager's budget. However, the budget may not have an allocation for coaching, and hence, it may stretch business unit resources. Perhaps for this reason or when alternative motivations come into play, the organisation may take steps to progress to the next stage of developing a coaching culture where the cost of hiring external coaches is born by the HR budget.

Overall, when an organisation is in the first stage of developing a coaching culture, coaching is delivered by an outsourced, professional, expert coach who has the required skill set to remediate an underperforming individual and resolve the situation. Coaching can be expensive and may not be included in the line manager's budget.

3.5 Summary of Stage 1

Coaching-as-Intervention

In summary, the *utilitarian conceptualisation* of coaching at the *Coaching-as-Intervention* stage is as a skill set or tool that is task-focused, providing an immediate solution to solve a particular problem or situation. The *instrumental motivation* for coaching is to fix a problem—usually an individual. The underperformer is required to become more capable and productive or risk being exited from the organisation. A stigma is often attached to remedial coaching, which is seen as a last resort since the manager may simply be going through the motions to comply with legislative requirements before they exit the individual from the organisation. The *individual drivers* of coaching in this first stage are line managers who may have used the organisation's performance management system to try to remediate the individual but with no success. In some organisations, performance management is just a 'box ticking' exercise. At other times, a difficult employee may be flicked to another department because of the manager's fear of being charged with claims of harassment or bullying as a result of their attempts to remediate the individual themself. The *outsourced delivery* of coaching is conducted by an external coach to resolve the issue or improve an individual's performance. However, engaging in external coaching services can be expensive and puts a strain on the line manager's budget, particularly when there are large numbers of individuals to be coached over a long time.

3.6 Case Studies

Stage 1
Coaching-as-Intervention

In this chapter and the three that follow, a number of case studies are presented to illustrate the predominant thinking and purposes for which coaching is conducted in a particular organisation at this stage in their development of a coaching culture. The case studies are included so that the reader can reflect on whether the stories in these case studies resonate with activities in your organisation, as a way of assessing which stage of development your organisation is at in terms of developing a coaching culture. Alternatively, the case studies may be used in an academic setting for students to discuss the different characteristics of organisations at the different stages, and ways that the organisation can progress to a more advanced stage.

Readers should note that, whilst the stages in the development of a coaching culture appear progressive, they are, in fact, dynamic. That is, an organisation can regress to previous stages if significant events cause progress to be halted, for example, by the exit of a committed CEO, lack of funding, or an organisational restructure or takeover.

These case studies were developed from interviewee reports of activities being undertaken in their organisation to develop a coaching culture. Readers will note that the number of case studies presented to illustrate each stage diminishes from the first to fourth stage which, from anecdotal reports, is consistent with the number of organisations in general which have been able to commit to, fund, maintain and sustain a coaching culture.

Pseudonyms are used in all these case studies.

Case Study 1

TotalCare is a not-for-profit organisation in the aged care/disability sector. The organisation has approximately 500 support workers. Bella worked in TotalCare as a Learning Consultant for six years but left the organisation ten months ago as a result of unresolved bullying. She claimed that she was unfairly treated and bullied by her manager, Lisa, who was a peer before being promoted. Lisa's adverse behaviour included having conversations with the team and not including Bella and cancelling the training that Bella had organised and not telling her. Lisa was treating another team member the same way. Bella did her best to *"stay out of her way"*. As a result of this treatment, the relationship between Bella and Lisa became *"non-existent"*. Bella knew that the CEO, Megan, was aware of Lisa's behaviour but didn't do anything about it, so there was *"no point in putting in a complaint"*. However, when she couldn't take it anymore, Bella went directly to Megan and asked for assistance. Megan engaged an external coach whom she had used before and who was, in fact, her coach (but Bella didn't know that at the time).

The external coach, Maryanne, had worked as a consultant/coach to TotalCare for a number of years. Megan had used her services before with staff who were experiencing issues. For example, the manager previous to Lisa, Eliza, was promoted to the manager role when she didn't have the skills or experience to do the job. As a consequence, Eliza did not provide all the necessary information to her team members, undermined certain staff who didn't agree with her, and created divisions within the team between those she favoured and those she couldn't control. As a result, one team member had developed mental health issues and was 'let go' rather than the organisation dealing with the problem. Another example was when Maryanne coached a 'delightful manager', Dave, but someone with poor management skills who was 'sent to coaching' to be remediated as a result of complaints from team members.

However, the coaching was ineffective and *"didn't end well"*, with Dave being *"managed out"*. A third example was in relation to the manager of TotalCare's day service, Trevor, who was quite dysfunctional and aggressive. He was 'sent to coaching' but the problem was 'not fixed' and is still ongoing —after seven years!

Bella and Maryanne started her 'supervision', which was then *"turned back on me"* with the mention of the possibility of dismissal. Six coaching sessions were conducted at Maryanne's home, which was being renovated at the time. The first session was all about the renovations that were being undertaken. In the next session, they talked about *"how Bella approached the world"*, and she vividly remembers Maryanne telling her that she had *"angry hair"*. From Bella's point of view, the best thing that came out of her coaching sessions with Maryanne was when she said, *"Every day, we paint a picture of who we are in the workplace"*, and people either say, *"Wow"* or *"It's not a good place to be"*. As an aside, Maryanne did say that when Bella's line manager, Lisa, was 'pushed', she would *"come out firing"*, which meant to Bella that she was *"not going nuts"*. Bella found out later that Maryanne had also coached Lisa, but in relation to Bella's situation, she *"made it my fault that we were in conflict"*. Bella derived no benefit from the coaching because her concerns were constantly *"swept under the carpet"* by Maryanne.

When another executive took over running the department, Lisa's behaviour *"accelerated"*, which resulted in a *"huge altercation"* between her and Bella, and there was talk of Bella being made redundant. The new executive, Jack, took over Bella's management, and Bella got more out of working with him than she did from working with Maryanne because, even though Jack was *"trying to performance manage me out"*, he did it in a way that Bella could *"leave on my own terms"*.

> Jack left TotalCare six months later because his numerous attempts to implement different practices, policies, and procedures had failed because the CEO, Megan, was unwilling to make any changes.

Case Study 2

> *BLGC Corp.* employs approximately 400 people and services five regional communities across its extensive, isolated, outback government jurisdiction. Tricia worked for BLGC for two and a half years in the role of Workforce Planning Coordinator responsible for organisational capability, succession planning, and current and future workforce scenarios. An incident occurred whilst she was in the role of Acting HR Director for two weeks when the HR Director, Rosy, was on leave. It involved the senior manager in charge of the asset team, Bill, who had approximately half the staff reporting to him. Even since he was appointed twelve months ago, Bill had been badly behaved—shouting at staff, not giving balanced feedback, embarrassing staff in front of others, and swearing. These behaviours were accepted by the organisation as *"that's just the way Bill is"* and *"don't worry about it . . . just get on with your work"*. As a result, some of his bad behaviours had filtered down to managers and team leaders in his department.
>
> However, as new employees were appointed to teams within his department, they began to question some of these behaviours. They were not used to this kind of management and enlisted the help of the union organiser, Mike, to *"push it up to HR"*. Mike phoned Tricia *"in confidence and off the record"* to see what could be done. They arranged to meet, and Tricia committed to *"get some more information and insight"* into the situation.
>
> Over the following week, Tricia met with the team members who had complained about Bill's behaviour and then brought the situation

to the attention of the General Manager, Ted who acknowledged the concern but said, *"That's the way Bill is. He's very passionate but gets very stressed"*. Tricia told Ted that she had spoken to Bill and informed him that there were *"lots of concerns about his blow-ups"* and that this behaviour was not appropriate. As Bill was well known to Rosy, who would be back to work the following week, Ted decided to leave it until then so that she could address the situation.

When Rosy retuned to work, Tricia completed a handover with her, and one of the top items to address was Bill's behaviour. She provided Rosy with the details that had emerged from her investigation of the situation, to which the Rosy responded, *"This has happened before, and it was not managed well"*. Tricia was *"pretty shocked about this"*. She was concerned that with union involvement, *"this could go pear-shaped and go further in terms of its effect on BLGC"*. Tricia suggested the option of coaching to 'fix' the situation, a suggestion which was *"taken very positively"* by Rosy. It took a month or two to gain an appointment with Ted (because of internal 'politics'—if Bill was more senior, the situation would have been dealt with more quickly), after which Tricia was asked to seek providers of professional coaching services.

Tricia met with a few external coaches to 'vet' them because the situation was sensitive and the coach would be dealing with someone with a *"strong ego"* who had not been managed well in the past. It was important to get the right 'fit'—someone who *"understood his ego"* and made a good connection with him. At the same time, Tricia had identified some team leaders who were showing promise from a talent management perspective and arranged for them to be coached as well. She may have been trying to defuse the situation in relation to Bill's behaviour, although she did recognise the need for *"that type of intervention"* (coaching) as a talent management strategy that would be 'proactive in helping these team leaders take the next step' and an especially good opportunity for them to develop *"self-awareness and insight"*.

Meanwhile, Ted spoke with Bill to see if he was *"happy to give it [coaching] a go"*. When Bill agreed, an external coach, Mitchell, was engaged to conduct the coaching with him. Mitchell was very subtle in his approach, but he also *"called it as it was"*, got Bill to see the bigger picture, and worked with him over the next nine months. Afterwards, they continued to meet for coffee for a while. Tricia admits that *"it was a risk . . . it could have gone either way"*. Bill could have just been 'ticking the box' to say that he had complied with the coaching intervention.

Towards the end of the coaching, Tricia asked Mike, in confidence, how things were going. She didn't mention that Bill had received coaching as it was something new to the organisation, and if the 'grapevine' got hold of this word, it would be associated with counselling, which was not highly regarded. Mike reported that there had been no concerns or complaints raised by staff about Bill's behaviour over the past six months. Hence, Tricia concluded that *"as an intervention, it [coaching] was very good"*. In addition, she reported that *"the organisation thought it was great too"*. However, coaching did not continue within BLGC as shortly after the coaching with Bill ended, the organisation underwent a series of restructures.

Case Study 3

HealthBubs provides specialist, medical intervention services to patients using state-of-the-art technology and equipment. The organisation employs 500 people in Australia and overseas. An external coach, Craig, was contracted to assist a team leader, Jack, who had a problem with one of his direct reports. It was a behavioural issue concerning how one of the scientists, Sharon, interacts with others in the laboratory environment. Scientists do not, in general, have good 'people skills', but this individual was even worse—rude, abrupt, and verbally aggressive. She railed at and questioned everything that was requested of her and wanted to know how everything was done.

In the first two coaching sessions, Craig let Sharon vent and waited until she had offloaded all her issues. She complained about everything, pushing blame onto everybody else. She was an *"angry young lady"*. In the third session, Craig asked her, *"What are you trying to achieve?"* There was a long pause, and Sharon started to cry. She said, *"I have so much to offer, and no one's listening to me. I can add so much value so we can get ahead of the game"*. Craig asked her what she had done to get people to listen to her and what she could do differently. She replied that no one takes her seriously and that her team leader, Jack, doesn't respect anything she says. The coach discovered that Sharon had the respect of another team leader, Melissa. He prompted her to meet with Melissa and chat about her ideas.

In the next coaching session, Sharon beamed, *"You would be so proud of me!"* She had met with Melissa, who was impressed with her innovative ideas and said that she would speak with Jack about them. Sharon then met with Jack, who was *"gobsmacked"* that she was *"laughing not attacking"*. They discussed her ideas and talked about the process of creating innovation. As a result, Sharon came to understand how things are done from an organisational perspective. As the weeks went by, Craig continued to work with Sharon to change her *"victim, attacking, aggressive"* behavioural style into more appropriate ways of behaving so that she would be heard in the future.

As a result of her changed behaviour, Sharon was appointed to head up a new innovation team and sent to the United States to compare ideas and learn best practice. She is now presenting to the national scientific community. From a person with aggressive behaviour, she has changed into a team leader working with innovation. HealthBubs was amazed at how personally transformative coaching can be, even in the technical space.

Craig subsequently discovered that even when Sharon was growing up, no one heard her, and her voice didn't count. He concluded that the value of the coaching program and the turning point for her was when she realised that "*I create my behaviour*". Consequently, as a result of her improved behaviour and interpersonal skills, people now listen to her. The benefit to the organisation was that they retained a talented scientist and team morale lifted, as did the organisation's reputation when they started working in the innovation space.

Case Study 4

StateTrans delivers statewide transport solutions. It was created twelve months ago as an amalgamation of a number of government departments with the intention of breaking the culture of existing 'silos' to form a modern, customer-focused organisation. The new entity inherited a large number of engineers who were 'old school' and not 'people persons'. They have never had another job and continued to be fiercely loyal to their previous department, holding onto old ways, traditions, and expectations. To them, coaching is a tool to 'fix' a problem or exit an individual, with no thought being given to identifying the underlying cause. Peppered within this 'old school' group of employees are new leaders who have been recruited since the new entity was formed, who are supportive of coaching for developmental purposes.

The continuing problem for the new CEO, Dennis, is that the 'old school' employees will remain in the new organisation until retirement age to ensure that they receive all their entitlements and defined benefits. Hence, cultural change will be five to ten years away. An additional concern is that his 2IC, Brian, who was retained from a previous organisation, has a bullying style. Hence, whilst Dennis is supportive of people's development and very approachable, Brian continues to display an aggressive management style in his interactions with everyone in the organisation, including key external stakeholders.

Worrying for Dennis is that Brian's aggressive style has been remarked on in government circles over the past twenty years, but no one has ever done anything about it. His behaviour has been accepted and gone unchallenged. The dilemma for Dennis is to decide if, how, and when he challenges Brian's behaviour before it starts to affect StateTrans's standing in the community. Or should he just hope that as the new organisational leaders 'make their mark', they will have a significant impact on Brian and the organisation's culture? Realistically, Dennis knows that this scenario is unlikely and that cultural change is going to be a long way off and won't happen until Brian and the 'old school' brigade have retired.

Case Study 5

ConCare is a small government department of approximately 1,500 employees who are mainly scientists in various fields relating to nature and conservation. The scientists are highly intelligent and well-educated people focused on their job and how they preserve the natural environment, but their 'soft skills' are limited. In ConCare, coaching is positioned within the culture and performance team, which is responsible for organisational culture and leadership development. ConCare has a long-standing mentoring program with senior executives as the mentors. The organisation is at the stage of delineating how coaching is different from mentoring. A few senior executives have been coached by external coaches so they understand the value and benefits of coaching as opposed to mentoring. They are open to coaching and overtly coach their direct reports.

Within ConCare, employees understand that leadership is not necessarily hierarchical but behavioural, and therefore, everyone can lead. Coaching is considered to be a highly effective way of developing people to be high-achieving as well as supporting a workplace culture that empowers individuals and enables success. Leaders believe that coaching is about unlocking an individual's potential by asking the right questions. Hence, coaching is an opportunity for individuals to look both inside and outside of themselves so that they're uncovering their inner wisdom to manage themselves and others more effectively.

ConCare has a performance framework which includes coach-type conversations to give employees formal one-on-one feedback which helps them perform better in their role. However, as it's early days, anyone searching for coaching on the intranet would find no reference to this service at all. When required, formal, matched coaching relationships are arranged for nominated individuals so that developmental coaching can occur. The cultural performance team knows that their task is to become more purposeful in developing more employees—giving them the skills to coach and understanding the value of it. And because the organisation will soon have five generations in the workplace who need to be coached, team members are considering instigating 'reverse' coaching into the organisation, that is, more senior people being coached by junior people - but that's just talk at the moment. If ConCare makes a decision to proceed with coaching, the culture and performance team will develop the infrastructure for coaching and establish a register of coaches from whom all employees can proactively seek to be coached.

CHAPTER 4

STAGE 2
COACHING-AS-HR-FUNCTION

The second stage in developing a coaching culture is labelled *Coaching-as-HR-function*. During this stage, coaching resides within the HR function, which is responsible for the training of leaders in coaching skills and the delivery of coaching to individuals in the organisation. Coaching is characterised by a *pedagogical conceptualisation* of coaching as a training and learning experience; a *developmental* motivation for coaching to change mindset and behaviour, improve individual performance, and support career progression; *functional drivers* for coaching positioned within the HR function to build the infrastructure and support for coaching; and *targeted delivery* of coaching to leaders and talented individuals within the organisation.

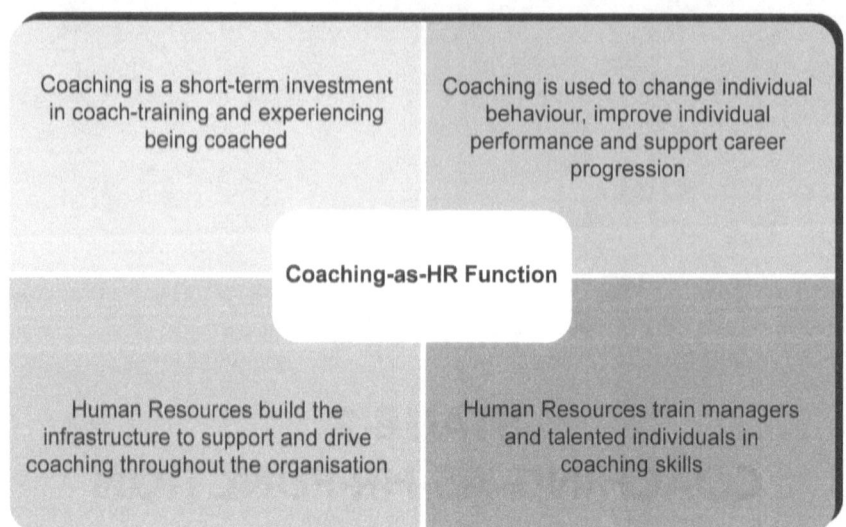

Figure 4.1: Coaching-as-HR-Function Stage

4.1 Pedagogical Conceptualisation

In the *Coaching-as-HR-Function* stage, coaching is conceptualised as a training and learning experience. HR professionals, selected organisational leaders, and talented individuals are trained in coaching skills or formally qualified as coaches by external coach-training providers and experience being coached. The training and coaching experience allows them to build stronger and deeper relationships with others. It is a short-term investment in valued employees who are committed to building the organisation's human capital as they transfer their skills to others in the business.

4.1.1 HR Professionals Are Trained in Coaching Skills or as qualified Coaches and Experience Being Coached

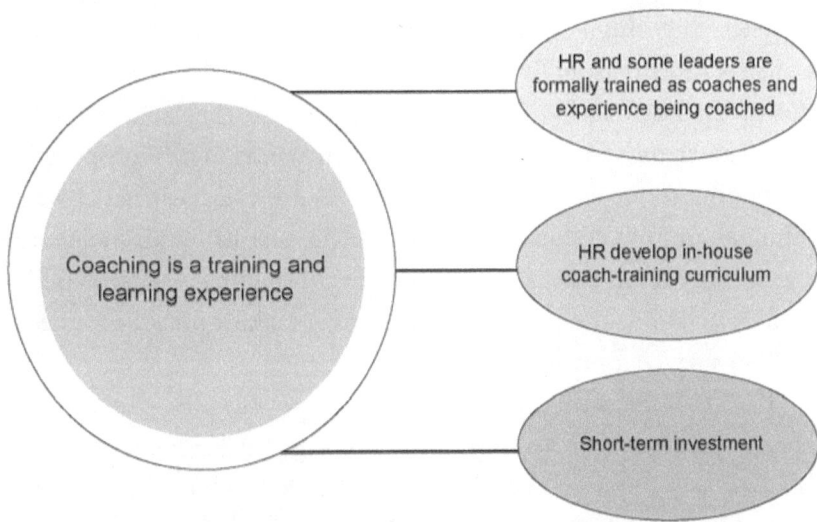

Figure 4.2: Coaching is a training and learning experience

Organisations which invest in formally training HR professionals, selected organisational leaders, and talented individuals as coaches have made a decision to bring coaching skills into the organisation in the most cost-effective, short-term way. These individuals learn what coaching is all about, develop coaching competencies, and learn how to coach their direct reports to help them resolve their own problems, goal set, and action plan. The coach-training that is conducted should be approved to international standards as proposed by organisations like the International Coach Federation. A additional component of the coach-training program is usually the delivery of individual coaching sessions so that participants experience being coached and come to understand what coaching is all about. From their experience, they *"get it in their heart and guts"* as well as in their head, which makes all the difference in terms of their understanding of how powerful coaching can be, and their subsequent advocacy for coaching as a valid developmental process for change.

During their coach-training, HR professionals and selected others develop an understanding of coaching as an instrument that promotes self-development by consistently, in every interaction, encouraging self-awareness and insight. Utilising coaching skills allows HR professionals to engage more personally with individuals to meet their specific needs, play to their strengths, and bring their best to the table, as well as appreciate the diversity that exists in their teams. Through listening, questioning for exploration and discovery, and summarising, coaching facilitates improved communication, collaboration, and cooperation among individuals and within teams. It enables conversations based on trust, motivation, and positive intent, which make it possible for deeper issues to surface for discussion.

The analogy of a horse-drawn carriage explains the coaching process: *"Back in the olden days, the coach was that horse-drawn carriage that took very important people—so you had to be rich—from one place to another. It takes people from where they are now to where they want to be."* This analogy supports the concept of coaching as a vehicle for forward movement to arrive at a particular destination, that is, a specific coaching outcome. In order to do this, coaches need to believe that the individual they are coaching is a most important person at that moment in time, whom they're going to help get from where they are now to where they want to be.

4.1.2 HR Professionals Develop In-House Coach-Training Curriculum

Organisations in this second stage of developing a coaching culture want to become self-sufficient in training all managers in coaching skills, which is understandable from a financial point of view. The way they do this is to fund HR professionals and selected others to become formally qualified as coaches by external providers, who then design coaching skills curriculum for all managers based on what they have learnt in their formal coach-training, and customise it to meet organisational needs. Thereafter, they provide follow-up support until coaching practice is fully embedded within the organisation. This strategy doesn't require the major investment that would have been necessary if the coaching skills training was delivered by an external coach-training provider.

The coach-training curriculum that is developed in-house may consist of, say, three key training programs based on leaders' tenure, functionality, and anticipated career progression within the organisation. The design of such programs takes time since there are many stakeholders to consider and functional groups within the organisation whose specific needs must be accommodated within these programs. The time taken to approve such programs within the HR function may take longer than in a customer-facing business unit because of the many policies and procedures to take into account within the HR environment. When the responsibility for coaching is positioned within a business unit, as it is in the next stage of developing a coaching culture, there is a sense of urgency to gaining approvals because every interaction counts towards a business win or loss.

4.1.3 Coaching Is a Short-Term Investment

In this second stage, the coach-training of HR professionals and selected others is a short-term investment in increasing their leadership capability and ability to coach. Unfortunately, in many organisations, once the budget for coach-training is exhausted, the programs cease and the funding has to be renewed year-on-year to keep the initiative alive. At this stage in the development of a coaching culture, it is rare that an organisation will allocate recurrent funding to the provision of coach-training unless it is on the path to developing a coaching culture, as this organisational leader explains:

> *I think that having such a program in place for five years is testament to the success of the program—testament to the impact organisationally and culturally that it's had.*

Overall, when an organisation is in the second stage of developing a coaching culture, coaching is conceptualised as a training and learning experience for HR professionals, selected organisational leaders, and talented individuals to develop their coaching skills and experience being coached. HR professionals may go on to design an in-house coach-training curriculum which can be delivered across the whole organisation.

4.2 Developmental Motivation

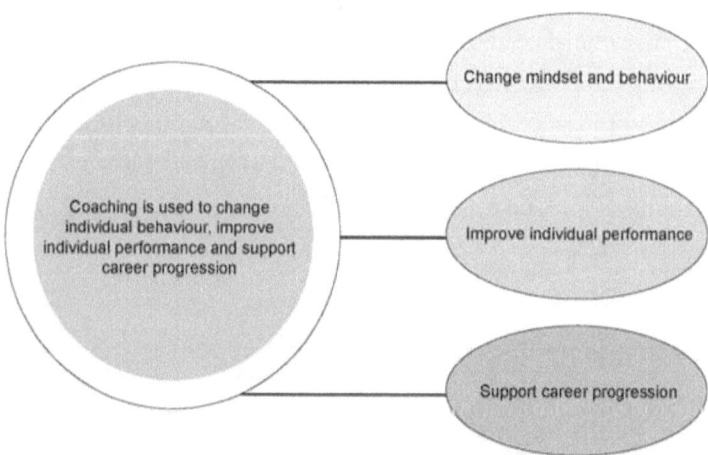

Figure 4.3: Coaching changes individual behaviour

In this second stage, the motivation for coaching is *developmental*. Coaching is specifically focused on assisting individuals develop greater self-awareness and insight so that they shift their mindset from a *management* style of interacting with their direct reports to a *coaching leadership style* which supports individuals to change their behaviour, improve their performance, and enhance their career progression.

4.2.1 Change Mindset and Behaviour

The *developmental* motivation for coaching is to train HR professionals and selected others in coaching skills so that they will coach their direct reports. Coaching has two key intentions: to ensure that individuals are serving a higher-order purpose and to help them translate that into behaviours that promote positive and effective action. Behavioural coaching that is conducted one-on-one with individuals can be revelationary, helping coachees achieve their goals and progress in their career faster than they normally would. As individuals start to better perform in their role, the focus of the coaching shifts to identifying the factors that support behavioural change and those that hold individuals back. Behavioural coaching is based on reinforcing the behaviours that lead the individual to be personally and professionally effective, and then asking what's going to stop them from being successful? The following story from an executive coach illustrates the reaction that some managers have when it dawns on them that they need to change their behaviour:

> *The guy basically was having massive behavioural issues, massive anger issues, and as he turned around, he went,* OMG! I've been doing this harm. I've affected my team. Come, please come and support my team.

During coaching, a behaviour profiling assessment may be used to identify the individual's strengths, weaknesses, and leadership style. However, even the use of this tool may be confronting to some individuals as this story illustrates: "*We just did a really light-on 360-degree assessment. It's nice. It's simple. People can relate to the colours, but my god! The pushback on that tool. It's just to start the conversation.*" Assessment is typically conducted with senior executives to improve their performance through behavioural change. It's also commonly used with individuals who have recently been promoted into a leadership role, particularly if they are transitioning from being in an operational to a strategic role or a technical into a more general management role. Coaching supports them to lead differently.

However, before an individual can change their behaviour, they may have to shift their mindset. This is especially true of managers who use a *command-and-control* approach to their direct reports. They may find it difficult to embrace a *coaching leadership style* of interacting with them instead. Managers who were brought up in the 'old school of management' see coaching as a sign of weakness. However, as coaching has been reinterpreted into a training and learning experience, they are encouraged to let go of their *command-and-control* management style and replace it with a *coaching leadership style*.

Many managers struggle when they are required to change from a *telling* to an *asking*, enabling, empowering, and supporting leadership style. Some readily change their style and thrive on the new challenge. Others may comply on the surface, but their *command-and-control* is still very much in play as an inherent, underlying behaviour even though very few employees have ever responded positively to such an approach. Hence, for those managers whose *command-and-control* style was previously an issue within their team, it may still be an issue after the training—just dressed up as coaching—and still problematic. This is especially the case when managers have resisted being personally coached.

When managers adopt a *coaching leadership style*, instead of telling employees, "*This is what I want done, and this is how I'd like you to do it, and this is when I'd like you to do it by,*" they would be asking open questions that support discovery so that their direct reports are working out what to do and how to do it by themselves. Their intention is to engage in more meaningful conversations with employees to enable and empower them to perform better and use their initiative. Three examples illustrate that the *command-and-control* management style is very much alive in organisations today, but changing. A large national telecommunications company was bought out by an overseas firm, which comes from a *command-and-control* cultural background. The new CEO had multiple strengths but no real understanding or appreciation of coaching. Hence, the coaching initiative, which had been ongoing for two years, was starved of funds and died. The second example illustrates what happened when a new CEO was appointed to an organisation which had been coaching for five years. She had no knowledge of coaching—what it is, how it is conducted, and what it can do. However, she allowed the coaching initiative to continue, which it did, supported by the dedicated HR professionals who knew and appreciated coaching. A third example illustrates the confusion of staff within a military organisation when the new commander, a leader who had just completed a formal coach-training course, used a coaching approach with his team: "*They were a bit taken aback. The guy who was in the position before me was very directive, commanding control, had a short temper, and you know, would just go ballistic at times with people.*" So when this leader sat down with his direct reports it was like, "*Wow! Nobody's ever done this before.*" It took team members a while to adjust because they didn't know how to respond to a more personal and empowering approach from their leader. They didn't know whether or not they could trust him based on their experiences with the previous leader.

A fourth example is indicative of organisations on the path to the next stage of developing a coaching culture. The leader of a HR function in a government department in which a coaching initiative has continued to be funded for five years describes coaching as "*exciting territory which is really shifting the public sector management and leadership from the old-school archaic* command-and-control *to where we need to be, to drive value for money and engage a motivated, adaptable workforce.*" He believes that coaching has the capacity to spread across the entire public sector in his state to influence and improve whole-of-government effectiveness.

> *I think that to move away from that old-school public sector mindset and really build that coaching environment is critical to neutralise the preciousness and sensitivity of the government environment and goes a long way to us being organisationally effective.*

4.2.2 Improve Individual Performance

In this second stage, coaching allows individuals to grow and their performance to improve in a safe environment. It reframes failures into learning experiences, which build the capability of individuals whose resilience encourages others to keep trying, perfecting, and reinventing their best possible future. Coaching provides valuable, constructive feedback, which enables individuals to move forward with greater clarity of role and direction towards agreed targets. "*So it would be for them, instead of,* Oh you're naughty. You got it wrong, *it would be,* Okay, well, that's interesting. What did you learn from that? What would you do differently? *And that would be the standard response of everybody to everything . . . a way to fail safely and learn for the future.*"

The desired outcome of performance improvement is the achievement of KPIs. When KPIs are not being achieved or the individual is not performing in a certain area, a scheduled coaching session is conducted to discuss the situation. The leader has a coaching conversation with the coachee that's very specific as to what the individual needs to do to better perform in their role because that's how they will be measured, and to discuss the impact on the team dynamic of their non-performance. For busy leaders, coaching needs to become a KPI in their position description lest it doesn't occur post-training, as one leader signals: "*If there's no KPI, if there's no report required. If there's nothing that I have to give to anyone to prove I've done something, I might get to it if I have time.*" Hence, it's not as 'black and white' as "*You've just done a [coach-training] program. Now you've got a KPI to coach.*" Measuring this KPI shows how leaders are progressing towards meeting this performance objective. If non-performance is detected, a developmental coaching session needs to happen to support the busy leader make the time to coach their direct reports.

A major responsibility of leaders who coach is to actively remove business or systemic roadblocks or barriers to individual performance. This allows the individual to be the best person and performer they can be. Hence, coaching is more than just about helping an individual meet their KPIs. It's also about recognising their needs as a person.

An organisational leader who is responsible for the HR function of a multinational corporation at a state level explains: *"You have to actually have people on board. You can't have everyone leaving and on stress leave and putting in complaints about you, but heck, you met your KPIs, so we don't care about that."* Moreover, coaching to improve performance doesn't have to be conducted within a scheduled coaching session. Coaching conversations can occur as part of any interaction, during which a leader asks insightful questions to guide the individual to find their own solutions.

When leaders learn how to motive their staff developmentally through coaching, coaching conversations flow through all aspects of daily business, including how employees relate to their colleagues, resolve differences, manage problems, and run meetings to improve their own and others' performance. Hence, coaching which has a developmental motivation also has an operational component in the day-to-day when leaders provide constructive feedback on individual performance. However, in organisations which do not train their managers in coaching skills, the way that feedback is given, particularly in some front-line services functions, is very transactional. The supervisor listens to calls made to the operative, gives feedback on the operative's performance, and then engages in a conversation with the operative which, *"to be honest, it's probably not what I would consider coaching. It's probably more of just feedback on performance and a performance management type of conversation which has the beginnings of having a coaching conversation with staff, but it's not the real thing."* To encourage the take-up of coaching according to the International Coach Federation's core competencies for effective coaching, an organisation's recognition system might consider rewarding leaders who coach on a regular basis, or at least provide supervision for their coaching to maintain its quality.

4.2.3 Support Career Progression

Coaching has been identified as an important process to support career progression and retain valuable staff. Leaders at all levels of the organisation need to understand that coaching is not a 'nice to have' but an essential component of a leaders' responsibility because if employees are not engaged and don't feel that they're valued, that's when staff turnover sets in. Leaders who don't coach their direct reports end up with complaints because employees are not able to get the support they need. Having line managers understand that coaching can prevent high employee turnover is a massive exercise in a large organisation of, say, 60,000 or 70,000 people. The challenge is to help managers see the value and importance of coaching and then embrace the coaching of their direct reports so that they don't end up approaching HR to say, "*Oh, I've had another resignation. Can you help me?*" Leaders who conduct regular developmental coaching conversations with employees prevent resignations from occurring by providing specific feedback on employee performance, exploring ways to unlock their potential, and providing opportunities to improve their career prospects. Together, they develop a plan that's related to the employee's personal journey, guiding them to find their own solutions because they have all the answers. They just need some help getting there.

Some organisations use coaching as a reward for high achievers who, like elite athletes, go on to become even better performers, entering the organisation's talent pool and becoming part of the succession plan. In these organisations, *"the personal development aspect of coaching is quite phenomenal"*, and for these talented individuals, organisations are prepared to find the money to develop them and their careers. Members of the executive team sometimes automatically qualify for a coach when they enter the executive level: "*We take the development of our senior leaders seriously and find them mentors or coaches.*" An executive coach may be engaged for a number of sessions to support a 'higher-end manager'. As an example of the importance of coaching in a peak-performance environment, one organisation became motivated to use coaching to support the development, progression, and retention of talented individuals after experiencing the loss of a highly valued employee (and others) to an international competitor, as this story illustrates:

> *Ten years ago, an Australian law firm had a candidate who wanted to become a managing partner. He was passed over for that promotion. Within three months, a law firm came from Great Britain and started an office here. This particular partner took twenty lawyers with their client lists and went over to the British law firm. At that point, the Australian law firm started investing in coaching because they realised that the person was not coached or communicated to properly around the promotion and the career cycle. So it has to be a significant crisis for an organisation to take investment in coaching seriously . . . It's an expense, but in my personal experience, organisations are willing to spend the money if they can see a return on investment quickly.*

The above example demonstrates the need for organisations in this second stage of developing a coaching culture to not just claim they are motivated to develop talented individuals but also to demonstrate this motivation through the timely and targeted provision of coaching focused on individual employee needs and opportunities for growth. Coaching from a developmental motivation removes the 'stigma' of remedial coaching interventions in the first stage of developing a coaching culture and the resistance of 'old school' *command-and-control* managers in this second stage. Indeed, the developmental motivation for coaching shifts employees' views to the extent that being coached may seem more acceptable and even *prestigious*. The example also suggests that an enabling mechanism for progression towards developing a coaching culture beyond the second stage is the conversion of a developmental motivation for coaching into a business performance motivation in which the organisation is able to see and calculate an economic return on their coaching investment.

When coaching is considered to be *prestigious*, this view may indicate a potential challenge for an organisation to progress beyond the second stage because coaching may be seen as a *badge of honour*, which creates expectations amongst individuals that once they've reached a certain level in the organisation, they'll be entitled to a coach without actually knowing what a coach can do for them or even what they want from a coach. Individuals who seek coaching as a measure of their prestige or for entitlement reasons are unlikely to engage with coaching in a way that maximises its benefits, creating a very different experience and outcome that may limit their ability to move away from *command-and-control* behaviours.

Another challenge to progressing the organisation beyond the *Coaching-as-HR-Function* stage arises when systemic factors undermine realisation of the developmental motives for coaching, such as when certain individuals have demonstrated really poor behaviour and they have not been held accountable for that behaviour. For example, coaching of a talented financial controller in an important small division of a federal government department was unsuccessful because the individual held such an important role in the system that his aggressive attitude to staff was continually accepted. Hence, there was no real meaning to the behavioural coaching that he received. If the wrong behaviours are rewarded, there will be insufficient improvement in the individual or commitment by the system to progressing beyond this stage in the development of a coaching culture. This is especially likely when *command-and-control* manager behaviours are rewarded.

Overall, when organisations are in the second stage of developing a coaching culture, the motivation for coaching is *developmental* to assist individuals shift their mindset and behaviour, improve their performance, and support career progression.

4.3 Functional Drivers

In this second stage, coaching is positioned within the HR function and driven by HR professionals as a centralised process because, in organisations with a 'strong people function', HR professionals are usually the ones who know most about coaching. However, not all organisations have a transformational HR focus. Some are primarily transaction-driven, and whilst transactional HR professionals have an important role to play within the organisation, they may have no, or very little, desire to coach or learn about coaching. Some may even believe that coaching will *"do them out of a job"*. In organisations with a transactional rather than transformational HR approach, the organisation may be held back from moving to the next stage of developing a coaching culture for this reason.

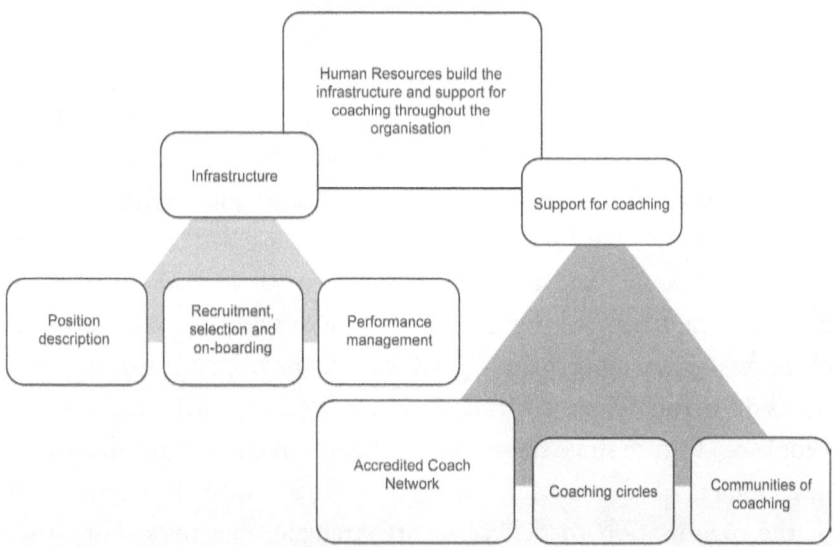

Figure 4.4: Human Resources build the infrastructure for coaching

4.3.1 Human Resources

In this second stage, coaching is driven by a transformational or professional HR function. The following story illustrates why a transactional HR focus is insufficient to develop a coaching culture. An executive coach was asked by a Learning and Development (L&D) consultant for a quote to coach a high potential in a functional business unit. He had a conversation with her to try to understand the situation and what was required before he submitted a proposal. He reports that the conversation was *"very linear, very boxy. It's very,* Do this. Do [taps table] that. Do this. Do that . . . *And that made me very cranky. She ended up saying,* All I want is your costs for 12 hours." Taken aback, he said, "*Okay.*" Later, on reflection, he sent her an email saying, "*Thank you very much for approaching us, but I don't think there'll be a fit for us, but best of luck. And if you need more coaches that might fit, then I can give you access to other people if you want. Otherwise, no, bye-bye.*" He now categorically refuses to work through the L&D function because he believes their focus to be tactical and operational, not transformational.

When transformational HR professionals display passion for coaching and the benefits it can bring to individuals, they are encouraged to drive the coaching initiative throughout the organisation. However, critics of HR taking this responsibility believe that it should lie at a more senior level with someone who has significant oversight of the strategic agenda as it does in a later stage. They believe that the function responsible for coaching needs to have a strategic overview of systemic factors and the business context so that the outcomes of coaching can make a significant difference to achieving organisational objectives. They suggest that if HR is to be the responsible function, it needs to partner with other functions like Workforce Development and People & Culture since these teams are instrumental in the design and development of organisational structures and assessing the requirements of the organisation to deliver on its strategic objectives. Plus, these functions may be driving some broader cultural agendas that can be supported by the uptake of coaching throughout the organisation.

4.3.2 Positioned within HR

Because coaching falls within the HR function in this second stage, the responsibility for developing the infrastructure to support coaching throughout the organisation lies within HR. HR professionals enact this responsibility by incorporating coaching within the organisation's HR policies and procedures, which apply from the time that leaders are recruited until the time they leave. The infrastructure that supports coaching throughout the organisation includes the establishment of specific mechanisms to support leaders who coach as well as fundamental changes to documentation relating to the leader's position description, recruitment and selection procedures, and performance management systems.

4.3.2.1 Infrastructure Support

Position description. In this second stage of developing a coaching culture, the requirement for leaders to coach is written into their position description and becomes a KPI, which is measured and reported against. The leader's span of control should be realistic to allow sufficient time and opportunity for them to coach. For example, if a leader's position is responsible for 100 people with no supervisory direct reports, the organisation is saying, *"We don't care. You have to coach all your direct reports anyway"*, which is an impossible task given the large number of direct reports. So it's important that the requirement to coach is written into the position description of leaders and reflected in the position's span of control.

Recruitment, selection, and on-boarding. In this second stage, when recruiting for a leader position in a coaching organisation, the position description specifies a coaching skill set as one of the selection criteria for leaders to have or be willing to acquire because *"we wouldn't hire them if they didn't have these skills or attributes"* as one organisational leader explains:

> *In my organisation, there's a requirement for a leader to have a bunch of skills, and that will include the technical stuff around what you do—planning systems of work and processes, developing your people, your role in a leadership team. But then just as importantly, it's coaching.*

If a suitable candidate doesn't have a coaching skill set but is open to learning and demonstrates an attitude conducive to developing others, these attributes are what the organisation hires for. Coaching skills can be trained. The recruitment process usually includes a behavioural-based assessment process and interview questions so that the selection panel can ascertain the candidate's degree of alignment with the organisation's values and coaching philosophy. After selection, an induction program covers 'common ground' requirements of the organisation and the role as well as expectations about organisational behaviour and professionalism. Ideally, the organisation has the first six months mapped out for the successful candidate in terms of what training they will receive either in coaching or in specific skills that the new recruit requires in the performance of their role. *Role coaching* through the first three months supports new leader development and delivers performance results more quickly.

Performance management. As well as the requirement to coach being written into the leader's position description, other non-performance-based indicators of performance may also be included, such as the requirement for leaders to develop their people and remove roadblocks to their performance. Team-based performance indicators include the requirement for leaders to support the development of colleagues as well as demonstrate support for organisational decisions and direction. When a *coaching leadership style* is adopted by managers, the performance management process becomes a meaningful exchange rather than a *"tick and flick"* exercise, which, at the very least, can be distressing and, at times, almost destructive when managers save all their feedback for this one hour in a year and then offload their negative feedback onto an unsuspecting employee. Sometimes, uninformed or untrained managers simply use this hour to gloss over any concerns, which leaves the employee with no valid feedback on which to base performance improvement. Rather, a coaching leader devotes regular four to six weekly coaching sessions to deliver constructive feedback to their direct reports and motivate them to keep doing more and better, which results in increased self-confidence as their performance improves.

4.3.2.2 Ongoing support for Coaching

HR professionals provide significant support for leaders who coach in three important ways by establishing: (1) an *Accredited Coach Network* for HR professionals and others who have been formally externally trained as coaches and who volunteer to coach back into the organisation in addition to their 'day job'; (2) *Coaching Circles* of leaders who have been internally trained in coaching skills to support the delivery of coaching to their direct reports; and (3) *Coaching Communities* to support coaching practice and supervision throughout the organisation.

Accredited Coach Network. In this second stage, HR professionals and selected others who have been formally trained as coaches by external coach-training providers volunteer to coach individuals who request to be coached, in addition to their 'day job', as coordinated by HR or L&D. This internal volunteer coaching service delivers coaching to individuals at all levels of the organisation. Executives and senior leaders may be funded to undertake formal external coach-training and then invited to become volunteer coaches. This establishes the credibility of coaching as an important developmental process within the organisation. Gaining access to senior executives who coach is a privilege because of the impost on their time and, for some employees, an incredibly powerful experience; the relationships that form may continue well beyond the coaching program.

Coaching Circles. A second way that the HR function provides ongoing support for coaching is by establishing coaching circles as a follow-up to leadership development programs which include a coaching component. After the training, leaders are assigned to cross-organisational groups to coach each other and continue their learning: "*I was part of the pilot three years ago. My coaching circle lasted longer than most. We came together, sort of* ad hoc, *and we just coached each other.*" However, for this leader, there was no follow-up to ensure that the Coaching Circle continued so after twelve months, his was the last remaining Coaching Circle. There were no recorded benefits or sustainable embedding of the coaching within the organisation as a result of their short-term investment in the coach-training of leaders.

Coaching communities. A third way that the HR function provides ongoing support for coaching is by establishing *Coaching Communities* to maintain the currency of internal coaching skills. A network of leaders who coach their direct reports is formed so that these leaders can self-audit their coaching delivery and receive supervision on their coaching practice. Formally, coach-trained HR professionals are injected into those discussions at various times to supervise leader's coaching practice and facilitate the extension of the coaching skill set into other areas of the business. HR may develop an online learning forum to support the *Coaching Communities*.

The challenge in this second stage is to convince managers that it is a requirement of their role that they coach. Unless this requirement is written into their position description and placed upfront during the recruitment interview, some managers may resist learning how to coach. However, as a KPI of their role, coaching practice is monitored and measured. Organisations which make attendance at coach-training programs voluntary may find that progression to the third stage in developing a coaching culture will take a lot longer to effect—if it is at all possible – unless they make the coach-training mandatory. In organisations which do mandate leader participation in coach-training programs, those who do not attend may find that their absence impacts on their performance results and may actually lead to their employment contract being terminated.

Overall, the findings indicate that when an organisation is at the *Coaching as HR-Function* stage of developing a coaching culture, the drivers for coaching are HR professionals. Coaching is positioned within the HR function, and HR develops the infrastructure and support for coaching to occur. However, there is some controversy as to whether HR professionals are the most appropriate people to drive the development of a coaching culture throughout the organisation given that many HR professionals are not formally trained as coaches and may, in fact, be transactional rather than transformational in their approach. Both these factors may hold the organisation back from progressing to the third stage in the development of a coaching culture.

4.4 Targeted Delivery

The final element that characterises the *Coaching-as-HR-Function* stage concerns how coaching is delivered within the organisation. Coaching is delivered in two ways: (1) via *Leader-as-Coach* programs to organisational leaders and talented individuals; and (2) as a contracted arrangement with an external coach to coach individuals for performance improvement or behavioural issues, and talented individuals on a developmental career path.

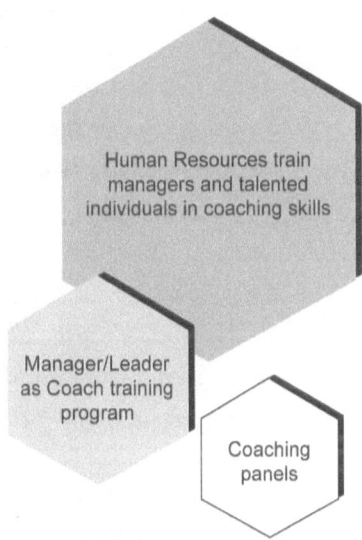

Figure 4.5: Human Resources train managers and talented individuals

4.4.1 Leader-as-Coach Training Program

In this second stage of developing a coaching culture, HR either delivers an in-house coach-training program as a stand-alone learning experience or includes a coaching component within leadership development programs. Typically, these programs are of two to three days' duration, although some organisations conduct more extensive leadership development programs consisting of fourteen days' face to face over ten months. Participants are paired across leadership cohorts for hands-on coaching practice and experience. *"So we ask them to do five hours' coaching with a pair-partner, and hopefully, they're using the skills in their workplace. Feedback from the last cohort was very positive about the coaching and how they've been able to implement it in their workplace."* This approach starts a process of *peer coaching* within the organisation. Alternatively, HR may contract the services of an external coach-training provider to deliver the training to increase the *"bench strength"* of organisational leaders.

> *The CEO took the stance that the* bench strength *of our leadership is too weak. They won't be able to cope with the messages that have to be delivered to the organisation. And this company is still really important, right, and we still had about 80 per cent of the nation's customers. So the organisation was important to this country. It couldn't fail. It couldn't just fall apart and become dysfunctional. So his view was to address it in your leadership, your line management.*

Coach-training allows leaders the time to reflect on their role and how they interact with their direct reports and to make the changes necessary to develop a *coaching leadership style.* These programs have the flexibility to be implemented consistently across the organisation but also to be tailored when they need to meet particular business needs. Where possible, the leader is included as a member of the delivery team so as to more quickly embed the learnings back into the workplace. The ideal is to conduct follow-up training and coaching sessions after the program has concluded to perfect coaching practise.

When individual coaching sessions with the coach/facilitator are included as an essential component of the coach-training program, participants report that being coached is the part of the program they value most. Many individuals don't have the opportunity for face time with their leader, so these sessions are especially important to recognise an employee as a person separate from their role as a team member and direct report.

One of the desired outcomes of conducting a *Leader-as-Coach* program is that managers, in participating in a few days of training in coaching skills and being coached, shift their awareness of self and others and come to an understanding that they are human beings just like everyone else. This realisation may happen gradually as the training progresses, or it can strike an individual like a *"thunderbolt out of the blue"*. By whatever process, the manager's views on the world have changed, and they realise that people are human, people make mistakes, and people are fallible—including themselves. With this realisation comes an acceptance of their own and others' imperfections and an acknowledgement that mistakes are really opportunities for improvement, provided they are handled constructively with specific feedback in mind. After their coach-training, the Leader-as-Coach's role is to assist their direct reports to develop their own self-awareness and assist them to self-manage to discover their own solutions within the responsibilities of their role.

Some people ask why in-house coach-training programs have not been successful in changing the mindset of all managers. Surely, a two- to three-day program would be adequate to make that shift? Not so, for many reasons: (1) although the motivation behind the coach-training is to be more developmentally focused and less *command-and-control*, two or three days is often insufficient to bring about a long-term mindset shift and produce real change; (2) in-house coach-training programs, whilst an important first step in developing a coaching culture, are unlikely to produce the desired change unless supported by the experience of being coached as part of this program; (3) managers are very busy—*"stretched to the max"*—and cannot give their undivided attention to changing the way they already operate; and (4) why would managers change the way they have been interacting with their teams for so long when they have been so successful in gaining promotion and being rewarded time and again for getting results for doing what they are doing right now?

Critics of in-house coach-training programs delivered by HR professionals believe that the outcomes of these programs are suboptimal because they are only as good as the understanding and experience that HR professionals have of coaching themselves. Some critics have even described the in-house coach-training delivered by (not formally trained) HR professionals as a *"car wash"*, the take-out, fast food version of leadership: *"I'm going to send you through the coaching car wash to clean you off, and you'll be clean for a little while. I'll spend some time buffing everybody's emotions and their abilities—but you'll be dirtier down the track."* To formally trained coaches who know and understand the benefits of the behavioural and performance shifts experienced during coaching, the programs designed and delivered in-house by HR professionals can appear *weak*—as if they've been *"dumbed down"* to appeal to a broader group of leaders with varying skill levels, backgrounds, and histories. They note that a *"caring conversation"* is important but not sufficient to bring about behavioural or performance improvements.

4.4.2 HR Appoints Coaching Panels

When individual coaching is to be conducted by an external coach or an executive coach is engaged to deliver in-house coach-training to leaders either as a stand-alone program or in collaboration with HR professionals, a procurement process is conducted to select and appoint the most appropriate external provider to deliver these services. The procurement process identifies a number of vendors and then shortlists a company to deliver the coach-training and conduct the leader coaching. Executive coaches are typically hired to coach the executive team and to coach in situations where an experienced coach is required. However, it is often difficult for organisations to know which external coaches to select onto a coaching panel because there are no standard criteria that organisations can use to guide their decision. The criteria for selection are usually based on the background and experience of the executive coach, and because the coaching industry is self-regulating, it should also be based on whether the external coach has been formally trained and accredited to international standards. An external coach should verify their formal coach-training qualification from an external coach-training provider plus their credentialing as a current member of a professional coaching association, such as the International Coach Federation, before being selected onto a coaching panel.

Overall, the findings indicate that when an organisation is in the second stage of developing a coaching culture at the *Coaching-as-HR-Function* stage, coach-training programs and coaching are primarily driven and delivered by HR professionals. Organisations in which HR professionals are formally trained as coaches are better able to assist the organisation transition to the third stage in the development of a coaching culture than are organisations which rely on the *"car wash"*, in-house coach-training delivered by HR professionals who are not formally trained as coaches.

4.5 Summary of Stage 2

Coaching-as-HR-Function

In summary, organisations in the second stage of developing a coaching culture at the *Coaching-as-HR-Function* stage have a *pedagogical* conceptualisation of coaching as a training and learning experience. The *developmental* motivation for coaching is to develop self-awareness and insight in HR professionals, selected organisational leaders, and talented individuals to assist them to make the behavioural changes they need to make to improve their performance and progress in their career. The developmental motivation also aims to achieve mindset shifts in managers so that they let go of a *command-and-control* mentality and replace it with a *coaching leadership style*. The *functional* drivers for coaching are HR professionals who drive coaching throughout the organisation from a centralised HR position and develop the infrastructure support for coaching. Coach-training is *targeted* at functional leaders and talented individuals who are trained in coaching skills so that they can coach their direct reports and others in the organisation.

4.6 Case Studies

Stage 2
Coaching-as-HR-Function

Case Study 6

ConnectHub is a large national technology company in an industry where the profit margins have been gradually dropping for years. The *"cash cow"* that was the telecommunications infrastructure is being reduced to a utility. Hence, ConnectHub had to rethink how to monetise the pipe, that is, how to make money out of basically a dead electric pipe. Under the previous CEO who was keen on coaching, one of the Big 4 consulting firms was engaged, at considerable expense, to train leaders in coaching skills. *Coaching Circles* were established after the training was completed but because no one was coordinating them or monitoring their activity, they were discontinued after a few short months.

Then the company was bought out by an overseas firm. The new CEO was not interested in coaching. He was more interested in the 'bottom line' and creating innovation in a market of declining revenues. Hence the 'coaching' that was being conducted in the organisation returned to one-on-one conversations which were basically problem-solving exercises based on asking a series of questions to promote self-learning. Using the coaching process, leaders would like to enable their employees to *"go deeper and own their solutions"* and learn from the experience, but the reality is that that rarely happens because, in the new environment, there are more important priorities, no budget or resources for coaching, and the CEO is pushing a different agenda.

Case Study 7

FedFinancial is a federal government organisation in the financial services industry with approximately 19,000 employees. The organisation is in its 'infancy' in terms of creating a coaching culture. Some of the executive team have external coaches and other senior leaders can access coaching from the *Accredited Coach Network*, which matches internal volunteer coaches with those who request to be coached. The *Network* consists of more than 200 volunteer coaches who have self-funded their formal training through various private providers. Any senior staff member can request to have a one-on-one coaching relationship with one of these coaches. However, this type of coaching is more aligned to a mentoring relationship rather than coaching, which, in this organisation, *"doesn't really matter as long as it's about the person's development"*.

General staff with direct reports have access to a two-day *Manager-as-Coach* program which has been conducted in the organisation for some years. The program is designed to train managers in how to use coaching conversations for developmental purposes, particularly around some of the technical areas for development. The program trains managers to ask, *"What are your goals?"* and *"What are your strategies to get there"* so that they can give direct feedback to their team members. Hence, the training is really in *performance* rather than *pure coaching*.

In their call centre operation, the 'coaching' that occurs is completely transactional, simply providing feedback on operator performance much as would occur under a performance management system. Full-time call centre coaches listen to calls with the operative, give feedback on their performance, and then assist them to do some development planning. 'Coaches' assist front-line team members in establishing their own goals and direction and keep them motivated and engaged to achieve their goals. In principle, the idea of *pure coaching* is still evident in that coaches try to guide staff to understand their capability gaps and set their own goals, but the actual *performance coaching* uses forms and templates so it's quite often, depending on who's doing the coaching, just a step-by-step directive process.

In other (senior) areas of FedFinancial, the coaching is more traditional. One-on-one coaching sessions over six weeks are conducted, driven by the senior leader. For the past twelve months, the HR function has been trying to gain approval to develop and roll out a *"middle of the road"* coaching program that sits between the performance management feedback currently delivered to front-line staff and individual one-on-one coaching sessions delivered at the executive level. This coaching program would be delivered to all staff for development purposes on the understanding that the approach would be *"a little bit more directive [than a client-led pure coaching agenda] in terms of building specific skills and capabilities"* but less performance-directed. It was only when a consultant reviewed the work of the unit and recommended coaching as a high priority that executives agreed to conduct a pilot coaching program at the middle-management level.

A working party was established consisting of representatives of various sections of the business which co-designed the program based on an analysis of the current situation and how the organisation wants coaching to be conducted in the future. After designing the generic components, the working party addressed: *"What's the extra bit that's specific to our section? What is coaching actually going to achieve as opposed to whatever else is out there?"* The pilot was then conducted in one of their sites. People who volunteered to become coaches were those who were one level below management, typically at the level of technical expert—for example, full-time call centre coaches or team leaders with the intention of helping junior staff succeed. These volunteers wanted more information about the coaching they were already doing informally, and to improve their coaching skills. They were then connected with individuals who wanted to be coached.

As a result of the success of the program, it *"got on the radar of the executive"* and will be extended across the business group, but how and when this will happen has yet to be determined. What is necessary to do next is to set up an evaluation process to gauge the effectiveness of the program, the coaches, and the coaching relationships, and to determine if the coaching is actually developing the coachee. After that, it's looking at the bigger picture to ascertain things like: *"How is the program actually delivering on our capability of the workforce as a whole?"* and *"How are we getting better at the types of things that we need to get better at?"* The working party is unsure as to how to address these questions, but at least they are part of the thinking and program design moving forwards.

Case Study 8

RRRIncorporated is a government authority that delivers infrastructure services to the general public at a state level. It employs 2,300 people directly plus numerous contracted staff. There's a strong mentoring culture and an emerging recognition of coaching which began two years ago when a new CEO was appointed. Since then, there's been strong encouragement for all senior executives to take on an external coach as modelled by the CEO and several executive directors. So from the very top, there's recognition that coaching is a valid component of employee development and a methodology to be embraced in order to become a fully functioning member of the organisation.

RRRIncorporated believes that coaching is a one-on-one opportunity to work closely with an individual to improve their performance and develop identified skills deficits. Coaching encourages individuals to be accountable for the decisions they make about how to do things differently within their leadership and collegiate teams. Coachees make a commitment to plan their learning so that when they meet with their coach again, they can discuss what worked, what didn't work, and how to move on to fully developing themselves and their people.

All the executive officers and senior leaders in RRRIncorporated have been trained in how to debrief a particular assessment instrument. In committing to fund this external training, the organisation made a decision that they wanted to be self-sufficient and use internal accredited coaches rather than continue to engage external consultants. All those who undertook this external training were assigned a coach with a clearly defined objective—to develop a coaching plan over the next six to twelve months around how they could improve as a senior leader and how that would be measured. The five or six 'coaching sessions' were structured in according with the 'guide' that executives received during their training on how to deliver individual feedback around the results of the assessment instrument.

In addition to this external training, RRRIncorporated conducts internal *Leader-as-Coach* training programs and provides support for leaders who coach. The facilitators who deliver the in-house coach-training programs have been accredited in the assessment instrument. The organisation is working towards embedding coaching as an understood requirement of leaders and an expectation that all employees will be coached at some time in their career. In the past, senior leaders who have not been able to focus their leadership on the development of others and become a contemporary, authentic leader have been exited from the organisation.

CHAPTER 5

STAGE 3
COACHING-AS-LEADER-CAPABILITY

The third stage in developing a coaching culture is labelled *Coaching-as-Leader-Capability*. During this stage, coaching is an expected capability of leaders which is often embedded within a leadership development framework. Coaching is conceptualised as a *practice* and an understood requirement of leaders who have a *performance* motivation to uplift team and business results. *Business units* are responsible for driving coaching throughout the organisation, and coaching is *internally delivered* by leaders to their teams and team members.

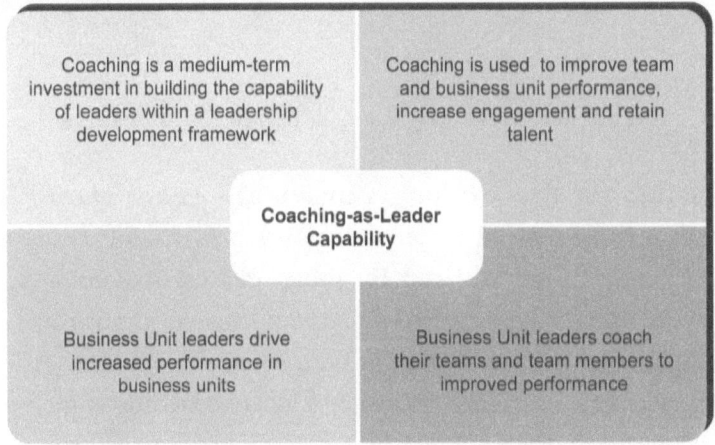

Figure 5.1: Coaching-as-Leader-Capability Stage

5.1 Practice Conceptualisation

In the *Coaching-as-Leader-Capability* stage of developing a coaching culture, organisational leaders have a *practice* conceptualisation of coaching as a requirement of the leader role and an expected capability for leaders to progress in their career. Coaching is a 'micro skill' in the leader's 'kit bag' that they can draw upon not necessarily as a formal coaching session but as the need arises in any conversation. It is a medium-term investment in building the leader capability and human capital of the organisation.

5.1.1 Coaching Is a Core Capability of Leaders

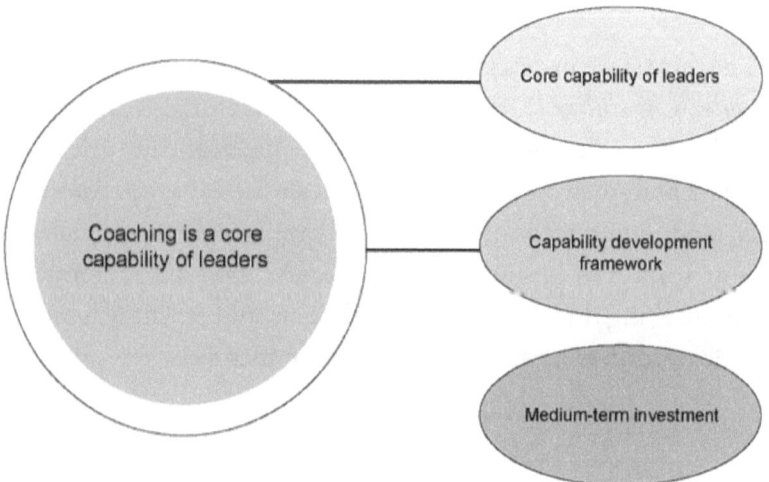

Figure 5.2: Coaching is a core capability of leaders

The first way that coaching is conceptualised as a *practice* is as a capability requirement of leaders in the performance of their role. In previous stages, it was difficult for some organisations to accept the value of coaching as an expected practice of leaders. In this third stage, coaching is a required leadership capability. Coaching is like Leadership 101—leaders have to be able to coach. Hence, coaching is included in a leader's position description which makes it crystal clear that leaders are required to coach their direct reports as part of their role. However, organisational leaders' conceptualisation of coaching is still not entirely well-formed at this stage. Hence, some coaching advocates may position *coaching* under the banner of *leadership* which employees are familiar with and see as being really important, whereas coaching is relatively unknown to them. Then, when leaders interact with their team as a coach, they may describe using the coaching skills as *leadership*, not *coaching*.

In organisations which have the funds to deliver consistent, ongoing leadership development programs which include a coaching component, the expectation that leaders will coach is a mandated requirement of their role. In other organisations which do not have the funds to ensure the training of all leaders in coaching skills, the expectation that they will coach is just that—an expectation that is not enforced. These organisations have limited resources and, hence, limited places in their development programs. In addition, the leadership development programs may be competing for funds with other organisational initiatives. Hence, in less well-resourced organisations, it is left to the individual leader to sign up to attend a leadership development program that includes a coaching skills component, and it will take longer for a coaching culture to develop.

Coaching is all about getting the best out of people. "*You just have to say a few words so that they understand that you understand, and that opens a lot of doors.*" Coaching entails listening, reflecting, affirming and supporting team members to create options for action. In coaching organisations, it is unacceptable for leaders to pass coaching on to an external coach unless the situation requires a degree of skill or expertise that the leader does not possess or the consequences of 'getting it wrong' are significant.

In this third stage, when leaders express a desire to develop their leadership capability through coaching, the business unit leader sits down with them to identify the outcomes they want to achieve and discuss options for doing that. Building the capability of leaders in coaching skills enables them to elicit better performance from their team as they create shared models of understanding based on a common coaching language and relationships built on trust, openness, and honesty. A shared understanding of coaching promotes *"a philosophy of coaching"* within the team and a way of interacting that the team accepts as malleable, mouldable, and built on foundational principles. The coaching philosophy is the agreed understanding of how the team communicates the levels of cooperation and collaboration required within the team and the support that's available for ongoing development and career progression.

Leadership capability is built on a coaching philosophy which supports leaders not only to lead for improved performance but also to nurture their employees' innate ability to grow. Building organisational capability has been described as *"exciting, fertile ground"* and a way of ensuring that individuals and teams are provided with regular, constructive, one-on-one formal and informal feedback on their performance. Leaders who coach, step back from the day-to-day 'doing' and *"hold the space"* for others to lead, which is difficult for those managers who have not made the mental mindset shift from *command-and-control* to a *coaching leadership style*. If managers cannot achieve this transition to leader, they may be exited from the organisation because in this third stage, a coach *"is not a person that you bring in to do it for you."* The responsibility to coach lies with the leader as a requirement of their role.

An example is of an organisation which needed their managers to be strong and provide coaching to their teams is of an organisation which was subject to severe competition in the marketplace. As a consequence, the organisation was restructured and forced to make thousands of employees redundant. The line managers needed to be strong not only because they had to lead the changes but also because they were the ones who had to stand up in front of their team and explain why it was necessary for half of the team to be 'let go'. Plus, they then had to put their team back together and keep it performing after the restructure. The view of the CEO was that their leadership was too weak and that they wouldn't be able to cope with the messages that had to be delivered to the teams. Hence, training in coaching skills was elevated to a level sufficient to support managers to deal with the issues at that important time.

5.1.2 Coaching Is Embedded within a Capability Development Framework

The second way that coaching is conceptualised as a *practice* is as a capability requirement coaching within the organisation's *capability development framework*. This framework guides the delivery of in-house training in coaching skills and establishes processes to monitor the quality of the coaching that is delivered—same way, right way, each and every time. Establishing a capability framework for leaders that includes coaching involves gaining executive agreement on what coaching means to the organisation (because each individual will have their own view) and the standards and quality of the coaching delivered within the organisation. It is in this third stage that organisations may decide to reshape their capability development framework to include an *employee life cycle continuum* of which coaching forms an essential component, particularly at the middle-management level.

As a designated leader capability with the organisation's capability framework, coaching can be applied to any conversation for any purpose, among a leader, their direct reports, and others in the organisation. For example, in one organisation, their capability development framework for leaders has six capabilities—all soft skills—with a strong emphasis on coaching, engagement, and connection to serve the organisation's broader goals. These leadership capabilities underpin the roles of the approximately 850 leaders in the organisation, all of whom have participated in the organisation's leadership development program which incorporates the coaching language and shared models of coaching as applied to the day-to-day leadership of their teams.

Another organisation has established a capability development framework for leaders that is a compilation of a set of principles around leadership and the expected behaviours of leaders in their organisation. Rather than conducting training programs to inculcate these principles and behaviours, the organisation is filtering them down through monthly team discussions about what these principles mean to individuals and how they should be enacted at the team level and then following through with peer accountability thereafter. These principles are statements of intent as to how a leader behaves in relation to their direct reports and others in the organisation. They're framed as questions to stimulate discussion at the team level. One of them, for example, asks how leaders provide the opportunity for team members to input into decisions. Each month, a new principle becomes the focus for discussion as a way of investing in their leaders to think about their roles and encourage them to approach their leadership responsibilities in the 'right' organisational way.

A third way that coaching is conceptualised as a *practice* is as a capability requirement of leaders to advance in their career. Coaching is included within a *career progression framework*. Leaders who wish to promote are expected to possess coaching capability. Pathways are developed which identify the skills and capabilities required to make the important transitions, such as from technical specialist to team leader to line manager to inspiring leader of people. Within some state government departments, career pathways have been developed at the various leader levels, which identify the *"stepping stones"* to executive leadership. These self-assessment tools give upwardly mobile team members the knowledge they need to make decisions about the capabilities they require to promote to their desired position within the organisation.

Within a clearly articulated framework for coaching and acknowledgement of its value, every leader new to the organisation in this third stage of developing a coaching culture undertakes in-house training in coaching skills and receives individual coaching if they haven't been coached before. Hence, every organisational leader develops their coaching capability—to different degrees for different levels. As part of the capability strategy for the organisation, the Workforce Planning function periodically *"core reviews"* coaching as a skill to ascertain the numbers that need to be included in future coach-training programs. Investing in the ability of business unit managers to coach is one of the most important decisions that an organisation can make in this third stage of developing a coaching culture.

5.1.3 Coaching Is a Medium-Term Investment

The in-house training of managers in coaching skills in this third stage is typically a medium-term investment in building organisational capability. Organisations usually only invest a few hours to a few days in dedicated coach-training programs; obviously, the more time invested, the better leaders will be at coaching. A few hours of training allows the organisation to say, "*We coach*", but in fact, it is an insufficient allocation of time to understand what coaching is all about and to become proficient in coaching skills. Time devoted to coaching is what is needed for leaders to practise coaching and become confident in their coaching. Some organisations offer a more comprehensive program of training, for example, three days of training a month apart with coach-training practice in between. A three-day program may include, say, one day on coaching skills, one day on coaching process, and a third day on coaching practice around issues of real concern to leaders. As part of the training, leaders may be allocated an external coach to focus on their development needs during the program and assist them to embed the learnings back into their workplace post-training.

An example of an organisation that cost-effectively implemented coaching throughout a business unit is a large national organisation in the technology service sector. It successfully transitioned from using external coaches to train and coach employees, to providing the funding for a number of selected employees to be formally trained as internal coaches by a private coach-training provider. Because they weren't going to keep the external coaches coming back interminably, these qualified internal coaches started delivering training and coaching throughout the business unit, cascading it from the senior leaders to team leaders. Now, approximately 90 per cent of their team leaders are far better coaches than most other leaders in the organisation. So, rather than relying on just five or six HR professionals to do the coaching, there are over 800 leaders in the business unit who have been trained in coaching skills, and they coach their teams on a regular basis. This has allowed the call centre to implement changes and shift mindsets more quickly than ever before, resulting in a greater impact on business results. An organisation starts to get traction when it invests in the coach-training of its leaders, who then deliver coaching to their teams within the business unit.

Overall, when an organisation is at the Coaching-*as-Leader-Capability* stage of developing a coaching culture, coaching is conceptualised as a *practice*. Coaching is a medium-term investment in building an organisation's capability by including coaching as a core capability of leaders and incorporating it into leadership development and career progression frameworks.

5.2 Performance Motivation

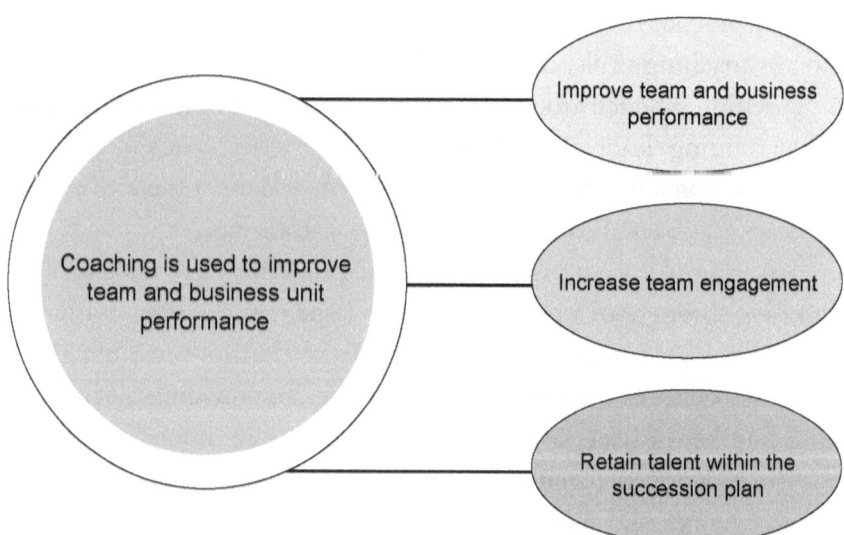

Figure 5.3: Coaching is used to improve team and business performance

Another element that characterises the *Coaching-as-Leader-Capability* stage concerns the motivation for why coaching *practice* is being undertaken by the organisation. In this third stage, coaching has a *performance* motivation as part of a suite of development tools at the leader's disposal so that leaders can improve the performance of their teams and team members, increase team engagement, and retain talent.

5.2.1 Improve Team and Business Performance

The first element of a *performance* motivation involves using coaching to enable employees to fulfil on the requirements of their role and deliver on their KPIs. This is *performance coaching* in which a leader works with a middle performer—where the leverage is, where the opportunity sits, and where the potential is—demonstrating an investment in that team member over and above the time that they've already spent with them. Performance coaching directs the conversation towards deliverables: How is the team member going to achieve their deliverables, and what will the impact be on them and the team when they achieve those deliverables?

Performance coaching also considers the external environment in which teams operate to identify what might be holding team members back from delivering on the requirements of their roles, for example, the pressure that they're under, the sensitivity of the assignment, and the complexity of changes in the team composition and roles. There is a *"latent demand"* for team members to have a specific conversation about performance and personal development with their leader, which adds to their motivation and level of engagement. However, if managers have not undertaken training in coaching skills, it's a *"hard sell"* to have them understand how powerful a coaching conversation can be when it provides specific and timely feedback in a supportive manner as opposed to the traditional performance management approach.

As a KPI of the leader's role, the coaching that leaders conduct with their teams and team members is scrutinised and the results input into job contract renegotiations. However, if the expectations around how and when the coaching will be conducted and to what standard have not been specified, the actual measurement of the KPI is less than meaningful and may become another *"tick and flick"* exercise. With this possibility in mind and being cognisant of the fact that an annual performance review can cause anxiety and stress for most individuals, some organisations are moving away from the *"redundancy of annual performance review as an artefact of a performance culture"* and replacing it with regular coaching sessions, as this story illustrates:

> *So we have a system in place where we no longer get performance ratings at the end of the year but we are required as leaders to have monthly one-on-ones with our people. So you have KPIs, and then you have the development part of it. And every month, you'd have a look at it and see where that person is going and give them feedback, give them coaching. And like I said, it goes all the way from the CEO down.*

Critics of individually-based KPIs would change the way that performance is measured. They would focus on how individual performance and behaviours impact on the team rather than just on the achievement of individual KPIs. Non-individual KPIs could relate to team performance and business effectiveness and may include indicators of, for example, communication, relationships, collaboration, and cooperation within the team as well as the demonstration of behaviours which are consistent with organisational values. Advocates of team-based KPIs believe that the focus of coaching should go beyond individual results into the achievement of collective outcomes at the team level.

When the coaching that is conducted is purely performance-driven - that is, *performance coaching* - it may become *"prescriptive"* and be used instead as a performance management tool. If coaching is used in this way, it could create defensiveness rather than being seen as *"reflective practice"*. When used as a prescriptive tool, coaching is all about shaping the performance of a team rather than it being about *"who* we are . . . and *how* we are in the workplace". However, there are times when a prescriptive approach does have its value as an enabler of performance, for example, in an environment in which business performance requires the achievement of specific tasks and supports *"CTR . . . coaching to revenue"* by, for example, using performance-enabling software in a performance-driven sales environment. If the performance needs to be lifted in certain business areas, *"prescriptive"* coaching can be applied within those areas to improve overall performance, as this story illustrates:

> *So we're working in the back-of-house with our finance team and our analysts to produce data, produce reports, and then we feed them up to the sales leadership team to help them make decisions, to help them drive performance to enable the sales leadership team to then be having meaningful conversations with their sales teams.*

This quote highlights how coaching practice is used to support a performance motivation for improved economic returns to the business. The expectation is that, after receiving training in coaching skills, leaders will go to a *"coaching place"* first before they adopt a *"performance management"* stance. Leaders believe that constantly giving feedback is one of the most valuable things they can do for their teams and, in return, seeking feedback as well. An example is of a managing director of a large company who establishes relationships with team members first before going to performance management:

> *He is a guy that I admire a lot because in his early forties, he's got an enormous job and high energy levels. He walks the talk around the most important thing I can do is deliver profitability, which comes through people.*

In this third stage, leaders focus not only on achieving business outcomes but also on ensuring *"care and concern"* for individuals as they drive team performance towards achieving the designated business targets. Balancing the need to look after people but also deliver on role expectations illustrates how leaders in this third stage of developing a coaching culture, coach not only from a *developmental* motivation but also from a *performance* motivation as well.

5.2.2 Increase Team Engagement

The second element of a *performance* motivation involves using coaching as a way to increase team engagement to improve business outcomes. Identifying the strengths of team members is a good first step to increasing job satisfaction but insufficient to ensure increased team engagement and business improvement. Rather, when team members are coached within a capability framework that supports and affirms individual and team performance, the business benefits from the increased productivity generated from the team's collective efforts. Leaders who use the coaching language within a productivity framework integrate coaching into everything they do with the team and team members, including how they communicate, relate, and interact with each other on a daily basis. When leaders adopt a *coaching leadership style*, it demonstrates that the business cares about the team members who work for them, and they have an objective and a goal to help them develop and do more to reach their potential. This ultimately leads to more engaged team members who perform better, which impacts on the organisation's 'bottom line'. In all aspects of the business relationship, coaching enables consideration for the people involved in driving and delivering the business transactions.

Team morale improves when team members are enabled and empowered to perform their best and contribute significantly to the performance and productivity of the team. An example of team collaboration is when team members participate in co-designing their own coach-training program. When this design method is used, organisations establish a working party of key stakeholders who represent the interests of different departments or sections of the business. They design not only for commonalities but also for differences pertaining to the areas they represent. The key is always to discover the *"additional extras"* that should be incorporated into the flexible part of the program specific to a particular group or team to ensure that the learnings are tailored and applicable to that group or team's business performance.

Some areas of importance to the organisation that may need a specific design modification include how to coach team members who work in different locations including overseas, and how to coach teams with specialist or technical expertise that is of particular value to the organisation. For example, a team leader in an international logistics firm who wants to become more engaged with his team and have team members feel more connected to each other requires infrastructure to support coaching his team members at a distance such as internet-enabled group forums and interactive webinars. A second example is of a leader attempting to create an empowered team when there are a number of high-performing team members, each with their *"ego on display"*. Coaching these individuals can prove challenging in itself. Coaching them as a team may require additional coaching capability because of team-related issues such as how to achieve collaboration and cooperation among individuals, especially if the team is very much a group and not a team.

An example that illustrates this situation is of a large federal government department where the work is fast and high-pressured. Each team member has a discrete area of responsibility and, at worst, they may be immediately dismissed for any errors of content or judgement since such errors will have a significant impact on key stakeholders and the reputation of the department. Team members are usually recruited because they are *"stars"* in their own right, used to working alone in their particular area of expertise with little direction and making huge judgement calls on a daily basis. These teams often have a very big remit. However, because team members are all *"stars"*, they're not used to working together as a team. Therefore, the focus of coaching is to transform this 'group' into a 'team' with interdependencies and support systems in place. The leader's role is to use their coaching skills to assist the 'group' members identify the ways they can improve the overall team performance by developing awareness of each other's roles and responsibilities using an open and honest coaching approach. They can then outline the areas of expected team performance and explore options to transition individual "*stars*" into team members.

5.2.3 Retain Talent

The third element of a *performance* motivation involves using coaching as a way to retain talent within the team or business unit. Coaching is particularly effective in developing people and recognising their true potential, enabling them to flourish, step into their greatness, and make a significant difference to their life and the lives of others with whom they interact. Organisations which develop the coaching capability of their leaders and talented individuals are well-positioned to utilise their skills and expertise as the organisation grows. Such individuals are included in the organisation's succession plan and receive coaching to prepare them for future positions within the organisation. The aim is to achieve a talent pipeline of individuals who have the potential for development over time, whom a talent champion can steward through the levels of the organisation until they reach the executive level. Employee surveys may be used to gauge the extent to which an organisation needs to support talented individuals whom they wish to retain within the organisation:

> *In my nine years with this organisation, nothing gets done just because it's a good idea. You have to have a reason. So the reason that they've put in place is the intention to leave survey results from people in their area where they can identify that a coaching conversation will help reduce that.*

When talented individuals are identified, resources are allocated to provide the potential leaders with opportunities that recognise their abilities and enhance their career prospects. A *Leader-as-Coach* program is something that aspiring leaders identify as of particular benefit and support to them in their process of transitioning to a more senior role. Individual career coaching may be offered to support individuals in making the transition from one position to another. External coaches may be used to work with talented executives who have confronted the 'glass ceiling' for a range of reasons or who may be competing with younger talent identified for promotion. An 'outside' perspective may be just what they need to help them transition into their next role. In fact, in some organisations, the only reason that external coaches are engaged is to support talent. Coaching by an external coach is an opportunity for the talented individual to have the *"impartial ear"* of someone to whom they can speak confidentially, which they may consider less likely with an internal coach who may not be seen as completely confidential. However, this level of external coaching support can prove expensive when large numbers of people are involved such as a cohort of twenty-five people of talent in the organisation.

Aspiring leaders may be recruited into the organisation via a graduate entry program which aims to identify potential in the early phases of an employee's career. Such individuals may be 'fast-tracked' within a talent management cycle as they transition from one position to the next based on a series of talent metrics driven by HR. *"I'm working with five early leaders who've just gone through psychometrics and, for want of a better word, developmental opportunities."* The talent management cycle looks at the *"end to end"* processes from the policies and procedures surrounding how the organisation recruits new employees through to how it plans for the workforce of the future and manages organisational talent through that cycle.

When external people are appointed to new positions, this may affect staff morale and possibly lead to resignations of team members who have been overlooked for the new positions, as illustrated by the story of a very large organisation which provides essential utility services to customers nationally. Initially, it only produced the product, but then the decision was made to move into distribution and retail of the product rather than using partner distribution networks and resellers. As the organisation grew the distribution arm of the business, the growth could be managed by existing staff supplemented with a manageable number of new recruits in a few specific areas. However, to develop and grow a completely new retail arm of the business in which the organisation had no expertise required some talent to be *"bought in from outside*" because no one in the organisation knew how to run a retail business. Growing the retail business from almost nothing to four million customers necessitated successive rounds of recruitment of people who had the expertise to fill these new roles. This proved to be a particularly challenging time for existing employees who were not selected for the available roles. The morale of some unsuccessful team members plummeted, and some talent left the organisation. Those who remained needed to be supported by coaching to understand the reasons for their non-selection to these roles.

Overall, when an organisation is at the Coaching-*as-Leader-Capability* stage of developing a coaching culture, *performance* motivations for coaching combined with *practice* conceptualisations of coaching have progressed organisational leaders from an emphasis on individual performance and motivation to team motivation and business performance. There are two challenges for organisations wishing to progress from a *developmental* to a *performance* motivation for culture. First, leaders need to work out how to combine individual human capabilities with strategies to embrace the diversity and different skill sets available within their team, to drive improved performance. Second, leaders need to decide whether their approach to talent management will include the provision of opportunities for more than the select few to receive coaching, and identify ways to do this when large numbers of employees are involved. Sceptics of a talent management strategy quip that "*it really amuses me because once you have a talent management pool, you're telling everyone else in the organisation that they're not talented.*"

To progress to the next stage in the development of a coaching culture, leaders need to intend that all team members, not just a few talented individuals, will be coached so that their performance can improve as much as possible, resulting in increased engagement and work performance because of the personal attention they receive. Not everyone can be included in the organisation's succession plan but if all team members lift their performance, it will result in improvements across the entire business unit.

5.3 Business Drivers

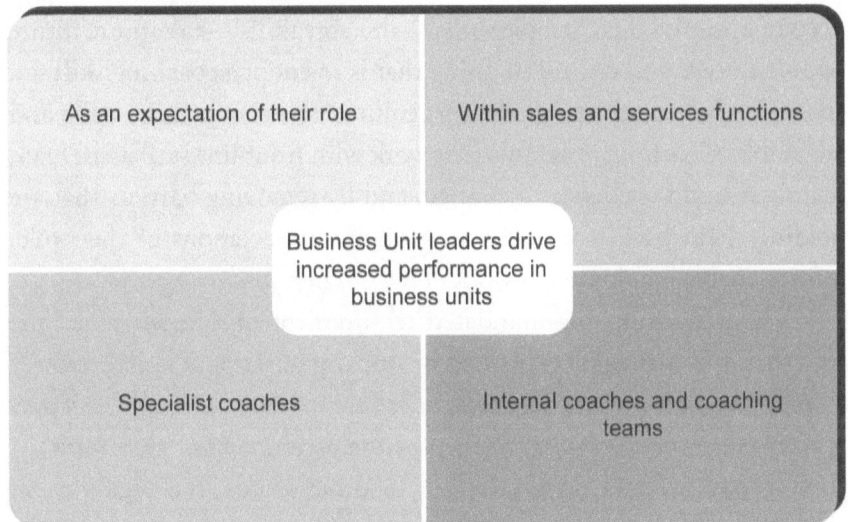

Figure 5.4: Business Unit leaders drive coaching to increase performance

A third element that characterises the *Coaching-as-Leader-Capability* stage concerns who in the organisation is driving the development of coaching capability throughout the organisation. In this third stage, the leaders of *business* units drive coaching as an expectation of their role to increase the performance of their teams. They use their coaching capability to motivate team members to greater levels of engagement, collaboration, and teamwork. When coaching is positioned within business units, the *performance coaching* may initially be "*formulaic*" and "*procedural*" to provide consistency and ensure product quality and "*same way delivery*" each and every time.

5.3.1 Leaders Drive Business Performance as an Expectation of Their Role

The first element relating to the business drivers of coaching in this third stage of developing a coaching culture involves leaders coaching their team members as an understood requirement of their role as leader.

In a digital economy, the workforce needs to respond quickly to changes in the marketplace. Reports on digital workforces point out that leaders need to optimise their 'people skills'—the 'soft skills'—to capture future opportunities, and critical to doing that is to adopt a coaching skill set. Increasingly, workforces are being required to become more agile and adaptable. Coaching programs that work with front-line staff assist team members build resilience to change, and by removing barriers that are holding them back from delivering on the expectations of their role, leaders enable employees to work *"better, faster, and stronger"*.

When coaching is a mandated requirement of a leader's role, the way that it is enacted is explained by one organisational leader thus: *"I set the scene from the very beginning when we recruit new leaders that part of their role is the coaching of their team and others, not just their team . . . from a 'pay it forward' perspective."* In other words, the organisation asks, *"What have you learnt from others, and how can you share that with somebody else?"* In addition, if the function has, say, 500 employees, the question is asked, *"is the leader able to manage that well, and are they actually able to coach within a leadership framework to make sure that people are performing?"*

Leaders are also expected to meet the needs of key stakeholders. For example, governments expect their workforce to respond to megatrends in the marketplace, adapting and responding quickly to the changing environment in which they work. Departments are increasingly expected to move towards a one-government approach to whole-of-government issues and challenges, working in multidisciplinary, multi-agency teams. If coaching is not a core capability of departmental leaders, *"we'll never meet the expectations of the Ministers in Parliament."* Governments require a workplace culture that supports sharing, working with each other, learning from each other, and guiding employees towards higher performance. Unless leaders coach their teams and team members, the expectations set by key stakeholders won't be met.

5.3.2 Coaching Is Positioned within Sales and Services Functions

The second element relating to the business drivers of coaching throughout the organisation at this third stage involves coaching being positioned within sales and services business units to improve team performance. These business units have accountability for the achievement of business targets focused on the generation of revenue for the organisation as a whole. Hence, the coaching initiative may start within the front-line sales and services functions which are directly customer-facing as these are the functional areas most likely to see an immediate financial return to the business from coaching. Within these business units, coaching is used to support team leaders and front-line staff win sales deals of substantial proportions. Leaders of these business units recognise how important it is to get the best performance from the teams they lead because the revenue that they generate supports not only their business operations but also the corporate services and regulatory obligations that are delivered by the rest of the organisation.

In a revenue-generating distribution or retail sales environment, things are fast-paced. There's urgency to the interaction. Decisions must be made quickly or even on the spot. Problems emerge which must be dealt with immediately. Front-line employees are familiar with this environment and trained to respond appropriately. Hence, in this third stage, coaching needs to be positioned within business units rather than the HR function so that leaders are ready to respond to emerging opportunities or to counter potential threats quickly. Organisations which continue to have coaching reside within the HR function with a learning and development focus will find that their organisation will have difficulty progressing to this third stage of developing a coaching culture unless the responsibility for coaching is transferred and positioned within business units.

Business unit leaders have a wealth of experience in front-line roles, so they can focus their coaching on both the behavioural aspects of interacting as a member of a team as well as on the performance aspects of meeting business targets. Behavioural coaching is used to break down the *"silo"* mentality that may develop in organisations, which tends to reduce the level of performance because of internal disagreement and conflict. *Performance coaching* is used to drive business improvement, for example, by demonstrating how coaching can be used to manipulate new technology which supports business growth. Technology allows common infrastructure to be built across organisations to leverage scale efficiencies, influence performance and underpin economic returns. At the same time, the leaders can use their coaching skills to have a specific conversation about personal development which means so much to team members and their level of engagement.

Within sales and services functions, high-performance teams engage in rigorous debate and use consistent, common language, which ultimately drives success. Team members listen to the various customer concerns and support each other to ensure that the team has options and is on track for a sales win and to review the win thereafter. Hence, high-performance teams are more than just utilising the strengths of individuals and the team as in *performance coaching*. They engage team members at a personal level as integral contributors to team performance. A business unit leader comments that, in his organisation, he found there was *"a real appetite for people to just really start a personal development conversation and create some self awareness"* and that coaching was the answer he was looking for to take his team to that place. Coaching provides the vehicle to enable the sales leadership team to have meaningful conversations with their sales team around the information that is generated from data analysis and reports, which helps them make decisions that drive performance. By embracing *pure coaching*, leaders discover that there's a whole other layer to coaching outside of a one-dimensional, strengths- or performance-based conversation to develop their teams and team members.

Overall, when an organisation is in the third stage of developing a coaching culture at the *Coaching-as-Leader-Capability* stage, they have progressed from *functional* drivers of performance being centrally located within the HR function where their remit is to develop a training and learning experience for leaders and talented individuals, to *business* drivers of coaching positioned within business units where performance has a direct impact on revenue generation. The *performance* motivation in this stage focuses on economic returns to the business from behavioural change and improved team performance. Combined with a *practice* conceptualisation of coaching, leaders in this third stage of developing a coaching culture foster team engagement and the retention of talent, which makes central to this stage the business environment and business performance.

5.4 Internalised Delivery

The final element that characterises the *Coaching-as-Leader-Capability* stage concerns how coaching is delivered. In this third stage, coaching is delivered *internally* by leaders as a requirement of their role in two ways: (1) by coaching each of their direct reports individually to change their behaviour and improve their performance and (2) by *team coaching* to achieve business outcomes. Coaching by leaders is a cost-effective way of spreading coaching practice throughout the organisation.

5.4.1 Leaders Deliver Coaching to Their Team and Team Members

The first element of an internalised delivery of coaching at this third stage involves leaders coaching their team and individual team members as a requirement of their role. Business unit leaders are the ones who are accountable for meeting business objectives within budget. They're also the ones who spend the most time with their direct reports. They direct their energy and focus of activities within their area of responsibility. External coaches have their value but are nowhere near the centre of action when it comes to the immediacy that can be exerted to change behaviour and performance almost immediately as this quote emphasises:

Oh, hell no! Coaching's got to sit with the line managers. No one else can do it.

5.4.1.1 Individual Coaching

In this third stage, leaders conduct one-on-one coaching and feedback conversations with their direct reports every four to six weeks. To commence the coaching, they may request that team members undertake behaviour profiling to identify individual strengths and opportunities for improvement and map the dynamics of the team. When a team member displays behaviours which are inconsistent with organisational values, a coaching conversation is conducted and as a result, the individual may decide to change their behaviour so that they can relate better to other members of the team, and the team can function more effectively, or exit the organisation.

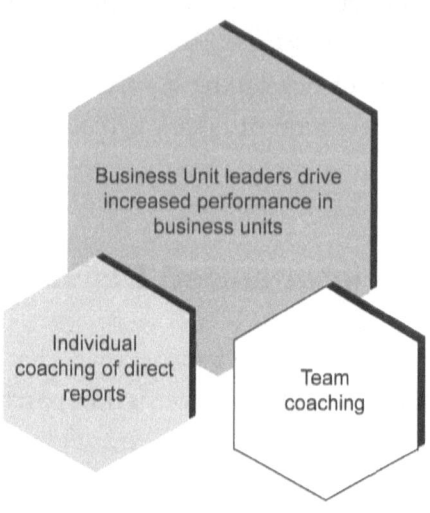

> *I remember a company once where the director of HR was a friend of mine. Every Monday, they had a directors' meeting. If the director of building and construction said* I've saved a million dollars out of that building in the city, *they would go,* Wow, isn't that fantastic! How did you do that? *He said, if I said I've saved a million dollars through staff turnover they'd go,* Well, isn't that your job? *He said the only reason staff turnover reduced in this company was that he got the CEO to tie staff turnover into individual director's performance bonus. Everybody had to have their staff turnover below 20 per cent, or it affected*

their bonus. That's the only reason why they even looked at staff turnover.

One of the biggest barriers for leaders to coach their team members is having time to coach. They are often so busy with their role and delivering on their responsibilities that they don't make the time to coach. However, when coaching is a requirement of their role and their span of control is realistic, the environment is set for them to fulfil on their coaching obligations. Their coaching is not just a *"car wash"* approach to say that *"I've done coaching"*. It's an investment of the leader's time in increasing organisational capability.

An example of the turmoil that leaders can encounter on a daily basis is provided by the story of a leader who wants to coach his direct reports and starts to, but then gets *"sucked back"* into the 'doing' and urgency of daily priorities. This organisational leader likens his situation to *"someone swimming in an ocean called coaching, but then there's this whirlpool of the daily reality of dealing with priors. I can be coaching for a while but, inevitably, I get pulled back into the reality of problem-solving."* When the urgency of the daily priorities has abated, the leader has to recreate his coaching headspace and recollect his thoughts to get back into the mindset of coaching—out of the day-to-day turmoil that seems to happen all too often.

Coaching, when used as a reflective practice, allows busy leaders the time and headspace to relax and think through their role—what they are doing and how they are doing it—and search internally for better ways of operating. It allows leaders to *"hit the pause button for an hour"*, examine the goals and challenges ahead, look at what's working and what's not, and identify what they need to do differently to create a more desirable future.

A factor that may determine the success of a leader coaching their team members is the degree to which they have confidence in their ability to coach, and a key component of this is whether they have received coaching themselves or not. Those leaders who have been coached have more confidence and inner strength to transition into a *coaching leadership style* because they know that as a *leader who coaches,* they don't have to have all the answers, whereas as a *manager of the business unit*, they do. Leaders who are very comfortable with themselves and understand the relative vulnerability of being a coach within a business environment will succeed in greatly assisting those whom they coach to find that comfort and inner strength within themselves.

5.4.1.2 Team Coaching

The second way that leaders coach within business units is by team coaching at the collective level —also a requirement of their role. The motivation is to increase team engagement and ownership of performance outcomes. Leaders who coach use an *ask* rather than *tell* methodology with their teams to generate ideas and options for improved performance. *Team coaching* can occur every day or every week as leaders focus their team on achievement of their 30/60/90-day plan, highlighting opportunities for forward movement. It's an ongoing discussion that incorporates coaching as an embedded skill in their day-to-day leadership of the team. Intelligence is shared, ideas for improvement are encouraged, and options for action are examined. Leaders use the team's perspective to identify if a new idea will be embraced and if the team is equipped to execute it. Team coaching is about helping each team member understand how they can leverage each other's strengths rather than *"hedging their own little turfs"*. If team members view coaching as a means to enhance their personal and professional improvement, it's likely they will shift the way they behave with each other from then on, which will influence changes in interaction within the team, and the result will be *"phenomenal"*.

When leaders model team coaching, they expect that each team member will go back to their team and do the same. In this way, coaching will cascade fluidly down the organisation with very little effort and no call on the business unit's budget for external coaching services. The response of team members may initially be mixed because they may not be familiar with coaching or may not have been exposed to a *coaching leadership style* before. However, over time, coaching practice becomes a regular feature of team and business interactions.

An example of team coaching is of a leader who has coached his team for the past five years. In that time, team members have changed but he has remained the constant factor in promoting the coaching agenda. When they meet, team members ask themselves, *"Is this the best value way that we, as a leadership team, can be spending our time at this moment for this business unit?"* As new recruits enter the team, an existing team member is assigned to *"bring them up to speed"* on the *coaching leadership style* and how the team coaching sessions operate. Using this approach, team interactions have moved from *"reactive to dependent to independent to interdependent"* over the five years, even with multiple changes in individual team members.

Another example is of an executive director who meets one-on-one with each of her direct reports every four to six weeks. Their individual coaching sessions focus on work in progress but also include discussions around how the team member is developing themselves through the work that they're doing and identifying any issues that may be holding them back. The coaching conversation asks, *"Have you thought about? Tell me how you see that. Oh, that's interesting. How would you play that? What would be the effect of that sort of decision?"* In this way, the coaching is simultaneously motivated by performance and development intentions, which demonstrate to the individual that they are a valued member of the team.

A third example is of a high-performing team in the hospitality industry which had *"distension within the ranks"*. The business owner was a talented general manager but someone who gave his team a little too much freedom. As they pushed the boundaries of that freedom, team members started to *"tread on each other's toes"* causing even more trouble. Adopting a *coaching leadership style*, the business owner conducted individual coaching sessions with his team members and then brought them together for two days of team coaching in which he reinforced the one-on-one individual coaching with *"team work"*. As a result, the group came together as a team and started supporting each other to achieve improved business outcomes.

5.4.2 Specialist Coaches "Coach to Revenue"

The second element relating to the internalised delivery of coaching at this third stage involves the appointment of specialist coaches to business units to coach team leaders in specific performance aspects of their role, for example, how to win more sales. These specialist coaches are well-experienced business operatives. They know their customers' needs and wants and are intimately acquainted with how the business works. They use their specialist knowledge and skills to identify the significant business levers that will make a huge difference in terms of identifying the best prospects to approach and how to approach them to ensure the best chance of success in winning a sales deal.

An example is of a specialist coach who works in a revenue-generating business unit of a very large telecommunications company with national and international clients whose leaders know about and support coaching. He works in a $7 billion division of the $26.5 billion organisation, concentrating on international opportunities particularly in Asia and the US. In Australia, his division manages the top 1,200 enterprise and government accounts including the major banks. With thirty-five years of sales experience in this industry, he is able to examine a deal impartially and objectively which gives him the authority to start coaching account executives in areas that they hadn't thought of before because they have *"emotional blinkers"* on. As a coach, he explores options with them about how to approach existing and potential clients in different ways to increase their organisational engagement and generate increased sales revenue.

This specialist coach uses proprietary organisational software with pre-set criteria which allows the user to determine the likelihood of success of a particular strategy or action to generate increased revenue. He relies on this software tool because, whilst opinions are good, they need to be tested, and the only legitimate way to test an opinion is to use coaching as a tool that puts a science behind a major opportunity. He trains account executives in a qualification and validation process before they engage with either an existing or new client. In a disciplined coaching session, they review the particular vulnerabilities of any deal and look closely at the relationships the executives have within those acquisition accounts. He uses the software tool to assist account executives in deciding how best to approach a particular client or target market. They appreciate his support because he uses a coaching approach and a sports analogy to motivate them to perform better in the field of work without actually doing it for them. Following the success of his employment as a full-time specialist coach, his organisation is now training additional specialist coaches in coaching skills so that they can work in specific areas of the business as part of their 'day job' to generate increased revenue in other business units.

> *I'm there because they can't see their swing—bit like a golf coach, you know. They're too into the trees and the bushes, and I need to bring them out and show them that the maze is not that scary and that if we do all the right things, we can orchestrate ourselves to go from point A to point B, which is a successful sale. But there's a lot of stage gates that we've got to get through to lift our performance and execute against an agreed set of goals.*

5.4.3 Internal Coaches and Coaching Teams Deliver Behavioural and Performance Coaching

The third element relating to the internalised delivery of coaching at this third stage is the appointment of internal coaches or an internal coaching team to support front-line staff through behavioural coaching that releases issues that are holding them back from improving in their role. The internal coach is formally trained as a coach by an external coach-training provider in *pure coaching* techniques as well as *performance coaching*. With the coachee, the internal coach may address relationship, interpersonal, or behavioural issues that are impacting on the team member's ability to perform, and then work with the team or other team members to identity actions to remove these roadblocks.

> Interviewer: What would you say to somebody who suggests that if you've got dedicated coaches, then you don't need the leader to be a coach because the dedicated coaches will do all the coaching?
>
> *Yeah, it's not true. Not true at all. Having a dedicated coach, in my belief and opinion, is in addition to any leader-based coaching. It's a very different conversation because it's an impartial conversation. A leader as a coach will always be perceived and bring content to that conversation in a different way than an internal or external coach will. So I would see a dedicated coach as an addition to leader coaching. This coaching might focus on a specific area of need over a particular length of time. It would complement the coaching that the leader, as coach, is doing. And the leader-as-coach would actually tap into that. They'd tap into that in their own coaching and their own conversations with their team member.*

Internal coaching teams may be created to support all the business units in the organisation. As an example, an organisation in the financial services industry has established an internal coaching team which can respond swiftly to emerging needs of the organisation in times of change. As a dedicated team, they have an opportunity to operate almost independently of the business unit as they are not involved in the day-to-day machinations of the business and can function akin to an external coaching service, which has many advantages in terms of confidentiality and the way that employees perceive the service within the business unit. Being able to report into a senior executive champion gives the internal coaching team a different level of engagement and enablement. Employees see coaching more as an investment in them rather than an imposition on their 'day job', which makes it easier for them to respond positively to the coaching process.

This internal coaching team now sits within a front-line sales and services business unit where coaching can be leveraged to obtain maximum performance from employees. However, that wasn't always the case. In one restructure, the internal coaching team was taken out of the business unit and placed within the HR function where their brief became very different. It was to develop three coach-training programs for all leaders based on whether they were new to business, middle performers, or moving from the middle to upper band, for which they won a CEO's award. However, the team became disillusioned and was nearly disbanded because of the amount of red tape, sign-off, and *"hoops to jump through"* when positioned within the HR function versus when the team was in a distribution area of the business where decisions are made more quickly. They stayed in the HR function for only twelve months before they were transferred back into the distribution area where they could make a greater impact and *"show it on the scoreboard"* sooner.

Overall, when organisations are in the third stage of developing a coaching culture at the *Coaching-as-Leader-Capability* stage, coaching is delivered by leaders to their teams and team members on a regular basis. Specialist and internal coaching teams deliver coaching to support the leader-led coaching, particularly in relation to front-line, customer-facing staff who generate increased revenue for the business.

5.5 Summary of Stage 3

Coaching-as-Leader-Capability

In summary, when an organisation is in the third stage of developing a coaching culture at the *Coaching-as-Leader-Capability* stage, the *practice* conceptualisation of coaching is as an expected capability of leaders within a leadership development framework. The *performance* motivation for coaching is for leaders to improve the performance of their teams, increase engagement, and retain talent. The *business* drivers for coaching are business unit leaders, supported by specialist and internal coaches particularly in revenue-generating business units, who *internally deliver* coaching to their teams and team members to generate increased revenue for the business.

5.6 Case Studies

Stage 3
Coaching-as-Leader-Capability

Case Study 9

> *GenAdvance* is a large public sector organisation that delivers basic utility services to the general public. It is on a journey to support individual leaders to improve their performance, and change their behaviour. A leadership framework which incorporates coaching as a required leader capability has been built based on a values-led leadership style. The leadership framework is underpinned by the agreed understanding of senior leaders that values-based leadership behaviours are expected at every level of the organisation and that these behaviours are as important as management skills, technical skills, and experience—an appreciation that leadership has technical elements particularly at the team leader level but not especially at the senior leadership level where technical skills are often so diluted as to be completely redundant.
>
> The leadership framework is balanced by a real understanding of *who* leaders need to be and *how* they need to 'show up' in the organisation in terms of their behaviour. The framework is focused on behaviours like connection and the ability to manage diversity, how to manage change effectively and communicate the changes in a humane way, and the ability to coach and develop employee capability. It's heavily weighted towards *behaviours-in-action* that flow through to every aspect of the business, including the language that leaders use, the way that performance conversations are conducted, and how behaviours affect team members as well as team culture.

GenAdvance uses the language of *leadership* in their development programs and promotional materials rather than *coaching* because their employees find *leadership* a more acceptable term than *coaching*. Hence, the conversations that leaders engage in have a strong coaching element but, principally, they focus on the 'bigger picture' leadership framework, which leads to improved performance and increased employee engagement. GenAdvance believes that the coaching initiatives they have put in place have started to achieve business and organisational goals more quickly and effectively than ever before.

Case Study 10

InnovationOne is a leading telecommunications and technology company offering a wide range of services within Australia and South East Asia from programmable networks to enterprise collaboration tools. Their Global Services Division (GSD) manages the top 1,000+ enterprise and government accounts worldwide and has an annual turnover of $25+ billion. The division creates transformative, innovative solutions for businesses using the most advanced technologies to liberate the workforce, reach growth markets, and secure new business. Using cutting-edge technologies and ideas, InnovationOne runs critical systems around the country, dealing with the 'top end of town'—very senior executives and senior public servants going right up to the Prime Minister. These sales engagements are critical to InnovationOne's business success. Not every deal needs to be coached but the critical ones do, particularly *"if you're bringing in junior people and putting them in development roles in sales organisations because if you don't coach them, you're just going to constantly be doing their job"*, which Ben, a specialist coach, notes a lot of InnovationOne's sales managers *"end up doing and that's why they don't have time for coaching. It's a vicious cycle"*.

Ben coaches sales account executives to win deals, some of which are worth hundreds of millions of dollars. He equips sales account executives with the necessary skills, attributes, and standards of proficiency to perform in their role. With thirty-five years' experience in sales, he knows selling, and he knows what customers want. Headquartered in Australia, Ben regularly liaises with counterparts in other locations in the Asia-Pacific rim. As a specialist coach in GSD, Ben's role is to give the sales team *"the confidence that the strategies, tactics, and techniques surrounding a particular deal"* will win InnovationOne the deal. He works with the sales team to help them see where they are going and how they can execute against an agreed set of goals.

As an essential component of how the GSD does business, a coaching methodology is used to facilitate analysis of the business intelligence and research that is made available to the team from InnovationOne's finance division. The sales team are not the usual *"spreadsheet jockeys, sitting there looking at the numbers, punching out reports, doing the cadence"* to generate sales. Rather, with Ben's coaching, the sales team data-mine the research on each client and create value propositions that will sell. But it's the *"coaching to revenue"* that raises ideas and options to maximise the acquisition of new and existing deals, supports the achievement of specific sales goals, and exploits revenue opportunities.

The account executives who are responsible for meeting sales targets meet with Ben whenever there's an important conversation to be had with a new or existing client - which is frequently as they're constantly sourcing new deals. The coaching approach that he uses has been so successful that twelve organisational leaders at the middle management level who are advocates of coaching have been selected to participate in the launch of a dedicated 'boot camp' to show them how to coach and to certify and accredit them in the use of the proprietary software tool that InnovationOne uses to meet the additional demand for the coaching that Ben does with sales teams. When trained, these new specialist coaches, who also have day-job leadership roles, will undertake 'deep dives' with their teams into prospective deals. They will also have the opportunity to 'cross-pollinate' their coaching services within other revenue-generating divisions in Australia and overseas. To ensure the quality of their coaching, they will have to undergo annual certification of their coaching skills so that they are *"absolutely at the top of their game"*. In developing additional specialist coaches, InnovationOne is *"raising the tide to raise all the boats"* not only to increase revenue generation but also so that the organisation is less reliant on external coaches.

The business drivers for coaching in InnovationOne are the sales executives who support team leaders and front-line staff to *"win sales deals that make a quantifiable contribution to revenue"*. The coaching methodology was adopted by business leaders to qualify and validate major deals better. It is now well entrenched in all GSD's sales divisions in Australia and the Asia-Pacific regions which is so very important because *"we can spend hundreds of thousands if not millions of dollars on the pursuit of a deal and lose it"*. Hence, the account executives have been quick to grasp the coaching approach and use it with their teams. However, non-revenue-generating divisions of InnovationOne have yet to adopt a coaching approach.

CHAPTER 6
STAGE 4
COACHING-AS-CULTURE

The fourth stage in developing a coaching culture is labelled *Coaching-as-Culture*. During this stage, coaching is an essential component of the cultural change process which aims to develop all employees in the organisation to reach their potential. This final stage is characterised by an *organic conceptualisation* of coaching as naturally occurring and a *transformational motivation* to achieve personal, business, and organisational change. The CEO and senior executives are responsible for driving coaching *top down* throughout the organisation via the *integrated* delivery of coaching into everything everybody does as they communicate and relate in daily business transactions.

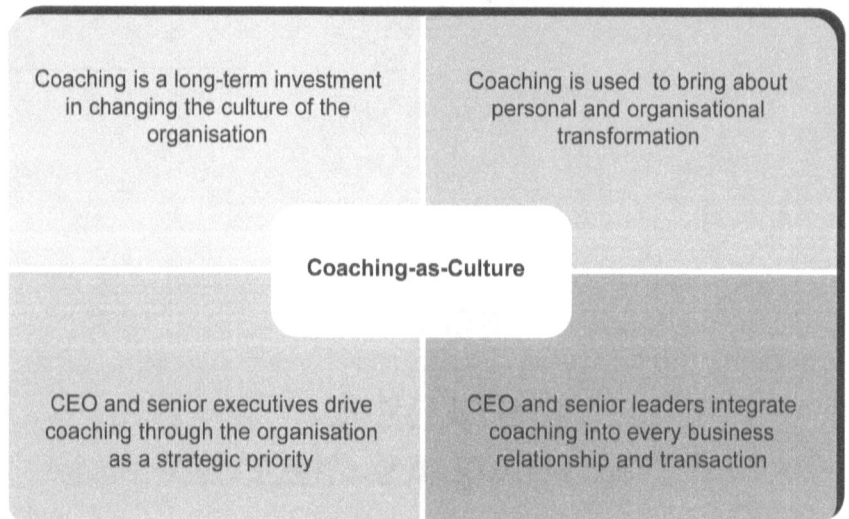

Figure 6.1: Coaching-as-Culture Stage

6.1 Organic Conceptualisation

In the *Coaching-as-Culture* stage of developing a coaching culture, organisational leaders' conceptualisation of coaching is as an organic and naturally occurring activity—just part of *"how we do things around here"*. Coaching is part of the DNA of the organisation and a lens through which to analyse all business transactions to achieve increased productivity and competitive advantage. Coaching is given meaning as part of the fabric of the organisation and a platform for cultural change.

6.1.1 Coaching Is Part of the DNA and Fabric of the Organisation

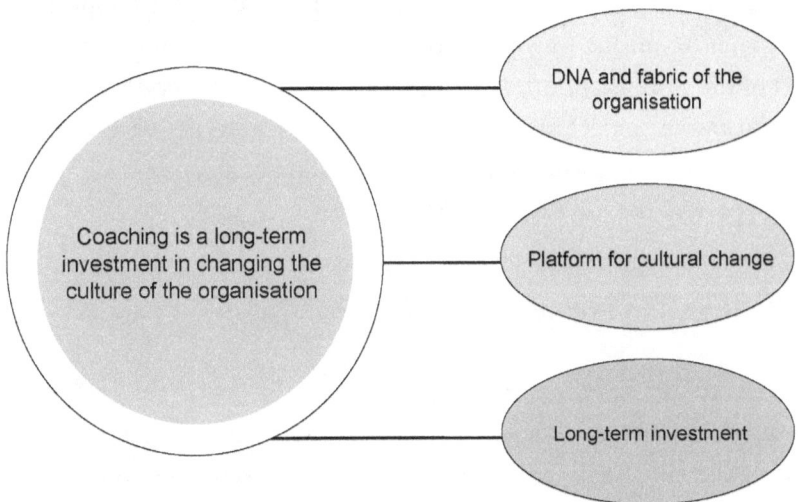

Figure 6.2: Coaching is a long-term investment

When coaching is conceptualised as *organic* and naturally occurring, it becomes part of the DNA and fabric of the organisation. Coaching conversations happen in the course of a day's work. They may be conducted formally on a scheduled basis or informally as the need arises. Formal coaching sessions are usually for an hour's duration; however, informal coaching conversations could last for just a minute or two or maybe ten to fifteen minutes depending on the issue or concern. As leaders are *"slow to speak"* and really listen to team members, they guide them on a journey to discover their own solutions. Leaders recognise the human side of their people assets and pay attention to the intent and potential of all their employees, recognising them as *"human beings first and then they do their work"*. With that recognition, leaders pay attention to *who* their employees are, *how* they are being in the workplace, and *how* that shapes their performance rather than the coaching conversation just being about the task.

As an accepted organisational practice in this final stage, coaching assists employees to do what they need to do to meet their individual, team, and business goals and objectives. Coaching is not something special or something that leaders do in addition to their daily responsibilities—it's just part of *how* they do business and *how* they lead their teams. In a coaching culture, every conversation is an opportunity for coaching in one way or another. Everybody is sharing as a normal part of the work that leaders do—just a little piece of everything that fits together with something else within organisational activities. Organic coaching is a standard inclusion in normal daily activities—a *"come to work"* part of the job - *"almost like exercise"*.

6.1.2 Coaching Provides a Platform for Cultural Change

A second way that coaching is *organically* conceptualised is as a platform for cultural change. In this final stage, coaching is an integral part of the culture of *"who we are and what we represent"* and *"the way we do things around here"*. Culture emerges from the stories that are told about the history of the organisation—whether that's culture in the sense of art, music, language, food, or people. That culture replicates into the workplace because employees are recruited from different walks of life and ethnicities and together, they form an organisational culture based on their shared experiences. The word *culture* is about *"our story—and coaching should just be part of that story—part of how we are."*

A coaching culture is developed from the common and shared understandings of organisational members in relation to how work is done and how they interact with each other as they perform their duties. When leaders and everybody coach each other on a daily basis in this final stage, a philosophy is developed, which guides all personal and business transactions and sets the foundations for a platform that supports human flourishing and business sustainability. The platform is the common coaching philosophy, coaching language, and shared coaching approach. There's a way of coaching that everyone understands, accepts, and adheres to, which includes compassion and a shared interest in outcomes which are of benefit not only to individuals and teams but to the organisation as a whole. Coaching is about *"what's done around here"* rather than *"what's done out there, for here"* (i.e. outsourced). A coaching approach guides and pre-empts the thinking before actions are taken. Once a platform for coaching has been developed, it can be applied to every situation including how decisions are made, how problems are solved, and how communication flows throughout and external to the organisation. When the organisation has a problem, coaching is recognised as the vehicle that enables the organisation to overcome it.

Leaders who enter an organisation with big aspirations and dreams about how they will shift the culture may become frustrated when they realise that all the history of that business may make it difficult to implement change. Take, for example, an organisation in the manufacturing industry with national service centres. The organisation is heavily losing money in its manufacturing arm. To change the culture, senior executives need to change their business model and how leaders interact with their staff. They decide to split the thirty-year-old manufacturing side of the business, which is highly industrialised, from the services side which is showing promise of profitability so that it can become more nimble and responsive to customer needs, and then work with staff in the production plant to change the leadership style and culture. However, changing the DNA of an organisation isn't something that happens just because executives say, *"This is what we're going to do now."* They need to consult with shareholders, staff, and unions to broker a deal that is acceptable to all parties and that will bring the majority of staff along with them to ensure continuity of production to feed their renewed services division after the deal is done.

The *fire* analogy presented in Stage 1 represents how conceptualisations of coaching have changed as organisations progress in their understanding of coaching and a coaching culture. In Stage 1, *Coaching-as-Intervention*, coaching is a *fast burn*. It's like lighting a match. It's gone out and forgotten very quickly. It's a transactional scenario within the organisation. In Stage 2, *Coaching-as-HR-Function* where coaching is a training and learning experience, coaching is a *slow-burn* fire. It's smouldering and ready to burst into flames but not quite yet. In Stage 3, *Coaching-as Leader-Capability*, coaching is a *moderate burn*, making an impact on some of the business units within the organisation but not all. In Stage 4, *Coaching-as-Culture*, coaching is a *raging bonfire* that keeps going and keeps everyone warm, creating light and comfort throughout the organisation. It's visible and can be seen, heard, and felt by everybody. As a raging bonfire, coaching is sustainably embedded into the organisation and can be leveraged within any area to bring about cultural change.

6.1.3 Coaching Is a Long-Term Investment

Cultural change takes time—eighteen months minimum, depending on the size of the organisation. To sustain cultural change takes a dedicated commitment, mindsets that believe in the potential of all individuals, and an ongoing investment in training, learning, and support for coaching practice. An example is of a CEO and senior executive team in a mining operation who were coached individually and as a group for three years during a cultural change process. The purpose was to build alignment across the organisation and a constructive coaching culture. The executive coach worked with the team and then with each of the senior executive's teams including their high potentials, around how to handle difficult situations and staff who had personal or professional issues to deal with but whom the organisation wanted to retain. She describes it as *"a real privilege to be able to work with leadership teams who are committed to developing and to being the best leaders they can be for an organisation"*. In every interaction with these organisational leaders, her challenge was to help them understand just how powerful coaching can be within an organisational setting.

To progress a cultural transformation throughout an organisation, there needs to be a significant investment in coaching based on a sound business case that outlines the major benefits for individuals, teams, and the organisation in terms of productivity and competitive advantage. The investment has to be related to the achievement of business outcomes, reinforcing the organisational values, leadership effectiveness, employee engagement, and how coaching can be used to drive business performance. A business case is usually developed, which specifies: *"What are the expectations? What do we hope to achieve? Who are the key people who have experienced coaching and its benefits? What are the gaps in our business that we are hoping coaching will fill?"* As a narrative to drive change, a business case can be powerful in the hands of a coaching advocate who invites executives to join in the conversation.

Once the business case is approved, support from the top has to be explicit because employees *"look up and follow"*. There has to be a commitment to developing a coaching culture and to lead by example to model the coaching behaviour. The push for coaching must come from senior executives who are passionate and enthused about culture and capability as a whole and are messaging the benefits of coaching throughout the organisation.

Overall, when organisations are in the fourth and final stage of developing a coaching culture at the *Coaching-as-Culture* stage, the conceptualisation of coaching is *organic*. Coaching is part of the DNA and fabric of the organisation and a platform for cultural change. Coaching conversations happen *"in the moment"* as the need arises to develop all organisational members. A coaching culture is embedded within the organisation when there's a *"look and feel"* of a supportive, encouraging, and enabling environment, and coaching conversations happen naturally on a daily basis.

6.2 Transformational Motivation

A second element that characterises the *Coaching-as-Culture* stage concerns the motivation for *why* coaching is undertaken by the organisation. In this final stage, coaching is motivated by the CEO and senior executives' desire for *transformational* cultural change. Coaching transforms not only individuals because it is such an effective way of developing people, but also the organisation as it attempts to increase productivity and create competitive advantage. Transformational cultural change is achieved when organisational leaders: (1) support the personal transformation of all employees, (2) identify the key business levers that increase organisational productivity, and (3) leverage the organisation's human assets to achieve competitive advantage.

6.2.1 Coaching Promotes Personal Transformation

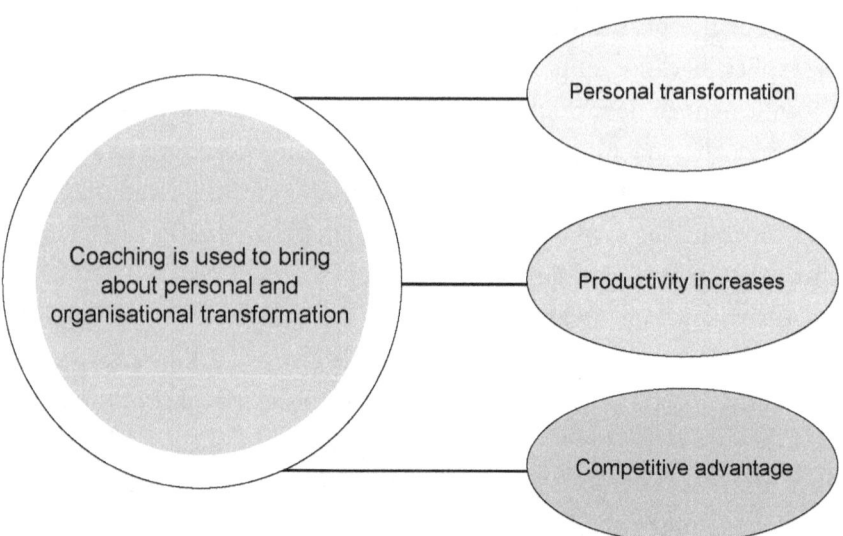

Figure 6.3: Coaching is used to bring about personal and organisational transformation

Under the *transformational* motivation in this final stage, coaching is seen as a way to unleash the potential of all employees, not just leaders and high-performing individuals, to bring about personal transformation. Organisations with a transformational motivation send a clear signal to employees that they care as much about their people and helping them reach their potential as they do about the goal and objectives for the team and business. In a transformational coaching culture, leaders provide all employees with developmental opportunities that are *"fit to role"* and *"fit to purpose"* in support of their professionalism and career development. This approach to team members ultimately leads to more engaged employees who are happier and more satisfied with their jobs and, when this occurs, leaders feel a greater level of job satisfaction too.

> *I think it's about having that growth mindset somewhere in the organisation where they realise people are able to be developed and wanting to be developed and the benefits of investing in them.*

A transformational motivation for coaching helps leaders shift their coaching practice so that it impacts on individuals and teams at both personal and professional levels. Coaching in this fourth stage supports individuals and teams to achieve a cultural shift, which is really *"about engaging the hearts and minds of employees'* as a *'visceral experience"*.

> *It's not something that's particularly granular. It's a shift of culture where consistently in every iteration, every interaction, you've got an approach to self-awareness and ongoing development, and leaders engage and develop people specifically.*

In this stage, coaching is used to unlock the potential of leaders who have attended a leadership development program but who have not been able to fully realise the benefits. These leaders need extra assistance in terms of not only their 'people skills' but also their own self-management within the leadership space. They may have had feedback like, *"You need to communicate more effectively"* or *"You need to build your reputation"*, but they have not had the follow-up support to achieve this. Or they may have attended generic coursework training programs which have given them the knowledge about what they should be doing, but not the ability to apply that knowledge into the everyday. They need coaching support to translate what they have learned in their 'head' into everyday 'heart' practice with their team and team members.

Not only does coaching in this final stage bring about personal insight and confidence but it also helps resolve interpersonal issues. An example is of a leader working in a regional hospital where there was a *"doctor/nurse-type issue"* in which an individual caused a number of team members to file a complaint. The complaint was sent *"two levels up from this team"* to the director of nursing and the director of medical, neither of whom had been in leadership positions before. The problem was that their roles and how they would work together had not been clearly defined, and so their professional relationship had to be sorted out first before the actual issue could be addressed.

Employees who are engaged and satisfied in their role perform better in the workplace which has a consequential, positive impact on the business 'bottom line'. Organisations which do not appreciate the value of all employees and are not motivated to develop the potential of all employees will find that they are held back from achieving cultural change because of their limiting belief in the ability of all employees to achieve peak performance. Coaching conversations are the way to unleash that potential.

6.2.2 Coaching Results in Productivity Increases for the Organisation

A second *transformational* motivation for coaching is to improve organisational productivity. In a coaching culture, coaching is viewed as an organisational activity integral to everything that occurs in a team and business unit. Coaching aims to transform workplace cultures to enable staff to become more successful and high-performing. To do this, leaders who coach need to take into account the complex system that surrounds people and the norming effect of culture. Coaching teams to increased productivity is a process that starts a chain of events in which individuals begin to interact differently with their environment to co-create a new system, a new reality with new behaviours that, in a coaching culture, foster increased cooperation and collaboration within teams. Leaders need to be aware of, and coach within, the different complex systems that are the team dynamic, the business environment, and the organisational vision and mission. At the same time, they must be aware of team members' coaching needs and guide them towards consciously navigating the realities of each system so that they can find their place as a force within each of these systems and influence the broader agenda.

At the organisational level, a coaching conversation with the executive team needs to identify the two or three key organisational levers that can be applied to reinforce business success, and ways to consistently use them until they are embedded within the organisation's culture. These levers may include for example, 'people levers', such as the inclusion of a coaching component in all training programs to ensure that the learnings are consistently applied thereafter in the workplace. A financial lever may be used to measure the impact of coaching programs in business units in which coaching has been rigorously applied to leverage productivity improvement. Another lever may be the identification of underperforming yet potentially new markets for exploitation or expansion and conducting a pilot program to measure the success of leveraging coaching into one of these areas. Challenging existing thinking can broaden the application of coaching into different areas of the business that had not previously been considered significant to business productivity.

6.2.3 Coaching Achieves Competitive Advantage for the Organisation

A third *transformational* motivation for coaching is to bring competitive advantage to the organisation. In a competitive market in which organisations have leveraged every physical asset, including all systems and technology, leaders start to consider leveraging their people. This is the hardest lever to pull because employees are not linear and cannot be easily manipulated. However, they can be encouraged and supported to look at things in a different way and embrace cultural change through coaching as a way of increasing their engagement and commitment to organisational initiatives. Even organisations in downturn, which have not invested in their people before, will invest in hard economic times. There is no doubt that developing a coaching culture will bring competitive advantage to the organisation during difficult times because,

Any time people can feel like they're supported and valued, they will get to a point where they can do their best. And any organisation which recognises that will far outperform the competition. I don't care if you're washing cars, planting bushes, or running a bank.

Within the private sector, the main purpose of achieving competitive advantage is to obtain financial gain. However, from a public sector perspective, the reason is less obvious. It is to ensure a supply of talented individuals who can lead within the government sector, thereby achieving government priorities and improving on the outcomes from government spending for the benefit of the general public. Competition for talented individuals means that government entities try to position themselves as an *"employer of choice"* with wages and conditions comparable to the private sector to attract the most suitable candidates. These organisations need to meet the expectations of multiple stakeholders, including Ministers who have to report in Parliament on how public funds are spent. Senior executives of government entities don't want their performance to be *"just average"* - they want it to be *"exceptional"*.

A coaching culture is particularly important when crisis situations arise in the external marketplace and organisational leaders need to act immediately to seize the opportunity or eliminate the threat. It assists organisations to *respond* to these situations rather than *react* to them. The crisis may have been precipitated by, for example, a rise in commodity prices or changes in legislation such as privatisation of a government entity. These externally driven, often unanticipated, events can have a major impact on an organisation such as threatening its profitability or forcing it to change direction or priorities. External events are often the triggers for organisations to do something different so that they can overcome the crisis and adapt to the changed situation. Coaching is a powerful way for leaders to overcome or indeed exploit a crisis for competitive advantage as the following story illustrates:

I was working with a large well-known national organisation, and they were given a report by one of the

Big 4 consulting firms that said, If you keep doing what you're doing, you're going to lose $12 billion in the next ten years. *So it's those kind of punches that get CEOs to wake up and go,* We've got to do it differently. This isn't working. *So they sent out a communication that said,* Look, we're not going to deliver [our product] every day. *You can imagine the revolt:* What do you mean? That's our DNA. That's what we do. *So they realised,* Oh, we can't just tell people. We've got to somehow win their hearts and minds.

Organisations generally accept the research that reports on the value and benefits of coaching. However, because budgets and time are limited, they have to make calls on where to focus their efforts. When margins are tight, they need to decide if coaching is one of the key skill sets to deliver on business targets. It's really a *"catch 22– chicken and egg"* situation. Productivity really needs to improve for the organisation to survive, but they need to spend money to achieve the productivity improvement. In some organisations facing new entrants into the market with advanced technology, there is an urgent need to identify the key levers that can be better utilised to at least maintain their current standing in the marketplace, if not improve it. Coaching may be the capability that organisations decide to utilise as they seek better ways to deliver on their vision and mission.

In the previous third stage of developing a coaching culture, coaching was recognised as a valuable capability of leaders who coach their team and team members. In this final stage, coaching is understood as the way to support all employees to achieve their best through coaching conversations that occur all the time, not just formally but informally as well. Anyone in the organisation can adopt a coaching approach to any conversation with any employee for any reason. Employees seek development, and if they cannot find it in their workplace, they'll look for it elsewhere. Like peeling back the layers of an onion, employees want to find out *"what makes them [and others] tick"*. A coaching culture enables them to find the answers.

Overall, when organisations are in the final stage of developing a coaching culture at the *Coaching-as-Culture* stage, the motivation for coaching is *transformational.* Coaching is an enabler of personal and professional growth for all employees and facilitates transformation of the entire organisation by improving the productivity of business units, creating opportunities for the organisation to gain competitive advantage in the marketplace and achieve transformational cultural change.

6.3 Top-Down Drivers

A third element that characterises the *Coaching-as-Culture* stage concerns who in the organisation is driving coaching throughout the organisation. In this fourth stage, coaching is driven by passionate and committed CEOs and senior executives who provide strong sponsorship for, and buy-in to, cascading coaching throughout the organisation. Coaching becomes a strategic priority. A coaching champion is appointed at the senior level. The CEO and senior executives speak publicly about the value of coaching and model coaching behaviour. Coaching is positioned within all business units to deliver the greatest ROI for the organisation.

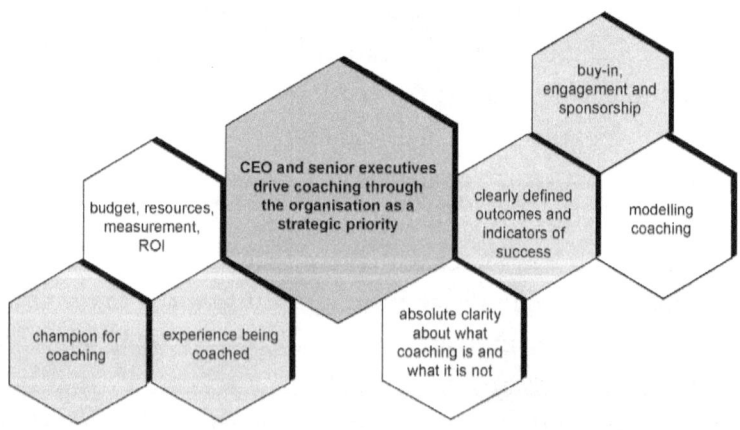

Figure 6.4: CEO and senior executives drive coaching through the organisation

6.3.1 CEO and Senior Executives Drive the Coaching Agenda

Coaching, in this fourth stage, is positioned within all business units. The executives responsible for business units are fully committed to the coaching agenda and cascading it down their levels. The *top-down* drivers of transformational cultural change are the CEO and senior executives who are passionate about coaching and delivering coaching as a core capability of leaders. In this final stage, a committed executive team has defined what coaching means to the organisation and how it fits with their desired culture. They recognise not only the opportunities but also the limits of their employees doing coaching, which requires a degree of trust, transparency, and confidentiality. They are clear on what their vision and values are and make explicit the kind of leadership they want and for why. Organisations which do not have *top-down* drivers for coaching will find that "*pockets*" of interest in coaching will spring up within various business units, but they will have difficulty in achieving transformational cultural change throughout the entire organisation. Moreover, if the senior executives are not passionate about coaching or don't see the value in it, then,

> *It's gonna kind of die in the arse. And we went through a period where we had a change of leadership, and you know, our senior leaders were people who just didn't believe in coaching. So it did die in the arse.*

> Interviewer: Who would be making that commitment [to develop a coaching culture] and deciding which place to start?
>
> *The highest level possible in the organisation. Absolutely C-suite. So if it's not the CEO, it would be an executive general manager who is absolutely passionate about developing people. Not necessarily someone from HR but someone who has a big job to deliver on, understands that coaching is not the only thing, but it's certainly something that can be used to leverage and get better return on investment of our other programs. You know, improve our engagement and our enablement. And you know, build resilience in people and support them through the change whilst at the same time helping them be better, faster, stronger, and deliver on the expectations of their role.*

6.3.1.1 CEO and Senior Executives Experience Being Coached

The most critical element in progressing to this final stage is the absolute and demonstrated commitment of the senior executives to being coached themselves. When senior executives talk openly about their experience of being coached and the benefits they have accrued, coaching takes on a credibility that wasn't afforded it before. If organisations do not have the top level displaying their commitment to coaching by coaching their team members and being coached themselves, there's little likelihood of transformational cultural change being achieved. The experience of executives being coached has been described as "*fertilising the ground*" for others in the organisation to see coaching as a developmental process to improve their performance as opposed to an intervention to support someone who needs assistance. Some executives may be formally coach-trained by an external provider and, hence, they may be even more committed to creating awareness of the value and benefits of coaching in achieving personal and organisational transformation.

> Interviewer: What do you see is the most critical element in getting a coaching culture together?
>
> *It would be the absolute and demonstrated commitment from the top. I think they need to be equipped with the skills to be able to do it. And they would have had to have been coached themselves to understand the experience.*

6.3.1.2 CEO and Senior Executives Have Absolute Clarity about What Coaching Is and What It Is Not

In order to change the culture of an organisation through coaching, the CEO and senior executives must have absolute clarity about what coaching is and what it is not, and what the organisation is trying to achieve by developing a coaching culture. Is it coaching or mentoring that the organisation wishes to engage in? Organisational leaders have become comfortable with the notion of mentoring but know less about coaching. They may not understand the purpose of introducing coaching into an organisation or know how coaching can change people's lives. Knowing about coaching and its capacity to impact powerfully on individuals, teams, and the organisation, starts with the CEO and top team. They are the organisational leaders who have to understand what *coaching* and developing a *coaching culture* mean and be fully committed to the coaching agenda for a coaching culture to develop, as this story illustrates:

An executive was sent to coaching by the CEO. In the first meeting with his coach, the steam was coming out of his ears, *and when he finally settled down, he said to the coach,* Look, I honestly don't know what to do. I have been rewarded all my life in this organisation for working the way that I have, and now my CEO gets up in a room and says, well, we don't want that, we want this, and I have no idea how to be this. *So, the executive had to unlearn past behaviours and learn a new set of behaviours more appropriate to how the executive role is expected to function today in* his organisation. Unlearning behaviours can erode confidence, especially in the transition stage from manager to leader.

6.3.1.3 CEO and Senior Executives Demonstrate Buy-In and Engagement with Coaching

For a coaching culture to exist and sustain, there needs to be high-level buy-in, engagement, and sponsorship of coaching by the executive team, which requires passion and enthusiasm for coaching to truly deliver on the cultural change. Role-modelling coaching has to come from the "*heart* not the *head*". There has to be honest, genuine buy-in and belief in coaching and its benefits. There are many reasons why change projects fail. However, when executives demonstrate total support for coaching and are seen to experience being coached themselves, there is less likelihood of failure.

An executive coach tells the story of working for two executive directors of a large national organisation with five geographic regions across the country over a period of five years. He was brought in to coach managers in the workforce. The executive directors who engaged him had been coached themselves and had an understanding of coaching, as had the CEO who supported the coaching initiative. Of the five geographic divisions, his two divisions plus one other were enthusiastic about coaching, the fourth somewhat, and the fifth not at all. There was *"no appetite for coaching"* in the latter division. They even changed the name from *coaching* to *performance management*. The person who was the designated coach in this division left because he couldn't get any traction for coaching. Unfortunately, the organisation had not put measures in place to record the benefits of coaching. Hence, there were no real business results from the coaching, and when the money ran out, so did the coaching. When the executive coach returned to his first division six months later, all the benefits had been lost because the director had been promoted, and his replacement was not interested in coaching. This story illustrates that unless coaching is embedded in organisational activities, it will only be sustained as long as a supportive executive is in place and sponsoring the coaching. When they leave, it will lose its organic nature and be relegated to, at best, an intervention or, at worst, renamed as *performance management*.

6.3.1.4 CEO and Senior Executives Model Coaching throughout the Organisation

When the CEO and senior executives are committed to developing a coaching culture, they are seen modelling coaching, messaging the importance of coaching and being coached, and *"walking the talk"* amongst employees at all levels of the organisation. The senior executives are approachable, amenable to listening and learning, and open to change suggestions. CEOs who truly understand that business success comes through their people make themselves personally available to employees who want to interact with them, for example, by chatting to employees to understand where they're coming from and what their needs might be, and then starting to address those needs. Once employees overcome their initial apprehension about intent, which is typified by, *"What? Why is this guy talking to me? I'm in accounts, and he's an MD,"* they will commit to *"walk over hot coals"* to help him and the organisation achieve its goals.

> Interviewer: Does the involvement of senior executives make a difference in developing a coaching culture?
>
> *Absolutely, yes. And with the latest cohort of the leadership development program, they found the coaching was the most valued part of the program. And bearing in mind that a lot of them are outdoor workers who are working in isolated areas. They don't network. They don't get face-to-face contact with anyone. And we had a really positive take-up rate of volunteer coaches ... and so these people were getting access to some very senior people who were very generous with their time. So for some of them, it was incredibly powerful.*

6.3.2 CEO and Senior Executives Make Coaching a Strategic Priority

When the CEO and senior executives are the *top-down* drivers of coaching throughout the organisation, they make coaching a strategic priority for the business. The momentum for coaching will take time to build—years even—to garner enough of a *"ground swell"* for it to cascade down all levels of the organisation. When there is complete commitment, the senior team looks to the budget to see how deep the coaching can go down the organisation. A strategy that is not only authorised by the senior team but one in which the CEO is personally involved, is devised to roll out the initiative and guide coaching culture development throughout the entire organisation. Other organisations which are not so committed will weigh up the value of investing in coaching as opposed to investing in other initiatives, and the decision they make is often dependent on the CEO's appetite for coaching. For example, some organisations which do not have the full support and endorsement of the CEO may decide to just train their leaders in coaching skills rather than attempt to develop a coaching culture.

6.3.2.1 Desired Outcomes and Success Indicators from Coaching Are Clearly Defined

In this final stage of developing a coaching culture, organisations are clear about what they are trying to achieve and have specified well-defined goals and outcomes from coaching programs. They have a clear *why* in terms of the purpose for introducing coaching into the organisation, *what* they want to change and *how* they want things to be, and a shared understanding of, *"What does coaching mean to us in this organisation? How does that connect with our broader values and goals as an organisation?"* This discussion takes place at all levels of the organisation as coaching is rolled out through the business units. In addition, the CEO and senior executives have a *growth mindset* and an absolute belief in providing transformational opportunities for all employees to reach their potential.

6.3.2.2 A Senior Executive Champion for Coaching Is Appointed

In this fourth stage, organisations appoint a senior executive as a coaching champion to promote coaching and steward the initiative throughout the organisation. The higher up the organisation that this champion sits, the more successful the coaching transformation will be and the sooner it will be realised. C-suite positioning is absolutely critical to success. If the champion is not the CEO, it should be a senior executive who is absolutely passionate about developing people, has a significant role to deliver on, and understands that if the organisation wants to assist people to navigate in a constantly changing environment, coaching is a formidable vehicle for doing that. The impact of a senior champion lauding the merits of coaching demonstrates the importance that the organisation places on coaching. Alternatively, a strong, transformational HR professional could be the champion for coaching if they have the full and demonstrated support of the CEO.

A cultural change project is not something that organisations "*hire out*" to external coaches to create alone, although executive coaches are usually engaged to design and develop the cultural change program from start to finish and assist with its implementation. The initiative and commitment has to start from somebody who authorises and embraces it at the top level of the organisation and appoints a coaching champion nearby. Unless the CEO determines the behaviours that they want to see displayed throughout the organisation—those that are consistent with the organisational values and those that are not—it's unlikely that coaching will be sustained in the long term.

6.3.2.3 Recurrent Budget Is Allocated for Coaching

When coaching is designated as a strategic priority for the organisation, a recurrent budget is committed to developing a coaching culture. It is insufficient and will not achieve the desired outcome if only a year-to-year allocation of funds is made. The CEO may leave and a new CEO may not support coaching. Funds may be redirected to other priorities or new initiatives. Training funds may be slashed in times of reduced revenue. This is where the dedication and commitment of a coaching champion are required to conduct an ongoing, convincing conversation with the senior team about the benefits of coaching. The champion can gain agreement for continued expenditure on coaching by one of the most convincing ways that executives know—providing evidence of the positive and tangible outcomes from coaching. Organisations which put measurement criteria in place and record data in relation to each and every coaching program are in an excellent position to display in hard facts, the benefits of approving the coaching expenditure, and the expected ROI that executives can look forward to in the coming year.

6.3.2.4 Outcomes from Coaching Are Measured, Including ROI

Organisations which establish measurement criteria and use this data to monitor and benchmark the effectiveness of the coaching that is being delivered across all coaching programs will answer not just these simple questions—*Is coaching happening?* and *What is the quality of those coaching conversations?*—but also, *What is the effectiveness of the coaching programs that are being delivered?* By answering these questions, organisational leaders will know *if* and *how* the coaching programs are delivering on the requirements of the workforce - that is, *Is the workforce getting better at the types of activities that they need to be engaged in in the performance of their roles?* The ROI is so important to organisations because:

> *Everybody is dollar-focused, so if they're going to spend $5, $10, $20 grand, then it's a very rare company that will spend that sort of money without expecting the executive you're working with to be more effective.*

As a strategic priority, leaders know that an ongoing budgetary commitment needs to be attached to the coaching strategy to transform the organisation's culture. Recurrent funding needs to be included in forward projections so that punctuated attempts to change the culture are not the result, as this story illustrates: "*We went one year from having a budget of $1.8 million to deliver a whole range of initiatives to help individuals and line managers to nothing the following financial year because there'd been a change of focus, a change of direction. I think there is an appetite for getting better at coaching, but like anything, it takes resourcing, and it takes time.*" However, in another organisation, "*That vision was clear about developing the capabilities of a line, and that stuck for many years. I could map out multiple programs that just year after year someone was able to find money in the budget to keep coaching going.*" Some organisations focus on developing the level below the CEO and senior executives because that's where things happen, and they assume that the people above them know and do coaching already—but maybe not? There is no doubt that organisations need to "*put their money where their mouth is first and foremost, otherwise the coaching initiative won't grow*".

One reason why organisations are reluctant to invest in coaching is because they don't know how to measure the ROI from coaching because the outcomes of coaching are not always easy to quantify. Indeed, the ROI may take some time to materialise because coaching often involves helping an individual break down barriers that have been built up over the years, so it's harder to ascertain the ROI until the individual has completed a coaching program and is practising new behaviours. However, in a sales environment where quantification can mean the difference between survival and extinction, measuring the success of coaching is relatively easy and critically important, as this story illustrates:

> *The issues we were grappling with were that we, as an organisation, were not very scientifically equipped to qualify and validate major deals, and that's a dangerous territory to be in as a sales organisation. So we've moved the needle. We're qualifying the deals better. Our win rates are up. Our execution is more efficient and effective.*

And they're doing all this using a coaching approach to winning sales.

As organisations prepare to transition to a *Coaching-as-Culture stage*, the reality of the size of the investment to be made may be daunting. Developing the coaching skills of all organisational leaders requires a significant investment, which many organisations cannot or may not be prepared to make. Investing in coaching within some business units is a good start. However, unless an organisation is fully committed to allocating the funds required to extend coaching into all business units, a lack of funds may starve the cultural change process. As well, unless organisations are prepared to take the time to identify the quantitative and qualitative measures of success from coaching, including positive and negative indicators, they will never be able to determine if the coaching programs have achieved the desired ROI, as an executive coach explains:

> *This particular organisation is coming to the end of a three-year program. We actually started doing a longitudinal study before the program started, and then we've checked in with interviewees every six months. So the organisation's got quite a bit of data now in terms of before and after on a whole range of measures. They can say that, for example, the effectiveness of leaders being able to give feedback to their people has gone from this per cent to that per cent. And we've got a whole range of measureable matrix data points.*

Overall, when organisations are in the fourth and final stage of developing a coaching culture at the *Coaching-as-Culture* stage, the key drivers of coaching are the CEO and senior executive team who are passionate about coaching and committed to driving coaching throughout the organisation. Coaching is designated as a strategic priority. The CEO and senior executives *"walk the talk"*, speak publicly about coaching, model coaching behaviour, and display buy-in and engagement for coaching by their sponsorship of, and dedication to, coaching programs. A recurrent budget for coaching is allocated, and the ROI is measured.

6.4 Integrated Delivery

The fourth element that characterises the *Coaching-as-Culture* stage concerns *how* coaching is delivered. In this fourth stage, everybody coaches and is coached. Leaders deliver coaching to their direct reports as an understood requirement of their role. Peers deliver coaching through informal delivery arrangements. Anyone, potentially, can be a coach. By starting the development of a coaching culture within the senior executive team, a coaching culture is cascaded down the organisation as executives model their support for coaching.

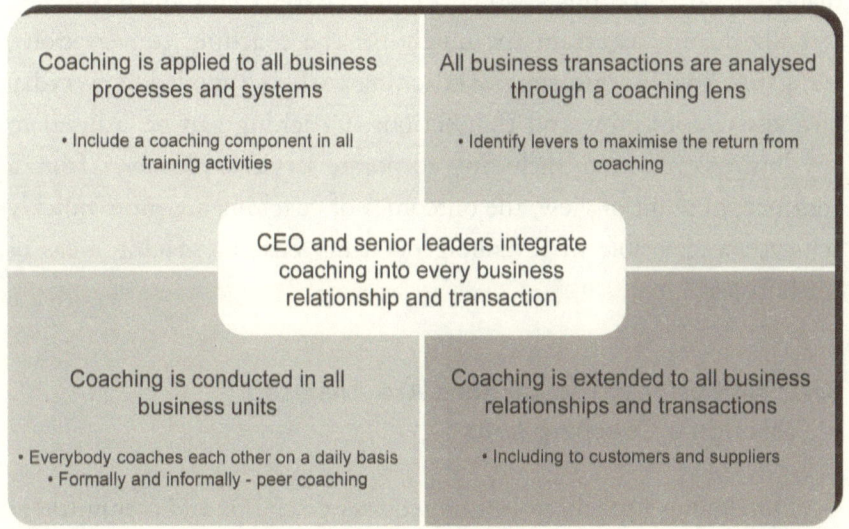

Figure 6.5: Coaching is applied to all business processes and systems

6.4.1 Coaching Is Applied to All Business Processes and Systems

When coaching is applied to all business processes and systems, a coaching approach is used to challenge existing thinking and extend coaching into other programs and areas of the business. The coaching approach is used to *"break free"* of restrictive mindsets, neutralise potential threats and biases that constrain forward movement, and contribute to the achievement of organisational initiatives, such as the introduction of diversity programs and working with millennials. If an organisation is serious about making coaching a strategic priority, coaching sessions are included in all training activities, even training for commercial and business acumen, as an effective means of embedding the skills back into the workplace. *"So all of our training no matter what the skill … comes with a coaching framework attached to it."* Coaching that occurs after training is closely monitored to see how much coaching actually occurs, ascertain the quality of the coaching conversations, and gauge how the outcomes of coaching are being applied to everyday business relationships and transactions. Coaching can be utilised in any business function, including corporate services. However, from a commercial point of view, the outcomes of coaching are more quickly achieved and visible in revenue-generating, customer-facing areas of the business.

6.4.2 All Business Transactions Are Analysed through a Coaching Lens

Developing a coaching culture requires discipline and commitment to analyse every aspect of the business and identify how coaching can be used to maximise the impact of current business transactions on the organisation's 'bottom line', for example, analysing how coaching can increase the number and quality of deals done, how leaders are selected, and how capability is transferred and applied to business situations. As organisations embrace a coaching culture, coaching becomes the lens by which the organisation analyses everything that it does. A coaching culture releases and harnesses the capability, knowledge, and perspectives of a diverse workforce in a way that is genuinely curious and exploratory. It sees expertise everywhere in the organisation and wants to build that up rather than turning everyone into a *"cookie cutter"*. In a coaching culture, organisational knowledge is distributed rather than centralised and controlled.

6.4.3 Coaching Is Conducted in All Business Units

In this fourth stage, coaching is conducted in all business units and can be delivered by anybody—leaders or peers or internal, specialist, or volunteer coaches. It's everybody's role to coach. It's an expectation that everybody will habitually and automatically coach each other, meaning that, if a situation arises in a meeting, there won't be combative challenge. Rather, there will be questioning such as, *"Okay, if we do this, what would that achieve?"* and *"How do you come to think that?"*—a much more collaborative and amiable approach to interacting at work. An example is of an AO5 HR adviser effectively using this approach in her daily activities as she just listened and used silence to help others work through their concerns and then assisted them to break down those concerns into chunks. In a coaching culture, it's not just the leaders who are expected to coach. Everybody, *"from the gardener to the Board chair"*, can conduct coaching formally or informally.

In this final stage, informal *peer-coaching* occurs as a supportive learning activity, no-matter what the content or when the coaching is delivered. Peer coaching has many benefits since employees don't need to be formally trained as coaches or even in coaching skills (although this is preferable), but they do need to exhibit *coach-like behaviours* as they interact with fellow employees. In a coaching culture, peer coaching is just part of how the business operates on a day-to-day basis. As a result, employees don't go to be coached. They experience being coached in the course of their everyday interactions with their peers and leader.

The way that leaders promote peer coaching is by modelling it with their colleagues and supporting team members who practice it within their team. As team members learn how to peer-coach, coaching cascades naturally and organically down the organisation and becomes the normal way of interacting with others in the business. When this occurs, a coaching culture becomes embedded into the organisation which means that peer coaching, in particular, has been embraced and is working internally—which possibly implies that the organisation has reached a level of maturity to realise and accept that coaching is something important that people do right across the organisation.

6.4.4 Coaching Is Extended to All Business Relationships and Transactions

Once coaching is conducted internally in all corporate and business units of the organisation routinely on a daily basis across all levels by leaders, peers, and everybody formally and informally, the challenge is to extend coaching relationships to customers and suppliers. Coaching enables the establishment of respectful yet robust and productive relationships among account managers and external customers and suppliers. A coaching account manager is somebody who knows how to listen, who has empathy, and who's not afraid to make the tough discussions. Account managers are focused on achieving mutually beneficial outcomes for the customer and the organisation. The conversation is based on an exchange of information that is open, honest, truthful, and concerned for the welfare of both parties. This approach reduces the possibility that conversations deteriorate into a *"talk fest"* rather than being used as a dedicated approach to achieving a specific outcome. To secure a business deal requires close attention to customer relationships, asking what the customer needs, and negotiating how best to meet that need within a business framework, using coaching skills that are effective in every business transaction, as this quote illustrates:

> *I think that most people don't realise the power of what coaching can provide. And that's unfortunate because it's a huge benefit I think. It was for me, and I'm seeing it in other cases both with my clients and in other people's clients. It's a challenging environment to both educate people in the value of it and to recognise, first, what it is, and, second, why it's useful or valuable, and then three, to embrace it.*

Overall, when organisations are in the fourth stage of developing a coaching culture at the *Coaching-as-Culture* stage, everybody coaches everybody else. Organisations wanting to transition to this final stage broaden their approach to coaching to embrace the entire organisation so that not just leaders but everybody in the organisation knows how to coach and is encouraged to coach each other on a daily basis.

6.5 Summary of Stage 4

Coaching-as-Culture

When an organisation is in this fourth and final *Coaching-as-Culture* stage of developing a coaching culture, coaching is conceptualised as *organic*. It occurs naturally as part of the DNA and fabric of the organisation. The *transformational* motivation for coaching is to assist all employees unleash their potential and for the organisation to culturally transform as it increases in productivity and gains competitive advantage in the marketplace. The *top-down* drivers for coaching are the CEO and senior executives who are passionate and committed to role-modelling coaching as a strategic priority of the business. Coaching is *integrated* into the *delivery* of everything that leaders, peers, and everyone in the organisation does on a daily basis, including into their relationship with external customers and suppliers.

The key elements of the four stages in the development of a coaching culture are outlined in Table 6.1.

Stages	Stage 1—Coaching-as-Intervention	Stage 2—Coaching-as-HR-Function	Stage 3—Coaching-as-Leader-Capability	Stage 4—Coaching-as-Culture

Conceptualisation of coaching (i.e. understanding of *what* coaching is)	Utilitarian conceptualisation
	• skill
	• tool
	• immediate outcome
	• one-off investment
		Pedagogical conceptualisation
		• training and learning experience
		  ○ HR are formally trained.
		  ○ HR experience being coached.
		• in-house coach-training curriculum
		• short-term investment
			Practice conceptualisation
			• leader capability
			• capability development framework
			• medium-term investment
				Organic conceptualisation
				• DNA and fabric of the organisation
				• platform for cultural change
				• long-term investment
				  ○ cultural change takes time

Motivation for coaching (i.e. belief in *why* coaching is done)	Instrumental motivation • 'fix' a problem • remediate an underperformer • comply with legislation	Developmental motivation • change mindset and behaviour • improve individual performance • support career progression	Performance motivation • business performance • team engagement • retention of talent ○ succession plan	Transformational motivation • personal transformation • productivity increases • competitive advantage

Drivers of coaching within the organisation (i.e. the *who* of coaching)	Individual drivers
	• line manager
	• positioned within line management structure
		Functional drivers
		• human resources
		• positioned within HR
		  ○ infrastructure for coaching
		  ○ support for coaching
			Business drivers
			• leaders as an expectation of their role
			• positioned within sales and services functions
				Top-down drivers
				• CEO and senior executives
				  ○ absolute clarity about what coaching is and what it is not
				  ○ clearly defined outcomes and indicators of success
				  ○ experience being coached

| Delivered by (i.e. *how* coaching is done) | Outsourced delivery
• external coaches
• expensive | Targeted delivery
• *Leader-as-Coach* training program
• coaching panel/s | Internalised delivery
• Leaders deliver coaching to their teams and team members.
• Specialist coaches 'coach to revenue'.
• Internal coaches and coaching teams deliver behavioural and performance coaching. | Integrated delivery
• applied to all business processes and systems analysed through a coaching lens
• delivered in all business units
  ○ everybody coaches each other on a daily basis.
  ○ formally and informally—peer coaching.
• extended to all business relationships and transactions |

(continuation of Integrated delivery column)
  ○ buy-in, engagement, sponsorship
  ○ model coaching
• strategic priority
  ○ budget, resources, measurement, ROI
  ○ champion for coaching

Table 6.1: Key Elements of the Four Stages in the Development of a Coaching Culture

6.6. Case Studies

Stage 4
Coaching-as-Culture

Case Study 11

SecureWealth is a top 20 ASX-listed company with approximately 15,000 staff who deliver financial solutions to 9 million customers in Australia and New Zealand through its network of banking, insurance, and wealth creation services. Since the early 1900s, the organisation has created value for stakeholders whilst being a responsible and resilient business. SecureWealth is a diversified, simplified, low-risk financial services group that delivers both high yield and above average system growth. Their goal is to create value for customers through their portfolio of market-leading brands whilst benefiting from the efficiencies of scale achievable as a large organisation. Its mission is to help people live the life they want to lead and plan for the life they want tomorrow. Peter heads an internal coaching team of ten coaches who deliver coaching services to customer-facing business unit team members. The organisation, headquartered in Australia, is five years into a strategy of embedding a coaching culture into the organisation.

In SecureWealth, coaching is regarded as *"just part of who we are and how we do business. It's not something special, or something we do in addition. It's just part of how we lead our people . . . to accelerate results"*. For Peter, coaching is co-achieving regardless of the environment, the business, or the individual. Coaching is concerned with understanding where an employee is performing now, helping them identify where they need to improve, and building a bridge between the two through powerful questioning. In recent years, SecureWealth hasn't needed to bring in external coaches for its business units and front-line staff because the growth of coaching conversations within the organisation has been organic.

Coaching was introduced into SecureWealth to deliver behavioural and performance improvements in individuals and teams to meet and exceed business targets. It was seen as the way to transform the business to create competitive advantage and facilitate cultural change. Peter is adamant that SecureWealth's competitive advantage has been derived from the presence of his internal coaching team, which works with front-line staff to remove barriers to their performance so they can deliver on the expectations of their role. The purpose of their coaching is to generate leverage within the organisation so that existing customers are retained and new business secured, with both strategies contributing to organisational sustainability.

The drivers of coaching in SecureWealth are the CEO and senior executive team who are absolutely committed to investing in coaching in the long term. The coaching initiative began from the enthusiasm and dedication of one senior executive who was instrumental in creating awareness of coaching and its impact at the organisational level. He's still a senior executive within SecureWealth and an influential member of the executive team who are all now passionate advocates for coaching. They have been trained in coaching and role-model coaching throughout the organisation. Peter's internal coaching team is sponsored by the initiating senior executive to whom they report. It gives coaching *"some clout . . . and an external feel"*. Peter believes that a senior level of sponsorship and buy-in is *"absolutely critical"* to developing a coaching culture.

There are three ways that coaching is delivered within SecureWealth. *Leader-as-Coach* training programs occur at all levels of the organisation, starting with entry-level managers. SecureWealth's policy is that all leaders are expected to coach their direct reports through scheduled one-on-one sessions. Peter's team assisted in designing all of SecureWealth's coach-training and leader development programs, which are focused on embedding coaching within the organisation. His team has also contributed a coaching component to several other development programs for leaders, for example, moving from frontline to business or business to strategic level based on employee's tenure and capability. The second way that coaching is delivered in SecureWealth is as an important component of the training that talented staff, identified via talent metrics and leader recommendations, receive as members of the succession planning pipeline. Third, coaching is delivered by a select panel of external executive coaches to executive-level managers and above. These three methods spread coaching throughout the organisation to the extent that Peter believes coaching is now *"integrated—it's part of what we do and how we do things here in our business"*. Coaching is also included to all extension programs - for example, to build resilience in employees and support them through significant change events - to increase employee engagement, support the application of key learnings back into the workplace, and obtain a higher return on investment.

Coaching by the internal coaching team is in addition to, and complements, the leader-led coaching that is routinely conducted throughout SecureWealth. Peter's internal coaching team works within the distribution area of the business—the front-line stores, first-line leaders, and business unit leaders who manage and oversee the regions—to increase business sales. In the customer-facing distribution area of the business, the impact of coaching can be seen almost immediately in the sales figures, which has a major impact on the organisation's bottom line.

From the coaching initiative which started five years ago within the front-line sales and services function, SecureWealth's coaching philosophy now extends to how the entire organisation does business with all its internal and external customers and suppliers. Coaching is particularly embedded in the sales and services business units, and there are "*pockets*" of coaching located in other areas of the organisation, including the corporate functions. Peter's estimate is that the organisation is about 60 per cent of the way towards embedding a coaching culture across the entire organisation.

Case Study 12

GlobalNetworks is a large international organisation which is steeped in hierarchy, bureaucracy, and compliance. Given the type of industry, everyone understands and accepts the need for rules and regulations. Twelve months ago, as a result of an employee perception survey, the CEO issued a global directive that the organisational culture had to change. The HR function, which for many years has delivered leadership development training to all leaders in the organisation, was charged with this responsibility. Their leadership training now includes a coaching component so that leaders understand what coaching is and how they can better engage with their staff to not only perform to the required level but also exert discretionary effort as well to achieve even more.

Everyone in the organisation receives coaching on a monthly basis as a mandated requirement of leaders. Outcomes of these coaching conversations are recorded in a HR metrics system together with performance and action plans. The monthly coaching replaces the annual performance review. There is no doubt that the coaching is conducted as required; however, the quality of the coaching that is delivered is variable. Leaders are recruited into the organisation with coaching skills, or they are trained during the induction period. Each business location has to submit a plan which details what the leadership team is going to do to shift the culture—one very specific thing that is tailored to shift the culture in that location.

GlobalNetworks's leadership development program is delivered worldwide, which signifies the importance the organisation places on leader coaching. The training runs for a couple of hours and looks at what a successful leader does and then replicates that—whether it's how to conduct core routines or run a successful staff meeting. It trains leaders how to engage staff and conduct one-on-ones with them so that they become excited about their work, solve problems more quickly, acknowledge the good things that their employees do, and improve in areas where they aren't quite meeting role expectations. Leaders take away a toolkit which has a number of items for them to refer to (which is also available for them online). Anybody who has a direct report must do the course. If a leader doesn't coach, it's considered a 'negative'. Everyone is coached even without asking for it.

A big part of the leadership development program is training leaders not only in how to coach but also in how to give constructive feedback. Employees are used to getting mostly negative feedback. However, in the last twelve months, GlobalNetworks has established a system whereby employees receive monthly coaching sessions rather than performance ratings at the end of the year. Their feedback is recorded in a real-time HR metrics system that is visible to, and interactive between, the individual and their manager and includes the individual's performance plan and actions to be achieved.

Because the leadership team is highly experienced, the focus of coaching in GlobalNetworks is on the line manager and team leader levels as part of the Enterprise Agreement (EA), which dictates that operators have an individual development and performance review discussion with their manager every year. The way this review is conducted is also specified under the EA as a compliance obligation using a designated template rather than as a coaching conversation. However, line managers use their coaching skills to assist employees to actively participate in the review process. To prepare for the review, HR team members meet with the operators to discuss any feedback they might have for their manager and how to give that feedback, including, at times, writing it down for those employees who can't express themselves well particularly under pressure. Employees then go into the meeting feeling much more confident.

Shadowing is another form of leader development in GlobalNetworks and something that's well-accepted. The HR team travels to a certain location, shadows the leaders, and gives them immediate feedback on what they are saying and what they are actually observed doing—for example, *Are the leaders being fair and consistent?* The leaders being shadowed love this process and really relate to this form of personalised feedback.

To conduct any 'heavy' individual coaching, GlobalNetworks engages the services of, say, four or five professional coaches from an external consultancy company to travel to a particular location to deliver comprehensive coaching to front-line team leaders and operators. The individuals who are coached are assessed pre- and post-coaching to see what the shift is and to understand whether they're taking on the coaching.

CHAPTER 7
TRANSITIONS BETWEEN STAGES

7.1 Foundations Underlying a Coaching Culture

In Chapter 2, the academic research underlying the educational, psychological, and management foundations of coaching was detailed. Figure 7.1 shows that the educational foundations for coaching lie in concepts related to mindset, malleability, and learning and development. Leaders must adopt a *growth mindset* to assist employees develop and reach their full potential. This mindset is inclusive of all employees, not just employees who are regarded as talent. With this mindset, leaders believe that all employees can, and are willing to, change their behaviour to become more adaptable and embrace new experiences which enhance their development.

Figure 7.1 also shows that the psychological foundations for coaching are based on the individual's ability to restructure their thinking and change their behaviour given feedback from their social environment, leading to self-regulation and emotional competence. When coaching is viewed from this perspective, managers must replace their *command-and-control* cognitive mindset with a *coaching leadership style* to empower and encourage all employees to excel. This shift creates a safe working environment for coaching to occur and shows due care and concern for direct reports as people. Cognitive reframing allows leaders and employees to restructure their social relationships with others, including customers and suppliers, so that they are more interpersonally effective. As employees are coached, they develop greater self-awareness and the ability to self-regulate their emotions, leading to more productive interactions with others in and out of the organisation.

Finally, Figure 7.1 shows that the management foundations of coaching focus on the acquisition of leader competencies to enhance employee motivation and performance, resulting in improved business relationships and increased productivity. In a coaching culture, everybody is able to coach and be coached, and have informal coaching conversations with peers. Equipping leaders with coaching skills and using the coaching language and philosophy throughout the organisation provide the platform for cultural change to occur. Coaching motivates individuals to engage in more open and honest conversations that are based on trust and a genuine desire for leaders and employees to succeed. Interpersonal skills improve with coach-training, and relationships flourish.

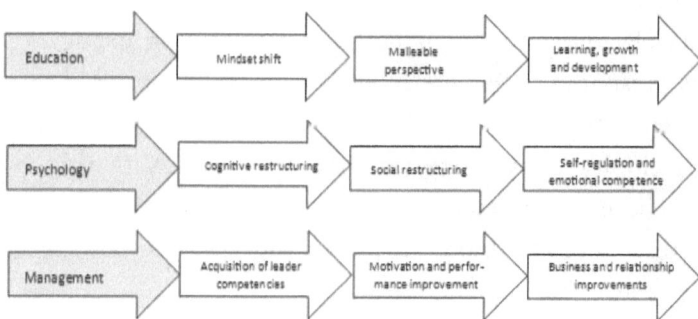

Figure 7.1: Foundations of Coaching Culture Development

7.2 Transitions between Stages

To move from one stage to the next in the development of a coaching culture, organisations need to implement strategies by which organisational leaders personally transform their mindset, attitude and beliefs from manager to leader, the business transforms its policies, practices and procedures by leveraging coaching within selected business drivers, and the organisation transforms culturally as all organisational members adopt a coaching philosophy and relationship style (see Figure 7.2).

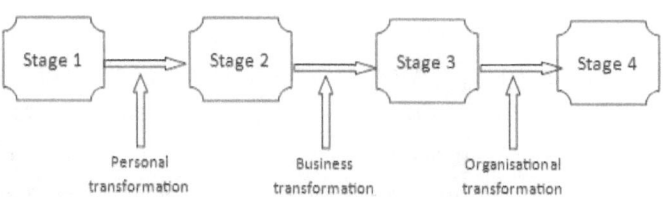

Figure 7.2: Three Transitions between the Four Stages

Management research provides the *strategies* that organisations need to progressively develop a coaching culture. However, it is the *psychological mechanisms* that enable managers to transform their mentality, and the *educational mechanisms* that support personal learning, that have been identified in this research study as the 'glue' that enables or inhibits strategy implementation at each transition. The ways that an organisation moves through these three transitions relate to the learnings, behaviour, and actions taken by HR professionals, organisational leaders, and CEO and senior executives, as they transition the organisation from one stage to the next (see Table 7.1). The numbers in Table 7.1 refer to the *strategies* and *mechanisms* that are detailed in Chapters 8–10. But first, a word about the difference between *strategy* and *mechanism* as used in this book.

Within the academic literature, *strategy* has been defined as a plan, ploy, pattern, position, or perspective (Mintzberg 1987). Strategic planning is undertaken by organisations to develop action plans to guide future business transactions. A ploy is a manoeuvre to confuse the competition into thinking that a certain action will be taken but maybe isn't. A pattern is the habitual way in which businesses operate, often giving comfort to consumers but making an organisation's next actions predictable. As a position, strategy indicates where the organisation stands in the marketplace in relation to its competitors, possibly predicting what its next actions will be. As a perspective, strategy is the way that the organisation views the marketplace and how it takes actions in relation to that marketplace. All these ways that *strategy* can be conceived relate to the actions that organisational leaders take to maintain or enhance their position in the marketplace, their standing in relation to customers and key stakeholders, their competitiveness and sustainability in the long term.

Stepping back from strategy and action is the intention in the minds of organisational leaders in relation to what they believe is happening, or needs to happen, to promote the best interests of the organisation. In effect, *strategy* is the door through which the organisation exerts its influence on the world. The key to that strategy—the key that unlocks the door to allow actions to take place successfully—is in the pre-thought and motivation that goes into the creation of the strategy and how it will be executed for optimal outcome. That key is the *mechanism* that underlies every decision, every motivation to achieve, and every desire to *be* and *do* the best by the organisations' customers, staff, and shareholders. Having the key opens the door that allows action to take place. Identifying the key—the trigger—that is the right *mechanism* to enact a great strategy is what this research study aimed to identify from interviewees' experience of working with coaching and trying to develop a coaching culture in their organisations or in the organisations to which they consult. *Mechanisms* are the keys that unlock the doors to organisational *strategy* and success.

For the purpose of this discussion, the mechanisms are the *experiences* that people have and the *learnings* they gain from those experiences. The strategies are what people *do* to achieve a desired outcome. The learning generally comes after the experience of doing. However, when organisations are preparing a transitional plan, they need to work backwards from learning (*what has been done before and how can that work for us?*) to experience (*how can I personally become involved so that I can see the benefits for myself?*) to the doing (*what do I need to do as a result of learning from my experience and the research that I have reviewed?*).

Coaching foundations	To *transition* from Stage 1: *Coaching-as-Intervention* to Stage 2: *Coaching-as-HR-Function* **Individual = individual change/transformation**	To *transition* from Stage 2: *Coaching-as-HR-Function* to Stage 3: *Coaching-as-Leader Capability* **Team = 'pockets' of cultural change**	To *transition* from Stage 3: *Coaching-as- Leader Capability* to Stage 4: *Coaching-as-Culture* **Organisation = 'whole' transformational cultural change**
Learn (Education) Adding to what we know and finding ways to incorporate new discoveries into existing frameworks so that they make sense to us	**Mindset shift** 8.1.1 HR professionals are formally trained as coaches 8.1.2 In-house coaching curriculum is developed	**Malleable perspective** 9.1.1 Coaching is a core capability of leaders and is embedded in a leadership development framework 9.1.2 Managers are trained in coaching skills to become leaders (Leader-as-Coach program) 9.1.3 Coaching is embedded in all Leadership and Executive Development Programs	**Learning, growth, and development** 10.1.1 CEO and senior executives are formally trained as coaches 10.1.2 CEO and senior leaders have absolute clarity about what coaching is and what it is not 10.1.3 CEO and senior executives model buy-in, engagement and sponsorship for coaching
Grow (Psychology) Thinking differently, embracing new perspectives, experiencing change, behaving in different ways	**Cognitive restructuring** 8.2.1 HR professionals experience being coached	**Social restructuring** 9.2.1 Leaders experience being coached 9.2.2 Leaders let go of command-and-control and adopt a coaching leadership style 9.2.3 Any unwillingness of leaders to coach is addressed	**Self-regulation and emotional competence** 10.2.1 CEO and senior executives experience being coached 10.2.2 CEO and senior executives adopt a growth mindset 10.2.3 CEO and senior executives believe in the value and potential of all employees and identify opportunities to unleash that potential
Lead (Management) Leading people and managing change in new ways to enable, empower, and "*hold the space*" for others to lead	**Acquisition of coaching competencies** 8.3.1 Coaching is positioned within HR 8.3.2 HR develops the infrastructure for coaching 8.3.3 HR establishes the support for coaching	**Motivation and performance improvement** 9.3.1 Coaching is positioned within business units 9.3.2 Leaders coach direct reports on a regular basis	**Interpersonal and relationship improvements** 10.3.1 Coaching is positioned at the organisational level as a strategic priority 10.3.2 CEO and senior executives align coaching with organisational vision, values and behaviours 10.3.3 CEO and senior executives define the purpose, organisational and business outcomes from coaching

• Accredited Coach Network • Coaching Circles • Coaching Communities 8.3.4 HR appoints a coaching panel to coach individuals throughout the organisation	9.3.3 Leaders create a safe environment in which to coach 9.3.4 Regular feedback coaching sessions replace the annual performance review 9.3.5 Specialist coaches are trained to coach within business functions 9.3.6 Internal coaches are appointed to work within business units 9.3.7 An internal coaching team is established to work across business units	• A recurrent budget and resources are allocated to coaching • The return on investment from coaching is measured 10.3.4 A senior executive is appointed as a champion for coaching 10.3.5 A communication strategy is developed to introduce and sustain the coaching practice 10.3.6 CEO and senior executives analyse every aspect of the organisation from a coaching perspective 10.3.7 Organisational levers to maximise the impact of coaching are identified 10.3.8 Coaching is applied more broadly across the organisation • A coaching framework is attached to all training activities • Coaching is conducted throughout the organisation • Peer coaching is conducted throughout the organisation 10.3.9 Coaching relationships are extended to external customers and suppliers

Table 7.1: Strategies and Mechanisms to Develop and Embed a Coaching Culture

CHAPTER 8

TRANSITION FROM STAGE 1 TO STAGE 2

In this chapter, the educational (*Learn*) and psychological (*Grow*) mechanisms that support the management strategies (*Lead*) that leaders need to take to transition their organisation from Stage 1 – *Coaching-as-Intervention* to Stage 2 – *Coaching-as-HR-Function* are detailed.

8.1 Learn (Education)—Mindset Shift

Since transformational HR professionals are typically the people in the organisation with the most knowledge of coaching, they are the ones who usually take responsibility for promoting coaching as a development tool. They may have read about coaching or spoken to a colleague who has been coached; hence, they may want to know more about coaching—what it is and what it can do for organisational members. By becoming formally trained as a coach and experiencing being coached, HR professionals change their mindset about coaching from being just a skill or tool in the hands of external 'expert' coaches to a powerful vehicle to bring about behavioural change and performance improvement in many employees, not just individuals who are 'sent' to be remediated by coaching. They come to see the positive benefits of coaching, which dispels the negative preconceptions they may have previously held.

8.1.1 HR Professionals Are Formally Trained as Coaches

Many HR professionals have not undertaken formal coach-training delivered by an external provider. They may have received in-house training in coaching skills ranging from a few hours to a few days either via dedicated coach-training programs or, more usually, as a component of leadership development programs. However, they're not feeling confident in their ability to train leaders in coaching skills or to conduct coaching themselves. Formal accredited coach-training enables HR professionals to build their coaching skills so that they are able to handle situations differently when they are faced with tough decisions, enabling them to increase their self-awareness and gain insight into the impact they have on others in their team and organisation. After receiving formal training as a coach, they realise that *"there's this great big thing called* coaching *that we don't have anywhere in our organisation"*. Alternatively, they may have undertaken training delivered by an external company in the use and debrief of a 360-degree assessment instrument which they believe to be *pure* coach-training. However, unless the training is approved by an organisation such as the International Coach Federation, it will not comply with the definition of coaching according to international standards.

8.1.2 HR Develops In-House Coaching Curriculum

When HR professionals attend external accredited coach-training programs, they may use this information and their experience to design an internal coach-training program, either as a stand-alone program or as a component of the organisation's leadership development program. The content is typically generic so that it can be implemented consistently across the organisation but also have the flexibility to be tailored to suit the needs of individual business units. Internally designed programs that 'fit' culturally are more acceptable to staff and effective in terms of their outcomes. Employees representative of different business units may be included in the design process to build the momentum for coaching within their business unit and work towards the broader organisation owning the coaching program as opposed to it being *"off the shelf"*. External coach-training providers may be engaged to work with HR on the design of the in-house training in coaching skills.

8.2 Grow (Psychology)—Cognitive Restructuring

In this first transition period, HR professionals experience being coached either during external accredited coach-training that the organisation approves as part of their development plan or by attending in-house training in coaching skills which includes individual coaching. The experience of being coached opens them to new insights about themselves and others. They gain greater self-awareness of who they are and their impact on others and use their learnings to make changes in their life and work almost immediately.

8.2.1 HR Professionals Experience Being Coached

Experiencing one-on-one coaching as part of a formal accredited coach-training program gives HR professionals the insight they need to transition from a *transactional* approach to the work that they do into a *transformational* appreciation of how effective coaching can be as a development tool. They develop their communication, relationship, and leadership skills and experience the transition from *transactional* to *transformational* leader of people. As a result of being coached, they come to understand and appreciate the benefits of coaching and how coaching can be used to enable and empower others on a broader scale, including all organisational leaders, to lead their teams more effectively towards behavioural change and performance improvement.

8.3 Lead (Management)—Acquisition of Leader Competencies

In this first transition period, HR professionals want to transfer what they have learned and experienced about coaching into the development of all line managers so that they may become *leaders* (rather than *managers*) who enable and empower others through coaching. Because line managers are busy people concerned about their leadership, coaching is typically woven into leadership development programs. Leadership is something that line managers know about, relate to, and are interested in. Hence, they will attend leadership development programs but may not be enticed to attend coaching programs, of which they know very little.

8.3.1 Coaching Positioned within HR

In the first transition period, the responsibility for coaching transfers from line managers being responsible for arranging coaching to remediate a single direct report, to coaching residing within the HR function as a *developmental* tool to support individuals perform better in their role. It is HR professionals who typically update their professional knowledge and skills to keep abreast of new ways to develop people. As a result of attending a formal accredited coach-training program, HR professionals have much to share with willing participants in leadership programs. They may also volunteer to coach line managers to practise their coaching skills before seeking credentialing from a professional association like the International Coach Federation. Such associations have a requirement that members accrue a certain number of Continuing Professional Development (CPD) credits to maintain their membership. Hence, most HR professionals are continually learning and growing in their ability to provide first-class service to their organisation so that they and the organisation can be at the leading edge in terms of employee growth and development.

8.3.2 HR Develops the Infrastructure for Coaching

So that the in-house training in coaching skills that is to be conducted with line managers in the next stage will be successful, preparation must be made in this first transition period to support its introduction and ongoing operation. In order to build the infrastructure to support a coaching culture within the organisation, HR professionals review and adjust all HR systems, policies, and procedures so that they reflect and recognise a coaching approach to employee development. This includes revision of all recruitment and selection documentation, performance management systems, reward structures, talent management, and succession processes. The first step is to write the requirement for leaders to coach into their job description as a KPI, include it as a desirable selection criteria, and provide training in the probation period if the successful candidate doesn't have coaching skills. The next step is to develop a HR metrics system to record how coach-training is being delivered in the organisation and how coaching is conducted thereafter within each business unit. This information includes data such as attendance at in-house training in coaching skills, for example, names, numbers, positions, and business units. Thereafter, the data metrics capture the number, frequency, and quality of the coaching sessions that are being delivered by leaders in business units.

In addition, in this first transition period, HR professionals revise organisational structures to address a leader's span of control so that it allows leaders the time to coach as well as fulfil on the requirements of their role. Leaders who have more than eight employees will find it difficult to coach individuals on a regular four- to six-week cycle. Job redesign processes can be utilised to make it possible for leaders to coach given the scope and complexity of the work that they do as well as the number of their direct reports.

8.3.3 HR Establishes the Support for Coaching

As awareness of coaching spreads throughout the organisation, the HR function will be required to respond to individual requests for coaching for *development* purposes. To manage such requests, HR establishes an intranet portal specifically for the purpose of providing information about coaching and its benefits. The portal holds a downloadable form for individuals to complete and email to HR to request that they be coached. Increasingly, these forms require the approval of the individual's line manager who attests to the coaching as a key component of their Development Plan. Having an approval process also ensures the commitment of the line manager to the coaching process. Individuals are matched to a volunteer coach within the organisation or to an external coach, depending on the nature of their coaching request.

HR professionals who are formally trained as coaches typically volunteer their services to coach others in the organisation via an *Accredited Coach Network* that they establish. Some CEOs, senior executives, and organisational leaders who have been formally trained as coaches may also volunteer their coaching services. Volunteer coaches are invited into this network not only because of their interest in coaching but also because of their personality style and proven ability as a leader. They are usually operational executives who understand how powerful coaching can be. They have high personal credibility and leadership qualities, are comfortable within themselves, and if not in the senior executive position, are able to coach upwards and relate well at that level. Not everyone who is interested in coaching will meet these criteria, especially if the organisation requires their volunteer coaches to coach up into the executive ranks. Volunteer coaches coach no more than two individuals at a time, delivering, say, six to twelve sessions over a period of six to twelve months, to fit in with their operational duties. Caution must be exercised during the coaching sessions that the more senior and experienced coach doesn't slip into a mentoring role without signalling a change of role and gaining permission from the coachee to switch intervention approaches.

Coaching Circles. In preparation for leaders coaching their direct reports post in-house training in coaching skills, HR establishes Coaching Circles to fully embed the learnings from the training into daily operational practice. Coaching Circles may consist of attendees from a particular training program, but more often, they are mixed cohorts from different training programs and business units. The conversations that occur on, say, a bimonthly basis, are opportunities for leaders to seek advice and support on any situations they have found difficult to coach around because, even though the session follows the same coaching process, the outcomes from each session may be very different. The Circle encourages self-reflection as the trained leaders ask themselves, "*What's working for me? What's not working? Where are my weaknesses? How can I become better at coaching? Tried this—worked well—share it with the group*". It is constant reflection and learning to improve coaching practice. Coaching Circles may last for, say, twelve months post-training but typically no longer unless they have ongoing support from HR to input additional training into the group.

Coaching Communities. To support volunteer coaches and leaders who have been formally trained as coaches, Coaching Communities are established to maintain the currency of their coaching skills and to explore opportunities for CPD and supervision. HR professionals are injected into these conversations to challenge current thinking and encourage the extension of the coaching skill set into other areas of leadership, training, and business transactions.

8.3.4 HR Establishes Coaching Panels

Because there will still be individuals in the organisation who need expert coaching for *remedial* purposes, or to develop executives, HR establishes coaching panels of external coaches who deliver refereed and affordable coaching services to these individuals. It is the responsibility of HR to manage the coaching engagements with external coaches who may be called upon for a specific reason, for example, performance improvement, role clarification, or promotion to a more senior role.

Individuals at middle management level and below are not usually coached by external coaches unless there is a particular need to do so, for example, talent management, or a particularly sensitive issue. Rather, middle managers are coached by the volunteer coaches in the *Accredited Coaches Network*.

To meet the particular coaching needs of senior executives, HR conducts a recruitment and selection process and appoints a number of external executive coaches to a coaching panel. When a request for coaching is made, meetings are arranged between the executive and several executive coaches to access the 'chemistry match' between them, which enables a trusting relationship to form and grow. Executives are often entitled to receive coaching when they enter the executive service either as a new external recruit or when transitioning from an internal manager to an executive position. An external executive coach may also be engaged when there is a performance or interpersonal issue with colleagues or staff, or when the coachee's focus is constrained by the complexity of their role and specific requirements of the job. The opportunity to be coached by an external coach opens up the possibility of 'bigger picture' thinking about their situation, and challenges them to think 'outside the box' in terms of how they 'show up' as a strategic leader in the organisation. Many senior executives use executive coaches to test out new ideas before they put them to the CEO or to a Board or to an overseas parent. They may use coaching to gain a different, neutral perspective on what they're proposing from a coach who will challenge them and maybe 'push back' on their ideas before they make a final presentation.

CHAPTER 9

TRANSITION FROM STAGE 2 TO STAGE 3

In this chapter, the educational (*Learn*) and psychological (*Grow*) mechanisms that support the management strategies (*Lead*) that leaders need to take to transition their organisation from Stage 2 – *Coaching-as-HR-Function* to Stage 3 – *Coaching-as-Leader-Capability* are detailed.

9.1 Learn (Education)—Malleable Perspective

In this second transition period, coaching becomes a valuable *development* tool that is included as a *core capability of leaders* within a leadership development framework and an essential skill for them to possess in order to progress in their career.

9.1.1 Coaching Is a Core Capability of Leaders and Is Embedded in a Leadership Development Framework

In this second transition period, managers learn how to replace their immediate, task-oriented understanding of coaching with an appreciation of coaching as a short-term investment in developing their ability to *coach* and *lead* their people—to transition from *manager* into *leader*—someone who is capable of coaching their direct reports with confidence on a regular basis. As a core capability of the workforce, *coaching* is embedded into the organisation's capability framework, leadership development framework, and/or career progression framework. For leaders to progress in many organisations, a coaching capability is required. Increasingly, the coaching capability of all organisational leaders develops the organisation's human capital, which contributes to the organisation's competitive advantage in the marketplace. Organisations become an *employer of choice* when they are renowned for their commitment to developing their people.

9.1.2 Managers Are Trained in Coaching Skills to Become Leaders

Generally, managers are trained in coaching skills, not to become coaches but to become *leaders* of people. HR conducts *Leader-as-Coach* programs for managers and talented individuals as an investment in developing the leader capability of the organisation plus as a way to increase employee engagement and retention of valuable staff. Managers learn how to become leaders who coach their staff to achieve improved performance, behavioural change, and career progression. Talented individuals are retained within the organisation's succession plan. On completion of their training in coaching skills, some *managers* who have made the transition to *leader* may be offered the opportunity to become formally trained as a coach by an external coach-training provider.

Increasing the leader capability of line managers is particularly important in times of change such as when an organisation is restructured, acquired, or merged. In such circumstances, it is the leader's role to make decisions about who should go and who should stay, and to tell their staff, plus support both groups thereafter. Leaders need strength and resilience to cope with the changes themselves as well as lead their new team back to the targeted performance levels, which may have slipped due to, what is often, months of interruption.

9.1.3 Coaching Is Embedded into All Leadership and Executive Development Programs

In this second transition period, organisations which are serious about reaping the benefits of coaching include a coaching skills component as an integral part of their leadership development programs. These programs support and align individual behaviours with the organisation's vision and values. Most organisations design their leadership development programs so that they are part generic, part flexible, and tailored to suit business needs and organisational culture. Executive coaches may be engaged to work with HR professionals and leaders to co-design the coaching component of the program. The way that programs are structured and delivered—the content, the language that is used, and the coaching model that is adopted—all reflect the purpose for which coaching is being introduced into the organisation and the desired outcomes. The program is structured so that it is highly relevant to employees and consistent with the strategic goals and objectives of the organisation.

9.2 Grow (Psychology)—Social Restructuring

In this second transition period, organisational leaders experience being coached. As a result of this experience, they come to view coaching not just as a way to change mindsets and behaviour but also as a valuable way to improve their leadership and the performance of individuals in their team. They adjust the way they relate to, and interact with, their team members and others in the organisation and create a more engaged workforce who feel individually and collectively supported and appreciated.

9.2.1 Leaders Experience Being Coached

When a coaching component is included in leadership development programs, an individual coaching program of, say, six sessions is usually attached to ensure that the learnings from the training are implemented back into the day-to-day working practice of each leader. This transfer of learning is essential if the organisation wishes to gain maximum traction from their investment in the training. External coaches may be engaged from a coaching panel, or qualified volunteer coaches may be sourced from the *Accredited Coaches Network,* to conduct the individual coaching sessions. Research shows that unless there is follow-up on the application of learning from training programs, up to 80 per cent of the learning will be lost. This is a huge, and unacceptable, bleed from an organisational investment to improve the leadership and capability of individuals and teams.

9.2.2 A Coaching Leadership Style Replaces Command-and-Control

A coaching culture can be described as one in which there is a commitment to *coaching* and *development* as opposed to *command-and-control*. The traditional management style of *command-and-control* changes in response to an organisation's need to become more competitive in global markets, and retain talent within an inclusive, engaging, and empowering culture. As expectations change, many managers have to relinquish what they know and the behaviours they have been rewarded for in the past, and replace this knowledge and behaviours with what is expected of them under a transformational cultural agenda.

A malleable mindset is required to shift from a *command-and-control* management mentality to one that is more supportive of individuals and their personal agendas for work and career. Leadership style change occurs when there is a will and the resources to utilise coaching as a vehicle to bring about a greater appreciation of the 'people skills' that are required of today's leaders. Coaching is a powerful means of shifting management from the old-school, archaic, *command-and-control* mindset to a *coaching leadership style* that organisational leaders need to possess in order to not only drive value for money but also engage a motivated and adaptable workforce. Coaching has been described as the "*engine room*" which unleashes discretionary effort and engagement, resulting in coaching relationships between people which are developmentally focused and positively intentioned.

9.2.3 Any Unwillingness of Leaders to Coach Is Addressed

Some line managers may welcome the opportunity to develop coaching skills, embracing the opportunity to learn something new as part of their growth and development as a *leader*. However, others may be sceptical that this is just the 'next big thing' being expected of them. This scepticism may be because they don't understand what coaching is, have no desire to coach, and see no reason to change. Managers who are most sceptical about adopting a coaching leadership style are more frequently those with a *command-and-control* style of interacting with their staff. These managers may see coaching as a threat to their established way of interacting with employees. They may not see that coaching is part of their role in a transformational organisational culture. They may understand mentoring but not what it is to coach. However, the consequence for managers who cannot change, or refuse to coach, may be termination.

One way to encourage line managers to change their *command-and-control* style is to use a 360-degree leadership/behavioural assessment instrument. The results deliver the evidence to support the need for a manager to make changes in their behaviour and/or method of interacting with staff. Feedback from the 360-degree instrument creates self-awareness of the impact a manager has on those in their team and others in their immediate environment. Debriefing these instrument results with the manager gives the coach an idea of how 'coachable' the manager is likely to be. Some managers may be deluding themselves that they are good leaders, and so providing feedback from a commercially available assessment instrument may give them insight into how to construct their social interactions with others differently in the future to achieve better outcomes.

9.3 Lead (Management)—Motivation and Performance Improvement

In this second transition period, the audience for coaching changes from an *individual* to a *group* focus on all managers in the organisation. The HR function has designed and now delivers training in coaching skills to all managers so that they acquire coaching and 'people' skills and become *leaders* who coach. Leaders create a safe space for regular coaching sessions to occur, during which time they provide valuable feedback to each member of their team on how they can improve. They use coaching as a way to incentivise employees to stay longer in the organisation and commit to a longer-term future supporting the organisation's vision and direction. When team members are more positive, greater opportunities exist for cooperation, collaboration, and teamwork to occur.

9.3.1 Coaching Is Positioned within Business Units

In this second transition period, HR professionals deliver training in coaching skills to organisational managers and talented individuals as a short to medium term investment in increasing leader capability. HR professionals who have been formally trained as coaches are equipped to develop and deliver these in-house training programs, possibly assisted by external providers. They have a comprehensive understanding of what coaching is and have acquired the technical skills to train managers in how to conduct both *performance* and *pure coaching* conversations. To transition through this period, organisations need to commit to building a strong coaching capability, actively supporting HR professionals in the delivery of in-house training programs, and providing funding for external coaches to be engaged as necessary.

As greater recognition of the importance of coaching spreads beyond the HR function, leaders of business units start to realise how coaching can benefit their teams and team members. The responsibility for rolling out coaching throughout the organisation transitions to business units. It is leaders of business units who must meet targets and budgets, and they start to see how they can use coaching as a way to improve individual and team performance. Those who coach their direct reports maximise the ability of staff to respond to emerging business needs and opportunities. Front-line staff, in particular, benefit from being coached to help them remove any barriers to their performance and assist them deliver on the expectations of their role.

9.3.2 Leaders Coach their Direct Reports and Others in the Organisation

In the first transition period, the requirement for leaders to coach their direct reports was written into their job description. This requirement is reinforced during the second transition period when training in coaching skills is conducted. After receiving the training, leaders are expected to deliver one-on-one coaching and feedback sessions to their direct reports on a regular basis as well as to their teams. In addition, leaders are expected to use a coaching approach in all their interactions with staff to enable and empower them to improved performance. Leaders who coach encourage discovery and forward thinking. The coaching may also reveal previously unknown risks or threats to the business which can then be immediately addressed. Team coaching is conducted at any time the team meets but principally at the start of each week as the leader encourages all team members to generate new ideas and options to progress their current workload. A coaching feedback approach shifts the leader's language and the way they address daily problems. Conversations are more developmental, meaningful, and constructive and serve to build up the individual and the team rather than take them down.

Leader delivery of coaching may prove to be a challenge in certain circumstances such as during an intense working schedule when time to coach is extremely limited, when team members are in different locations, or when the team is really a group of *"stars"* rather than people with a collective mentality. In this second transition stage, leaders need to make the coaching of their direct reports a priority even when their weekly schedule is busy. They will reap the benefits when individuals know what to do, and go do it, without having to come back to them again and again. Initially, leaders' coaching efforts may appear to be 'weak' but with practice and feedback on their coaching skills, they will quickly gain in confidence.

In a coaching culture, leaders adopt a *coaching leadership style* first before they action the organisation's performance management process. In doing so, they build relationships with their direct reports based on knowledge of them as people as well as team members. This understanding allows leaders to provide timely and considerate feedback to their direct reports on their performance, which is often linked to the team member's Development Plan. These plans are individually tailored so that the team member knows exactly where their performance sits at any point in time from their leader's perspective. Leader-led coaching, when delivered as and when needed, is fast-paced and inspires far greater performance by virtue of the individual and team's engagement because they perceive themselves to be valuable contributors to the end result.

9.3.3 Leaders Create a Safe Environment in Which to Coach

When coaching is positioned within business units, leaders create a safe place for coaching to occur, for example, rooms can be booked to provide a quiet space for coaching. For a coaching culture to grow, employees need to feel safe in a space where there is no judgement. Leaders who role-model coaching in a safe place demonstrate the importance they attribute to coaching and reinforce coaching as a process in which they and the employee can express anything and everything about what's working for them and what's not, in a respectful way. They encourage active dialogue to resolve issues in that private, confidential, and secure space. Individuals become *coachable* when they feel it's safe to take a risk in order to be heard.

9.3.4 Regular Feedback Coaching Sessions Replace the Annual Performance Review

In a coaching culture, annual performance reviews become a thing of the past as the usual *"tick-and-flick"* system gives way to constructive feedback on a regular basis. Annual performance reviews typically focus on *"what's gone wrong"* with an employee rather than on what they have achieved during the year. In a coaching culture, the regular focus is on, *"What's going well?"* and *"How can you improve your performance, yourself, your career?"* month by month. When leaders start their coaching conversations using these broad questions, it *"dials down"* the negative messages. Leaders can pre-empt their concern for an individual when a difficult conversation is about to occur by saying, *"This is something that you might feel a little uncomfortable hearing, but I am approaching the discussion with positive intent because I have faith that this might be an issue, but I want you to know that there is general support from me."* The emphasis changes from 'box-ticking' to meet organisational requirements, to 'people-ticking' to equip individuals with the feedback and skills they need to perform better in their role. In a coaching culture with regular feedback coaching sessions, there are no surprises because it's constant feedback throughout the year. When leaders deal with failure from a coaching perspective as a learning opportunity, the organisation is beginning to change its culture.

9.3.5 Specialist Coaches Are Trained to Coach within Business Units

In this second transition period, an important way that organisations are able to increase the productivity of their teams is by the appointment of internal full- or part-time specialist coaches positioned in revenue-generating business units. These specialist coaches typically have years of front-facing experience, understand customer needs, and have identified the key triggers that make a sales pitch more likely to succeed. They coach front-line team members who interact directly with customers to generate sales. These specialist coaches may or may not be formally trained as coaches, but they are generally trained in coaching skills and understand people and how to interact with team leaders to achieve their best performance. The impartiality and independence of the specialist coach is an advantage in examining a possible deal. The specialist coach has the authority to start interrogating organisational data and the ability to consider other ways of operating or areas of probability that the teams hadn't thought of before because they're *"emotionally intent"* on winning the deal. Coaching is a particularly useful tool to use with staff in a call centre environment to improve their customer interaction and increase sales.

9.3.6 Internal Coaches Are Appointed to Work within Business Units

Large global organisations like technology and media companies, banks, and superannuation organisations tend to be more *"sophisticated and au fait"* with coaching than most other organisations. These organisations have been around much longer than most and tend to be more developed in their coaching culture. They see coaching as important and have checks and balances to make sure that the coaching programs they conduct deliver on what's required. In such organisations, a dedicated position of *Internal Coach* is often established as a full-time support to leaders in a particular business unit. The role of the internal coach is to challenge current thinking and guide employees into different ways of behaving and performing in their role to achieve better outcomes.

One of the selection criteria for appointment as an Internal Coach is that the preferred candidate has been formally trained as a coach to international standards with a proven number of logged coaching hours. From their formal coach-training, internal coaches have a deep understanding of what *pure coaching* is (as well as *performance coaching*) and what differentiates these forms of intervention from others such as mentoring, training, and supervising. Internal coaches need to maintain their coaching currency by being supervised and attending CPD events.

Leaders who have attended the *Leader-as-Coach* in-house training are not eligible to apply for the designated position of Internal Coach unless they have a formal coaching qualification as well.

Internal coaches focus on the individual whom leaders believe, with encouragement and support, can maximise their potential. They work with 'middle performers' or above to identify any behavioural or performance issues that are holding them back as well as to identify opportunities that will unleash their potential. Appointing internal coaches is a clear sign that the organisation is investing in the potential of individuals *"on the edge"*. It also means that, over time, leaders can spend more time with other team members whose performance they may have been neglecting. However, there are challenges to being an internal coach which relate to their ability to remain independent of the internal politics of the organisation and to coach upwards with executives where privacy and confidentiality are major concerns. In these instances, the services of an external executive coach may be required especially when credibility is important in terms of the coach's background and experience and their proven ability to deliver coaching results.

9.3.7 An Internal Coaching Team Is Established to Work across Business Units

Organisations in advanced levels of developing a coaching culture establish not only a dedicated Internal Coach position but also an *Internal Coaching Team* of formally trained coaches to work within all business units to support teams and team members. The internal coaching team is separate from, and in addition to, organisational leaders who coach. The purpose of the team is to conduct *pure coaching*, which leads to the elimination of limiting beliefs, creation of mindset shifts, and the provision of support for behavioural changes that underpin performance improvement. This allows leaders to focus on *performance coaching* of teams and team members to meet business unit targets and deliverables.

To begin the process of engaging an internal coaching team, organisations develop position descriptions not only for *Internal Coach* but also for *Senior Coach* (in charge of the team) which specify the level of coach-training and experience required to be appointed to the coaching team. The position description, selection criteria, and interview formats can be used to recruit dedicated coaches and coaching teams into any business unit of the organisation. The position description also specifies the ongoing professional development required for the incumbent to continue in their role along a clearly mapped pathway of the learning, experience, and competencies that an *Internal Coach* needs to acquire to progress into a *Senior Coach* role.

Because the internal coaching team is costing the organisation money rather than making it money, the team is well-aware that they must assist the business unit to increase productivity to a level which will at least equal, if not exceed, the dollar value spent on their employment and overheads as a team. One of the keys to the sustainability of internal coaching teams is that they operate close to the business end of the organisation where they can have most impact. Hence, they can quickly evaluate the effect and the impact their coaching has on, for example, the sales results and service outcomes of the business unit in which they operate. The other important key to success of internal coaching teams is that they can respond quickly to support the business unit leader in managing change events as they occur as opposed to taking some time to respond, for example, if they were positioned within HR, which gives the organisation a competitive advantage in the marketplace.

CHAPTER 10

TRANSITION FROM STAGE 3 TO STAGE 4

In this chapter, the educational (*Learn*) and psychological (*Grow*) mechanisms that support the management strategies (*Lead*) that leaders need to take to transition their organisation from Stage 3 – *Coaching-as-Leader -Capability* to Stage 4 – *Coaching-as-Culture* are detailed. It is during this transition period that an internal, passionate advocate for coaching agitates for its introduction into the organisation.

The blueprint for transformational cultural change is depicted in Figure 10.1. It shows that the impetus for the development of a coaching culture can originate from any level of the organisation, and if not from the top, most frequently from within the middle management level. If it starts at the middle management level, the passionate leader must convince the senior executive of the value of introducing coaching into the organisation. They might do this by developing a business case for coaching, outlining what coaching is and why it would be beneficial to the organisation. Finally, they might appeal to the ways that the benefits can be measured to evaluate the ROI from the coaching initiative, and indicate that a pilot program would produce preliminary data.

To learn more about coaching, the senior executive team may conduct a workshop to better understand what coaching is, and what it is not, and experience being coached themselves. They may receive training in coaching skills, or become qualified as a coach by an external coach-training provider. If the decision is made to commence the coaching initiative, funding is allocated and a senior executive nominated to steward the program. A business unit will be agreed in which to conduct the pilot program.

Communication about the pilot program will be made available within the business unit. Coaching skills training will commence at the senior levels, to be cascaded down to all front-facing employees. A coaching approach will be encouraged in relation to interactions with customers and suppliers as well as all employees. Once the program is completed, the measures previously agreed to determine the success of the coaching program will be evaluated to determine the ROI from the coaching spend. If successful, coaching will be progressively adopted by all business units within the organisation. Details of these *8 Steps to Transformational Cultural Change through Coaching* are included in 10.1-10.3 below.

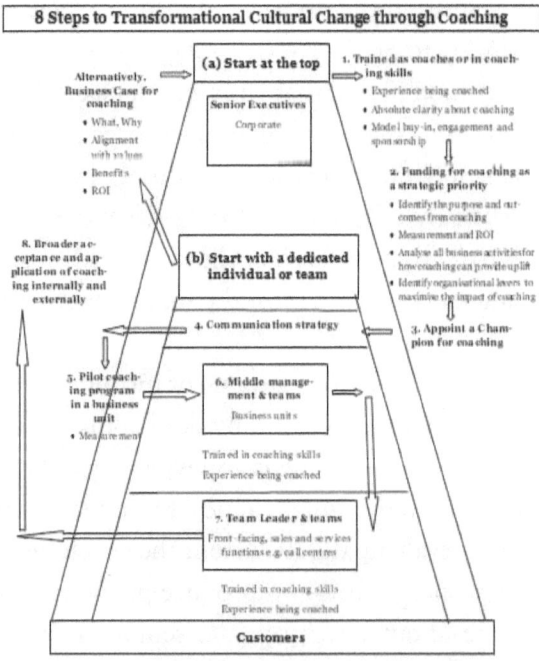

Figure 10.1: 8 Steps to Transformational Cultural Change through Coaching

10.1 Learn (Education)—Learning, Growth, and Development

In this third transition period, the CEO and senior executives are formally trained as coaches. They progress their understanding of coaching from a capability requirement for all leaders to a platform for organisation-wide, transformational cultural change. Responsibility for coaching lies with the CEO and senior executives who determine that, as a strategic priority, coaching is to be embedded into all business units, relationships, and transactions so that it becomes part of the DNA and fabric of the organisation.

10.1.1 CEO and Senior Executives Are Formally Trained as Coaches

In many organisations which aim to develop a coaching culture, the CEO and senior leaders have coaching capability. This capability may have been developed by attendance at in-house training in coaching skills or, increasingly, by completion of a formal coach-training qualification delivered by an external coach-training provider. In the former case, the CEO and senior executives may rely on internal expertise, such as within the HR function, to assist them in driving the coaching agenda throughout the organisation. However, it is unlikely that a coaching culture will embed unless the executive team members have been formally trained as coaches so that they fully understand what *pure coaching* is (as opposed to *performance coaching*) and how it can benefit individuals, teams, and the organisation.

10.1.2 CEO and Senior Executives Have Absolute Clarity about What Coaching Is and What It Is Not

For the coaching initiative to be successful, the CEO and senior executives need to have absolute clarity about what coaching is and what it is not and what the organisation is trying to achieve by developing a coaching culture. *Is it coaching or mentoring that the organisation wishes to engage in? Organisational leaders may be comfortable with the concept of mentoring but know less about coaching. What is the purpose of introducing a coaching culture? What is the motivation behind building leader coaching capability?* With this knowledge and understanding, they can become fully engaged with how coaching can change an individual and team's work life and performance for the better. But unless the CEO and senior executives are 'on board' with coaching, it is unlikely that the coaching initiative will be successful.

10.1.3 CEO and Senior Executives Model Buy-In, Engagement, and Sponsorship for Coaching

Buy-in, engagement, and sponsorship by the CEO and senior executives are absolutely critical to ensure that a coaching culture is developed and embedded in the organisation. If not the CEO or a senior executive, the initiative may start from somebody near the top level of the organisation who embraces coaching such as a business unit leader. Alternatively, it can start from someone at the core who is authorised and able to roll out a cultural change program on behalf of the CEO and senior executives. Typically, the leader of the business unit would take on this responsibility. However, in large organisations in which senior executives and business unit leaders are extremely busy, and the HR professionals are transformational, it makes sense for an HR professional to manage the roll-out of the coaching initiative throughout the business unit and ultimately the organisation. The HR professional will need senior executive support but not day-to-day 'interference' in the management of the cultural change program.

During this period, the CEO and senior executives role-model the importance of coaching and signal coaching as a valid investment in an individual's growth and development. When the CEO and senior executives are committed to developing a coaching culture, they are seen *"walking the talk"* amongst employees at all levels of the organisation and messaging the importance of coaching and being coached. Opportunities to interact with senior executives are rare; however, such occasions can help employees who maybe had not thought about coaching before, realise that they have the skills to be a good leader who coaches. It's absolutely critical that leaders are role-modelling the behavioural change they expect in their direct reports so that employees at lower levels of the organisation can see the changes that are possible and the performance improvements that are being achieved when everybody is on the same coaching journey.

10.2 Grow (Psychology)—Self-Regulation and Emotional Intelligence

In this third transition period, the CEO and senior executives commit to the experience of being coached. They adopt a *growth mindset*, believe in the potential of all employees, and identify opportunities to unleash that potential.

10.2.1 CEO and Senior Executives Experience Being Coached

The CEO and senior executives develop a better understanding of what coaching is and an appreciation of the benefits of coaching by having the experience of being coached themselves. Those who have experienced coaching are passionate and enthused about culture and capability as a whole and see the value of coaching in improving their professionalism and ability to manage difficult situations. It's only by having the experience of being coached that the CEO and senior executives really commit to developing a coaching culture with conviction. Individuals can know about and understand coaching from a cognitive perspective, but it's only when they experience being coached that they *"get it with their heart and their guts"*. They need to have an experience of, *"What's the difference between* command-and-control *and* telling, *and* curiosity-and-harnessing *and* asking?*"* Once a CEO has had that experience, they will start to understand and explore: *"What's in it for this organisation to adopt a coaching culture? What needs to change? Why does that need to change? How can coaching help my employees in their day-to-day job?"* It's a coaching intervention that will assist the CEO in making the decision to invest in developing a coaching culture.

Senior executives are typically coached by executive coaches rather than by internal coaches who are best suited to coach at the middle manager or team leader levels. This is because coaches at the executive level need currency across different organisations in order to bring rigour to the conversation. Executives need to be able to step out of their organisational thinking into a safe space for them to dialogue with an external coach about their issues, challenges, or concerns and gain a deeper understanding of what they need to do differently. Executive coaches provide exceptional value because they have an external perspective and can genuinely coach with no agenda other than to support the executive in any way that's possible.

10.2.2 CEO and Senior Executives Adopt a Growth Mindset

During this third transition period, CEOs and senior executives adopt a *growth mindset*, which means that they continually seek new horizons and ways to expand on the performance and productivity of their teams, recognising that such gains can only be achieved with and through their people. A *growth mindset* embraces new opportunities and challenges, facilitates the achievement of organisational deliverables, invests in learning and development opportunities specific to individuals and teams, connects individual aspirations with organisational vision, and harnesses the power of the team not only at the leader level but at all levels of the organisation.

To adopt a *growth mindset*, some managers may need to make a significant shift in how they think and behave especially if they rely on a positional power base where they are acknowledged for their authority as a manager or have a technical power base where they are acknowledged for their expertise. When a manager's authority is based on their title, they are inclined to be directive. Managers with technical expertise tend to have poor 'people skills' and little patience, so they may rely on their expert knowledge to manage their staff. Managers whose personality type is introverted may not want to spend time with people and expect others to understand them intuitively. Hence, some managers may embrace coaching as an important way for them to grow and develop, but others may see coaching as an imposition that they don't want. It may take longer for these managers to shift to a *growth mindset*—seeing people for all they are capable of becoming. Unfortunately for these managers, the essential requirement of leaders who coach is to have a *growth mindset*, which supports the view that employees want to be developed, want to have open and honest conversations with their leader, want to be able to put forth their views, and want to be empowered to make changes. Leaders with a *growth mindset* see the benefits of investing in employees who are able to *"lay everything on the table"*, check their biases and assumptions at the door, and acknowledge their limitations in a safe space.

10.2.3 CEO and Senior Executives Believe in the Value and Potential of All Employees and Identify Opportunities to Unleash That Potential

In a coaching culture, all employees are supported to develop self-awareness and insight and unleash their potential. Leaders can assist in this process by *"stepping back"* at times to allow employees to gain in experience and then *"hold the space"* for them to lead. Self-development starts with self-awareness of one's own strengths, and self-management continues with recognising and supporting the development of others' strengths. As individuals start to *"peel back the layers of self"* to find out *"Who am I and what makes me tick?"* the focus of coaching becomes how to help the individual understand the behaviours that are holding them back and the ones that are propelling them forward.

Research has shown that individuals who are provided with developmental opportunities to expand their skills and experience remain longer in an organisation. Leaders who coach identify opportunities for employees to grow—whatever is needed for them to get from where they are now to where they want to be. Unleashing employees' potential allows them to grow personally and professionally whether that's at a skill or resource capability level. Coaching shifts employees' perception of how they are valued. Individuals who are coached feel acknowledged and appreciated because the organisation is investing in them and their potential.

One way to unleash employees' potential is to encourage them to apply to work in different parts of the business to obtain a broader perspective on organisational activities and reduce the 'silo' effect. Another way is to provide them with the opportunity to 'work up' in their area of expertise as people leave, go on holiday, or accept promotions. A third way is to seek ideas for innovative projects from employees. After the ideas are scrutinised and a decision made to fund a particular project, the employee who puts forward the idea is placed in charge of a project team to drive the idea through to successful completion. Organisations can also unleash potential by providing opportunities for employees to undertake additional skills training or enrol in external professional development programs related to their career path.

Organisations which believe in the potential of all employees use coaching to attract and support new entrants to their leadership ranks and position them as future leaders responsible for managing change and implementing new initiatives. The aim is to identify potential in the early phases of an employee's career and then nurture that potential. Leaders are encouraged to recognise and utilise the diversity of their direct reports and use coaching to assist team members embrace that diversity too. Organisations recognise that the only way that they're going to keep growing and satisfying shareholders' terms and looking after their customers is if they promote skill development and performance improvement in all their people.

10.3 Lead (Management)—Business and Relationship Improvements

In this third transition period, coaching is positioned as a strategic priority of the organisation. Goals and objectives for the coaching program are defined and measured. A coaching champion is nominated to steward the coaching initiative across and down all levels of the organisation. As coaching practice progresses, every business transaction is analysed through a coaching lens, and the two or three key business levers that can be enhanced though coaching are identified. Everybody is able to coach and be coached as scheduled or as the need arises, and coaching relationships are extended to all customers and suppliers.

10.3.1 Coaching Is Positioned at the Organisational Level as a Strategic Priority

Organisations that make a decision to develop a coaching culture make coaching a strategic priority—in which case *"it will be done"*. Coaching becomes a key component of the organisation's strategy as it is cascaded down the levels to achieve its vision and mission. As a strategic priority, the coaching initiative is publicised in all corporate documents, such as the strategic plan, and incorporated into all internal documentation, such as job descriptions, recruitment and selection processes, and performance management systems. Coaching is a particularly important tool to use when an organisation needs to reshape its organisational strategy in response to external opportunities or threats, for example, when transitioning from public to private sector ownership or downsizing as a result of loss of revenue, market share, or changes in commodity pricing levels.

Organisations which have a transformational HR function use their coaching capability to drive cultural change throughout the organisation. Everyone new to the organisation is coached and develops coaching skills. Employees share a common coaching language, and coaching becomes part of the way of *"being and doing"* things in the organisation, which makes the business *"unstoppable"*.

10.3.2 CEO and Senior Executives Align Coaching with Organisational Vision, Values, and Behaviours

During this third transition period, before committing to the development of a coaching culture, the CEO and senior executives need to be very clear about their vision and values for the organisation, make explicit the kind of leadership they want in the organisation, and define how coaching can contribute to the achievement of business outcomes. *Do they know what their vision is? Do they know where they're heading? Do they know what they stand for? Do they know what their values are?* Coaching is a developmental and performance-enhancing intervention that enables the answers to these questions to be achieved.

Leaders who behave according to the organisational values are *"living the values"*. The minute employees see someone behaving in an inappropriate way, who is not reprimanded for behaving in that way, will say, *"What's changed?"* Therefore, everyone in the organisation has to *"live the values"* to develop the culture that the organisation desires, and coaching is an effective means of creating and sustaining the cultural change. When coaching becomes part of the organisation's value proposition as well as a powerful means of developing people, it contributes to organisational sustainability.

10.3.3 CEO and Senior Executives Define the Organisational and Business Goals from Coaching

Organisations need to be clear about what they are trying to achieve by introducing a coaching culture. There needs to be a well-defined goal and outcomes in terms of what the coaching can do for the organisation, how coaching fits with the vision, goals, and objectives of the organisation, and what strategy to use to achieve them. The CEO and senior executives need to engage in discussion about,

"What's going to change? What's that going to mean?" and *"How does that connect with the broader values and goals of the organisation?"* Ideally, this conversation happens at multiple levels across the organisation, starting with the senior executive team.

One of the best ways to identify desired outcomes from coaching is to formulate a business case that defines the problem and opportunity and predicts an investment result—*"What are the expectations? What, specifically, does the organisation hope to achieve from coaching? Who are the key people who have experienced coaching?"*—and try to identify the gaps that coaching can fill. The next step is to interrogate the organisation's development processes and people management systems to discover how coaching can be incorporated into these activities to leverage opportunities through to business units, teams, and individuals.

10.3.3.1 A Recurrent Budget and Resources Are Allocated to Coaching

Organisations which accept the value and benefits of coaching have taken the first step towards developing a coaching culture. As a strategic priority, a considerable investment is made in skilling leaders in how to conduct coaching and feedback conversations. However, budgets and resources may be limited. Therefore, an organisation's investment in coaching must be both cost-effective and proportional but also a long-term commitment to building internal coaching capability. Even though coaching is becoming a more acceptable activity in organisations these days, actually putting the dollars behind it becomes a more difficult decision as budgets decline. Consequently, some organisations are choosing to put resources into employees at the level one down from the top because that's where operational decisions are made based on the assumption that the CEO and senior executives know all about coaching—which is not always the case.

10.3.3.2 The Return on Investment from Coaching Is Measured

The majority of organisations don't know how to measure the ROI from coaching because the outcomes are not always easy to quantify. They are often qualitative, not quantitative. Also, the ROI from coaching may take some time to become visible because one-on-one coaching relationships built on trust may become intense at times, especially if there are barriers to be broken down that have been formed over a period of years. Hence, it's harder to determine the ROI until the individual has completed an entire coaching program and is applying the new learnings.

Positive and negative metrics can be used to record both 'hard' and 'soft' data from the coaching program. Hard positive data may include financial indicators like sales figures and employee satisfaction ratings. Soft positive data may include self-report of improved leadership ability, other-report of improved personal relationships with team members, and observations of team morale. Hard negative indicators may include reduction in staff complaints and turnover. Soft negative indicators may include less observed conflict and fewer communication issues within the team. A typical way to assess a coachee's progress in an individual coaching program is to use a commercially available assessment instrument such as DiSC or LSI pre- and post-coaching, which allows the coach to see shifts in the individual more obviously and understand how they're benefitting from the coaching.

Organisations are encouraged to take a customised approach to measuring the outcomes of coaching programs based on acceptable outcomes which are negotiated upfront. Once these outcomes are determined, the coach and individual or team can be held accountable for getting the results. For example, a company may say that they want a 90 per cent success rate from a coaching program as determined by specific measurements pre and post. However, when the coaching is of a generic nature, for example, learning how to 'manage up', or learning to manage internationally, or not being so stressed in a management meeting under pressure, the ROI is more difficult to measure. In such instances, organisations can have the sponsor who has been appointed to monitor the coaching program report from an observational perspective on whether they believe that the individual has changed, for example, is less stressed in meetings.

10.3.4 A Senior Executive Is Appointed as a Champion for Coaching

During this third transition period, it's important that a coaching *champion* be appointed at the top level to steward through the coaching initiative. This person needs to be a strong advocate for coaching and the promotion of employee potential. They must be completely dedicated to transforming the organisational culture through coaching, be prepared to take the time to circulate through all levels of the organisation, and be approachable to address issues that employees raise to their attention. The coaching champion should already be formally coach-trained and have experienced being coached themself.

The impact of a coaching *champion* at the senior executive level lauding the benefits of coaching indicates the importance the organisation places on coaching. There is merit when the coaching champion publicly speaks from their own personal experience about the benefits of being coached. It can be inspiring and encourage others to do the same within their networks and business units. The champion liaises with organisational leaders to identify the networks they can use to start spreading the news about the benefits of coaching. They are also responsible for measuring the success of the coaching programs as they are cascaded down the organisation.

10.3.5 A Communication Strategy Is Developed to Introduce and Sustain Coaching Practice

When coaching has been declared a strategic priority to which people and resources have been allocated to implement coaching programs, a communication strategy is devised to inform all employees of the value placed on coaching by the organisation and the intention for all leaders to coach their direct reports. For example, an information statement may announce that leaders will be trained in coaching skills as part of their leadership development program. Attendance at these programs by the CEO and senior executives, even for a short time, clearly demonstrates their support for coaching. Senior executives then share the message with their direct reports, who cascade it down their business units.

It's important that every member of the senior executive team is 'on board' with the coaching initiative; otherwise, the message is diluted. The message says something like, *"Coaching is important to this organisation and to me, and I think that, ultimately, it will be important to all of us, and here's why."* Stating how coaching will be conducted and the benefits of coaching is important because there's not always clarity around what coaching is. Employees may think of coaching as another way of managing their performance, in which case they will anxiously believe that they are *"on the edge"* and ready to be *"let go"*, whereas if the message is presented positively and in a way that demonstrates leadership commitment, any misconceptions will be quickly dispelled.

10.3.6 CEO and Senior Executives Analyse Every Aspect of the Organisation through a Coaching Lens

When organisations embrace a coaching culture, coaching becomes the lens through which the organisation analyses everything that it does to identify areas where coaching can provide uplift. This process requires discipline and commitment to ascertain how coaching can be used to maximise the impact on the 'bottom line' from all its activities. It may involve, for example, examining how training is conducted and how leaders are selected, scrutinising how deals are done, and questioning the processes by which capability is transferred and applied to business situations. When coaching becomes the lens through which all business transactions are viewed and reviewed, leaders assess and analyse every aspect of their business systems and processes to incorporate coaching as appropriate, to increase productivity and achieve cultural change.

10.3.7 Organisational Levers to Maximise the Impact of Coaching Are Identified

When an organisation adopts a coaching culture, coaching is used to leverage the benefits of every business relationship and transaction into multiple areas of organisational activity. Business unit leaders examine every major focus area to identify the two or three levers where a coaching approach can be applied to increase productivity and competitive advantage. These levers may include, for example, incorporating coaching into the training of individuals in business acumen, including coaching as a selection criteria for leaders (including for a technical role), managing external stakeholders strategically, and increasing the organisation's ability to exert influence in the external marketplace. The reputational currency from externals who know that coaching is an integral component of all development activities and business transactions gives enormous credence to the organisation as a caring community which looks after the interests of its people.

At the senior level, coaching has been used as a lever to bring about improved commercial outcomes through behavioural profiling and constructive feedback on executives' management and leadership style. When coaches work with executives, the quality of the conversation is raised to a higher purpose level, together with a higher consequence level about *"getting it right, or getting it wrong"*. Businesses that conduct robust conversations at the executive level gain from the transparency that emerges, which can be harnessed by all the executives to improve the productivity of their teams and, in turn, cascade that learning down the organisation.

10.3.8 Coaching Is Applied more Broadly across the Organisation

Coaching can have broader application than one-on-one formal coaching sessions and team coaching meetings. At any time, whilst performing any business activity, coaching can be used to challenge existing thinking, break free of limiting beliefs, unlock fixed mindsets, and neutralise the potential threat associated with discussion of politically sensitive issues. Although coaching can be utilised in any business function, including corporate services, from a commercial standpoint coaching is highly applicable to revenue-generating, customer-facing areas of the business. This is because in these areas, the results of coaching are more quickly realised and visible in both 'hard' and 'soft' terms, for example, winning a sale, pacifying an angry customer, or passing a driving test. Coaching programs can also be used to support the introduction of new initiatives into the organisation, such as diversity programs and how to work with millennials—helping leaders to understand the cultural gap in terms of managing expectations, providing feedback and exploring significant development opportunities.

10.3.8.1 A Coaching Framework Is Attached to All Training Activities

When an organisation is serious about having coaching as a strategic priority, coaching is applied to all kinds of training activities that are conducted to transfer the learnings into workplace practise. For example, coaching can be applied to training front-line staff in how to increase sales from individual customers and generate increased revenue from corporate customers. Coaching sessions thereafter are used to support attendees in transferring the learnings into day-to-day activities and sustain their improved capability in the long term. All training conducted within the organisation, no matter what the skill, would be delivered with a coaching framework attached to it and supported thereafter by coaching conversations.

10.3.8.2 Coaching Is Conducted throughout the Organisation

When a coaching culture is embedded in an organisation, coaching is conducted throughout the organisation across all levels starting at the CEO and senior executive level. Unless there's investment from the top, a coaching culture will only be developed in *"pockets"*, that is, in some business units whose executives believe in coaching, but not across the entire organisation. Starting at the top is definitely important because if the top level is not completely committed to coaching and actually displaying their commitment through delivering coaching to their direct reports and others in the organisation and being coached themselves, the chances of developing a coaching culture are slim.

A coaching culture which promotes the development of all employees must be embedded in the organisation for it to survive when a supportive CEO leaves because a coaching culture is leader-centric and will only last as long as that leader is in place. For a coaching culture to be embedded, the executive team needs to own it, drive it, and role-model coaching. When key stakeholders including the CEO are committed to coaching, it becomes embedded in the organisation as a developmentally focused and supportive practice to grow all employees, which means that it will survive longer in the organisation even though a new CEO may not be fully supportive of coaching. Changing an organisation's culture takes time—maybe five years or more. Indeed, some organisations have been constantly *"chipping away"* at developing a coaching culture for fifteen or sixteen years as the organisation has restructured and made significant changes at the CEO and senior executive levels.

10.3.8.3 Peer Coaching Is Conducted throughout the Organisation

In organisations with a coaching culture, it's everybody's role to coach and an expectation that everyone will receive the coaching they need. Coaching has become an accepted practice to assist individuals to do what they need to do to meet their goals. Organisations may start establishing *peer coaching* relationships within a leadership development program either by pairing participants within that program or across other program cohorts. Within a coaching culture, people habitually and automatically coach each other, that is, assume the role of peer coach. When peer coaching occurs throughout the organisation from the executive level to front-line leaders and their team members, that's a coaching culture in action. Coaching occurs at all levels of the organisation in different ways depending on the individual's level of responsibility, the issue to be resolved, and the goal to be achieved.

10.3.9 Coaching Relationships Are Extended to External Customers and Suppliers

In this third transition period, coaching relationships extend beyond organisational boundaries to include customers and suppliers. The interaction is both relational to cement long-term engagement and satisfaction, and business-oriented to achieve targeted results. When coaching is extended to improving relationships beyond the organisation, commercial outcomes are aligned with customer needs as well as with the organisation's strategic goals. All business transactions are underpinned by the commercial or strategic outcomes that the organisation is seeking.

Customers and suppliers may, at first, be unsure of the change in approach from organisational representatives. They may need to be assured that extending coaching into the external stakeholder environment is part of the cultural shift occurring within the organisation, and be encouraged to come on-board with the initiative. Within a political environment, coaching is an effective way to manage multiple agendas and navigate higher-order changes, for example, the legislative requirements of hiring and employing staff. In an industrial relations-driven environment, there's a whole raft of consultations that need to happen before cultural elements can be shifted, and coaching is the means to manage these consultations effectively.

In a rapidly-changing global environment, organisational leaders must be adaptable to respond quickly to emerging needs, keep up with technology, grasp opportunities to maximise the productivity of the organisation, and consolidate social connections with external stakeholders. Coaching can be used to assist employees embrace change, promote innovation, and increase revenue. CEOs and senior executives know that their most valuable asset is their human resources who protect the organisation's intellectual property, safeguard its products and services, and maintain organisational culture. Employees do this by displaying the behaviours that uphold the organisation's values, being flexible and adaptable to change, and supporting the organisation's vision and direction. All of these activities are critical in helping the organisation achieve its mission. Unfortunately, the majority of leaders don't realise that they can use coaching skills more broadly than for individual and business performance to give them greater influence and leverage in the wider business community.

CHAPTER 11

TO THE END

11.1 Insights from the Research Findings

In this final chapter, the insights from the research study are summarised, which may alert organisations to potential pitfalls as they progress on their journey to developing a coaching culture. The first area of insight relates to *coaching* and how this term is understood by organisational leaders.

The findings reveal that there is still a *stigma* attached to coaching in some organisations, which has caused some external coaches to refer to a coaching intervention by another name, for example, *"meeting"* or *"honest, open conversation"*. Organisational leaders may couch the term *coaching* within a leadership development framework, which is more palatable for leaders to understand and accept. In addition, developing generic training in coaching skills allows all leaders to understand and gain the basic coaching skills, but unfortunately, it does not allow leaders to delve into the depths of personal experience, self-awareness, and insight (the *pure coaching*) that a formal accredited coach-training program delivered by an external coach-training provider would enable them to do.

An important distinction emerged as the research progressed in that organisational leaders are not typically trained to be coaches but rather are trained in coaching skills. They are trained in the techniques of how to coach from a performance and feedback perspective (*performance coaching*). Moreover, in-house training in coaching skills are mainly conducted over just a few hours or possibly one day, and are unlikely to address anything more than a surface-level understanding of coaching and the techniques of how to coach. Unless there is follow-up support for leaders who practise coaching, they may feel abandoned if their efforts falter. Investing in formal coach-training by an external coach-training provider takes time and requires a considerable investment, so it is understandable that unless there is complete commitment to developing a coaching culture from the top level, such an investment would be an unsound business decision.

Because organisational leaders are trained in *performance coaching*, it is questionable whether they have an appreciation of individual differences, what motivates individuals, and how behaviours can be changed—unless the educational and psychological components of coaching have been included in the in-house training program. Like an iceberg, these key underpinnings of how people learn and how change is enabled and enacted, sit below the surface of many short training programs and are not discussed unless time and expertise permits. Hence, managers who do not have prior leadership knowledge gain no deep understanding of coaching, or of the rationale for coaching, or of the need to park their own thoughts, judgements, and preferred behaviours to embrace a new way of engaging with their team. Being trained in coaching skills at the technical level is the first positive step towards developing a coaching culture, but additional training is required to progress leaders' understanding and experience of exactly how powerful coaching can be.

The *performance coaching* typically conducted within organisations is a subset of the formal *pure coaching* delivered by external coach-training providers. External accredited coach-training programs address the educational, psychological, and management aspects of coaching, as it is delivered within organisations to meet business needs. These programs are often approved by a professional body which sets international standards for coaching, such as the International Coach

Federation. Some external training companies 'coach train' around certain methodologies, that is, DiSC or LSI. However, these training methodologies train only to debrief the results of their online assessment instruments or to manipulate proprietary sales-training software tools. Hence, they do not constitute *pure coaching* as defined by the International Coach Federation, which can be summarised as *partnering with a client to help them progress their own agenda with no pre-determined outcomes*. Organisations should check international approvals for coach-training programs before investing in external coach-training for their leaders.

This research study revealed that larger organisations generally have a better understanding of coaching than their smaller counterparts or newer organisations because they may have overseas affiliates which have been around and involved with coaching for a longer time, or they may be headquartered in the northern hemisphere where coaching is more well-known and accepted. Their conceptualisations of *coaching* are typically more mature; hence they may value *coaching* more highly and may employ dedicated coaches and coaching teams. The emphasis in many of these organisations, however, still tends to be on coaching for problem remediation and performance management rather than on investing in all employees to grow and develop their potential.

Generally, executive coaches should be engaged to coach at the CEO and senior executive level rather than having internal coaches coach upwards. This is because executive coaches have a wealth of experience, expertise, and (hopefully) formal coach-training, which gives them credibility at that level (as opposed to other coaches, e.g. business or life coaches). In addition, executive coaches have a wider perspective on the external marketplace and more experience gained from working across many organisations. Internal coaches who coach upwards in an organisation are not seen to have the same credibility or skills and may not be trusted with private and confidential information.

As an internal coach, it's a 'hard sell' to convince an organisation to engage in developing a coaching culture. Organisations have limited budgets and need to prioritise their spending. They tend to invest in tried and proven ways of improving their business. The outcomes of coaching are not easily measured, being mainly qualitative in nature. To prove the benefits of coaching and hence influence organisations to develop a coaching culture, the desired outcomes of a coaching program need to be predetermined before the program begins and measures of success quantified and recorded. A pilot program may be conducted to test the effectiveness of the coaching.

Even when a coaching culture is embedded in an organisation, the initiative may die very quickly if a new CEO is appointed who does not value coaching—unless there is a strong proponent of coaching who occupies a senior position within the organisation and who is sanctioned to continue with the initiative, that is, a senior champion or another influential individual with a *"seat at the table"*, like a transformational HR professional. Organisations gain competitive *"speed to respond"* and *"speed to market"* advantage when internal coaches or internal coaching teams are positioned within business units and report directly to a senior executive champion who can smooth their way if necessary.

Cultures take a long time to shift—often years. Organisations which decide to embark on developing a coaching culture need to be prepared to invest in the resources required to develop coaching skills in all existing and new leaders as the coaching programs cascade down the organisation. Leaders who are trained in coaching skills display improved leadership capability, which positions the organisation well during times of external change, for example, commodity price changes, stock market fluctuations, and legislative, environmental, or regulatory changes. In addition, as organisations attempt to change their culture, their efforts may be significantly impacted by political and union influences, and other external agendas that can get in the way of leaders taking the actions they want to take to change the culture. Navigating these particular environments calls for the use of coaching and negotiation skills to inform, influence, and persuade to achieve the organisation's agenda.

A coaching culture in which everyone is able to coach and be coached includes *peer coaching*. Peer coaching is not often mentioned in association with the delivery of coaching throughout an organisation. This may be because not all employees are trained in coaching skills, which, initially, could prove to be an expensive exercise—however with long-time benefits. As peers adopt 'coach-like behaviours', the culture changes and becomes more inclusive and accommodating of individual differences and accepting of the values and beliefs that build cooperation and teamwork. Leaders step back to *"hold the space"* for others to lead. Coaching appears to be particularly effective at transition points, for example, when an organisation is in turnaround or when a team member promotes into a leadership role.

Organisations with a coaching culture fit the description of a *deliberately developmental organisation* (Kegan et al. 2014), which is one in which coaching skills are deliberately applied to all conversations, meetings, training programs, transactions, interactions, and relationships throughout and external to the organisation. The culture is open and supportive of the growth that employees experience when they are developmentally coached. Employees who do not feel comfortable with this level of 'exposure' may not remain long in the organisation. Those who remain, experience a rate of personal and professional growth that is intense and potentially life-changing.

Leadership style, personality preferences, and cultural differences must be taken into account when attempting to develop a coaching culture. A *command-and-control* management style may become more malleable if managers are willing to be coached or if they are willing to allow a coaching champion to lead; the coaching initiative may go ahead successfully. However, if neither of these conditions occurs, it is unlikely that a coaching culture will be developed and embedded into an organisation. *Coaching-as-Intervention* or *Coaching-as-HR-Function* may remain the predominant coaching approach in such organisations.

These areas of insight from the research highlight the interplay and dynamics between the four stages that organisations go through as they transition towards the development of a coaching culture.

11.2 Implications of This Research

11.2.1 CEO and Senior Executives

Findings from the research indicate the criticality of having a CEO who understands what coaching is and what it isn't and supports the introduction of a coaching culture into the organisation. The CEO may have experienced being coached, in which case they really appreciate the benefits of coaching and the value it can add to individuals, teams, and the organisation itself. If not, they and all the senior executives should experience being coached so that they can credibly role-model the importance the organisation is placing on leaders coaching their direct reports and others, and promoting coaching throughout the organisation.

The CEO and senior executives need to have a *growth mindset* and an absolute belief in providing *developmental* opportunities for all employees to reach their potential. They need to be absolutely committed to developing a coaching culture and make this outcome a strategic priority with an allocated budget and recurrent resources. The desired outcomes from investing in coaching and developing a coaching culture must be defined in measureable terms. A senior executive sponsor who has experienced being coached should be nominated to steward the coaching initiative; a transformational HR professional who has a *"seat at the table"* may be a viable alternative champion.

As coaching cascades down the organisation from the *"gardener to the board chair"* and the benefits of coaching become more well-known, coaching should be extended into all areas of the business, including into interactions and relationships with customers and suppliers. The CEO and senior executives must be aware that cultural change takes time, often years, before it becomes embedded in the DNA and fabric of an organisation.

11.2.2 HR Professionals

When coaching is designated as a core competency of leaders, a *transformational* HR approach is required to take on the responsibility to train all leaders in coaching skills. HR professionals benefit from becoming formally trained as coaches so that they feel more confident in passing on their knowledge and skills to leaders when delivering in-house training in coaching skills. This training may be conducted as a stand-alone program, but more frequently, it is included as a component of the leadership development programs that are delivered to all functional leaders across the organisation. An *Accredited Coaches Network* of volunteer coaches is established and includes formally trained coaches who, in addition to their 'day job', deliver coaching on request to others in the organisation. Leaders at transition points may receive *"role coaching"* to settle them into their new role, for example, team member to team leader or technical specialist to team leader. *Coaching Circles* are established to support leaders who have attended in-house training in coaching skills, and subsequently deliver coaching to their direct reports. *Coaching Communities* support coaching practice, coaching supervision, and the extension of coaching into all areas of the business.

When coaching is designated as a strategic priority for the organisation, the ability to coach is written into all HR systems and processes, including recruitment and selection, performance management, reward systems, talent management, and succession planning. Hence, the requirement for leaders to coach their direct reports is assessed against their KPIs. Candidates for leadership positions who have coaching skills are highly regarded. A HR metrics system is developed to record the quantity and quality of coaching being delivered within the organisation to evaluate the effectiveness of coaching programs and measure the ROI from coaching.

11.2.3 Organisational Leaders

Organisational leaders are increasingly expected to coach their direct reports and others in the organisation on a regular basis. By providing timely feedback to employees, leaders are signalling the importance of supporting their growth, development, and career aspirations. The focus is no longer on just the most talented of employees; the focus is on *all* employees. Under a *growth mindset*, every employee given the encouragement, opportunity, and support can reach their potential.

A position of *Internal Coach* may be established and an internal coaching team formed of internal coaches positioned within business units. The team reports directly into a senior executive sponsor/champion who can facilitate *"speed of response"* to current and emerging situations. Internal coaches are formally trained in *pure coaching* skills that meet international standards of coaching and ethical practice, so that they can provide motivational, behavioural, performance and career coaching to individuals and teams within business units. Specialist coaches may be appointed within revenue-generating business units to *performance coach* front-line staff in how to identify which clients to approach to maximise the return on their time, effort, and investment, as well as how to build better business relationships with potential or existing external commercial partners. A pilot coaching program may be conducted within a business unit to prove the benefits of coaching, after which all employees may engage in peer coaching whereby everybody in the organisation coaches each other on a daily basis.

APPENDIX 1

SUMMARY OF THE PSYCHOLOGICAL AND EDUCATIONAL EVIDENCE FOR COACHING

Theory and Exponents	Description
Behavioural Theories	
Law of Effect (Thorndike 1911)	Thorndike found that when a stimulus results in a satisfying response, the stimulus is likely to be repeated.
Classical conditioning (stimulus–response) theory (Pavlov 1927)	Pavlov's research on conditioned reflexes influenced the rise of behaviourism in psychology. His experimental methods helped move psychology away from introspection and subjective assessments to objective measurement of behaviour.
Observation of human behaviours (Watson 1931)	Watson is often referred to as the father of behaviourism. His focus on observable behaviours and objectivity had a strong influence on psychology. The behavioural perspective dominated the field during the first half of the twentieth century.

Operant conditioning (Skinner 1938)	Skinner discovered that one reinforcement of an arbitrary response is enough to develop a conditioned response. Intermittent reinforcement continues to shape the behaviour. His behaviour modification and intervention techniques are used to change problem behaviours or reinforce new ones.
Cognitive Theories	
Cognitive-based therapy (Beck 1976; Neenan 2008)	Cognitive-based therapy (CBT) is short-term and focused on helping the individual identify limiting beliefs which are holding them back from achieving their goals.
Solution-focused coaching (Grant et al. 2012; Grant and O'Connor 2010; Nagel 2008; Wakefield 2006)	Solution-based therapy aims to accurately identify the problem and quickly conceive of possible solutions to it. It is a collaborative, future-focused approach to get the client back in control of their own life.
Rational emotive behaviour therapy (Ellis 1962, 1995)	Rational emotive therapy (RET) is an action-oriented approach to addressing thoughts, emotions, and behaviours that are unhelpful to the client and can create self-sabotaging routines.
Goal-setting theory (Locke and Latham 2002, 2006, 2013)	Goals which are specific, measurable, time-bound, and relevant are more likely to be achieved than those which are not. Self-efficacy is a supportive precursor to achieving difficult goals.
Motivational Theories	
Need hierarchy theory (Maslow 1943, 1954)	Maslow is perhaps best known as the founder of humanistic psychology. His hierarchy of needs and concepts of self-actualization and peak experiences remain influential to this day, especially in the field of positive psychology.

Human motivation theory (McClelland 1967)	McClelland proposed that every person is primarily motivated by one of three drivers: n-ach (achievement), n-affil (affiliation), or n-pow (power). McClelland believed that most people possess and exhibit a combination of these characteristics.
Two-factor theory (Herzberg, Mausner, and Snyderman 1959)	Hertzberg identified two major factors affecting job satisfaction and dissatisfaction, which he called hygiene factors (e.g. status, job security, salary, and fringe benefits—which do not contribute to employee satisfaction at work) and motivator factors; (e.g. challenging work, recognition, and responsibility—which lead to positive satisfaction with work).
Theory X and Y (McGregor 1960)	McGregor proposed that managers relate and behave in different ways to their employees depending on whether they believe the employee dislikes work and won't accept responsibility (Theory X) or is self-motivated, likes work and assumes responsibility for their work (Theory Y).
ERG need theory (Alderfer 1969)	Alderfer proposed a threefold conceptualization of human needs: existence, relatedness, and growth (ERG), which, contrary to Maslow's hierarchy, does not assume satisfaction of lower-order needs before achieving self-actualisation.
Expectancy theory (Vroom 1964)	There are three components of this theory: *valence*—the value a person places on achieving a specific outcome (positive or negative); *expectancy*—a person's subjective probability that his act will (one) or will not (zero) be followed by an outcome; and *instrumentality*—the person's perception of the probability that his/her performance will lead to a specific outcome if s/he behaves in a certain way.

Equity theory (Adams 1963)	Adams proposed that people attempt to maintain fairness by comparing their inputs (and outputs) with that of others performing the same behaviour. As long as the ratio between the two inputs and outputs is equal, people will perceive the situation to be fair.
Self-theory (C. Dweck 1990, 2000)	Variations in students' engagement, persistence, and achievement can be attributed to whether they view their intelligence (ability) to be fixed or malleable.
Developmental Theories	
Education (Dewey 1938)	Dewey's emphasis on progressive education has greatly contributed to the use of experimentation rather than an authoritarian approach to learning. His theory links the mind and body via primary and secondary experiential learning.
Cognitive development theory (Piaget 1950)	Piaget was one of the first thinkers to suggest that children think differently from adults, a concept that was considered revolutionary at the time. He believed that development of the structures of the brain is key to the ability to accomplish tasks.
Psychosocial development (Erikson 1959)	Erik Erikson's stage theory of psychosocial development helped generate interest and inspire research on human development through the lifespan, including events of childhood, adulthood, and old age, reinforcing the influence of parents, family, social institutions, and a particular culture.
Personality Theories	
Personality theory (Jung 1921)	Jung developed a typology of personality functions or attitudes which was later adapted to construct the Myers–Briggs Type Indicator (MBTI) (Myers 1980).

Personality psychology (Allport and Allport 1921)	Floyd Allport was one of the founding figures of personality psychology. He developed a trait theory of personality that described three broad categories of personality traits.
Personality factors (Cattell 1947)	Cattell is best known for his use of multivariate analysis and his sixteen-factor questionnaire, which has been widely used in career coaching.
Humanistic Theories	
Analytical psychology (Jung 1917)	Jung broke away from Freudian psychology to develop the concepts of individuation, archetypes, and the collective unconscious.
Self-psychology (Horney, 1950)	Karen Horney was a prominent psychoanalyst best known for her theories on neurosis, feminism, and self-psychology, which includes concepts of self-confidence and personal assets (autonomous convictions, self-reliance, realistic appraisal of and assuming responsibility for self, having strength and capacity for feelings, and establishing good human relationships).
Individual psychology (Adler, Ansbacher, and Ansbacher 1956)	Adler's research investigated areas such as the creative self, lifestyle, family constellation, and social and community interest. His concepts included horizontal interpersonal communication, reasonable cooperation, unconditional respect for the individual as a member of a democratic society, and social equality.
Person-centred theory (C. Rogers 1959, 1961)	Rogers was one of the most influential psychologists of the twentieth century. He developed the non-directive, client-centred approach to counselling and therapy in non-medical settings and founded the professional counselling movement.

Social Theories	
Sociocultural theory (Vygotsky and Cole 1978; Vygotsky 1934)	Vygotsky is the founder of sociocultural theory. He researched the relationship between learning and development in general and special education populations. He studied the interaction of the natural, individual, and social forces leading to mind consciousness and how humans make meaning from their environment. His concepts of the zone of proximal development and guided practice continue be highly influential in educational settings.
Social psychology (Lewin, 1935, 1943, 1944)	Kurt Lewin is often referred to as the father of modern social psychology. His pioneering theories argued that behaviour is caused by both personal characteristics and the environment. Lewin's emphasis on scientific methodology and systematic in-depth study of concrete examples had an enormous impact on future research in social psychology.
Social pressure (Asch 1951, 1955, 1956)	Asch's conformity experiments demonstrated that people will claim that something is correct when it obviously is not due to social pressure from peers. Asch also had an important influence on psychologist Stanley Milgram, whose own obedience experiments were inspired by Asch's work.
Social comparison theory (Festinger 1954) Cognitive dissonance theory (Festinger 1957, 1964)	Festinger was an influential social psychologist who is well known for his social comparison theory as well as his theory of cognitive dissonance. Cognitive dissonance occurs when a person holds two or more elements of knowledge that are relevant to each other but inconsistent; indecision results.

Psychological modelling (Bandura 1971), social learning theory (Bandura 1977), self-efficacy (Bandura 1997; Bandura and Locke 2003)	Social learning theory posits that all learning takes place in a social setting, for example, at school, work, family environment. Learning takes place by inspection of the situation and observation of models. Bandura is a known for his famous 'Bobo doll' experiment in which children were exposed to violent role models whose behaviour they emulated, especially when it was modelled by a same-sex adult. He introduced the concept of self-efficacy to describe the inner belief in oneself that one could perform a task, especially a difficult task, to achieve a specific goal.
Social cognitive theory (Bandura 2006; Bandura, Davidson, and Davidson 2003; C. Dweck and Leggett 1988; Mizokawa and Koyasu 2015)	Bandura's work is considered part of the cognitive revolution in psychology that began in the late 1960s. His theories have had tremendous impact on personality psychology, cognitive psychology, education, and therapy. Dweck's theory applies to motivation and personality as precursors of goal achievement. Mizokawa and Koyasu investigate social relationships and emotional competence from a social cognitive perspective.
Social modelling (Zimbardo, Goldstein, and Utley 1971)	Zimbardo is an influential psychologist who conducted a famous experiment during the early 1970s known as the Stanford prison experiment. He is also widely recognized for his research on shyness, cult behaviour, and heroism.

Positive Psychology Theories

Flow theory (Csikszentmihalyi 1990) and optimal experience (Csikszentmihalyi and Csikszentmihalyi 1988)	Csikszentmihalyi is an important contemporary psychologist, noted for his work in relation to the study of happiness and creativity. His theory of flow describes the state of deep mind concentration when a person is so involved in an experience or situation that time passes without notice. A successful flow experience results in self-affirmation, increased confidence associated with perceived competence, creativity, and a feeling of lifelong happiness.

Positive psychology (Csikszentmihalyi and Csikszentmihalyi 2006; Seligman and Csikszentmihalyi 2000; Seligman, Ernst, Gillham, Reivich, and Linkins 2009), authentic happiness (Seligman 2002, 2011), and learned helplessness (Seligman 1972; Seligman and Altenor 1980)	Seligman is considered to be one of the most influential psychologists of the twentieth century and is often described as the father of contemporary positive psychology. He has extended the work of Csikszentmihalyi into the area of authentic happiness, and his work on learned helplessness is highly applicable to the helping professions. He and colleagues have written on the empirical validation of positive psychology interventions (Seligman, Steen, Park, and Peterson 2005), application of positive psychology to coaching (Seligman 2007), and the benefits of a positive mindset to your health (Seligman 2008).

REFERENCES

Abington, A. (2013). 'Croydon Health Services NHS Trust Creates an Internal- Coaching Culture: New Skills Promote Organizational Change and Performance'. *Human Resource Management International Digest*, 21/4, 6–11.

Adams, J. (1963). Towards an Understanding of Inequity. *Journal of Abnormal Psychology*, 67, 422.

Adler, A., H. Ansbacher, and R. Ansbacher (1956). *The Individual Psychology of Alfred Adler: A Systematic Presentation in Selections from His Writings*. New York U6: Basic Books.

Alderfer, C. (1969). 'An Empirical Test of a New Theory of Human Needs'. *Organizational Behavior and Human Performance*, 4/2, 142–175.

Allard-Poesi, F. (1998). 'Representations and Influence Processes in Groups: Towards a Socio-Cognitive Perspective on Cognition in Organisation'. *Scandinavian Journal of Management*, 14/4, 395–420.

Allport, F., and G. W. Allport (1921). 'Personality Traits: Their Classification and Measurement'. *The Journal of Abnormal Psychology and Social Psychology*, 16/1, 6–40.

Alvesson, M. (2002). *Understanding Organizational Culture*. London: SAGE.

Anderson, D., and M. Anderson (2005). *Coaching That Counts: Harnessing the Power of Leadership Coaching to Deliver Strategic Value*. Amsterdam, Boston: Elsevier/Butterworth-Heinemann.

Ann, C., and A. Carr (2011). 'Inside Outside Leadership Development: Coaching and Storytelling Potential'. *Journal of Management Development*, 30/3, 297–310.

Antonsen, S. (2009). *Safety Culture Theory, Method and Improvement / Stian Antonsen*. Farnham: Ashgate Publishing Ltd.

Argyris, C. (1992). *On Organizational Learning*. Cambridge, Massachusetts: Blackwell.

Asch, S. (1955). 'Opinions and Social Pressure'. *Scientific American*, 193/5, 31–35.

—— (1956). 'Studies of Independence and Conformity: I. A Minority of One against a Unanimous Majority'. *Psychological Monographs: General and Applied*, 70/9, 1–70.

—— (2008). 'Effects of Group Pressure Upon the Modification and Distortion of Judgements'. *Managerial Psychology*, 193–203.

Ashkanasy, N. M., C. P. M. Wilderom, and M. F. Peterson (2011). *The Handbook of Organizational Culture and Climate* (2nd vol.). Thousand Oaks: SAGE Publications.

Avolio, B. J., and W. L. Gardner (2005). 'Authentic Leadership Development: Getting to the Root of Positive Forms of Leadership'. *The Leadership Quarterly*, 16/3, 315–338.

Babío, N. C., and R. G. Rodríguez (2010). Talent Management in Professional Services Firms: A HR Issue?' *International Journal of Organizational Analysis*, 18/4, 392–411.

Bachkirova, T., and C. Kauffman (2009). 'The Blind Men and the Elephant: Using Criteria of Universality and Uniqueness in Evaluating Our Attempts to Define Coaching'. *Coaching: An International Journal of Theory, Research and Practice*, 2/2, 95–105.

Bandura, A. (1971). *Psychological Modeling: Conflicting Theories*. Chicago: Aldine-Atherton; New York.

—— (1977). 'Self-Efficacy: Toward a Unifying Theory of Behavioral Change'. *Psychological Review*, 84, 191–215.

—— (1977). *Social Learning Theory*. Englewood Cliffs, New Jersey: Prentice Hall.

—— (1997). 'Self-Efficacy: The Exercise of Control'. *Freeman: New York*.

—— (2006). 'Toward a Psychology of Human Agency'. *Perspectives on Psychological Science*, 1/2, 164–180.

——, H. Davidson, and J. Davidson (2003). *Bandura's Social Cognitive Theory: An Introduction*. San Luis Obispo, California: Davidson Films Inc.

——, and E. Locke (2003). 'Negative Self-Efficacy and Goal Effects Revisited'. *Journal of Applied Psychology*, 88/1, 87–99.

Baron, L., and L. Morin (2009). 'The Coach-Coachee Relationship in Executive Coaching: A Field Study'. *Human Resource Development Quarterly*, 20/1, 85.

Batson, V. D., and L. H. Yoder (2012). 'Managerial Coaching: A Concept Analysis'. *Journal of Advanced Nursing*, 68/7, 1658–1669.

Bawany, S. (2015). 'Creating a Coaching Culture'. *Leadership Excellence*, 32/2, 43–44.

Bax, J., M. Negrutiu, and T. Calota (2011). 'Coaching: A Philosophy, Concept, Tool and Skill'. *Journal of Knowledge Management, Economics and Information Technology*, 1/7, 320–328.

Beattie, R., S. Kim, M. Hagen, T. Egan, A. Ellinger, and R. Hamlin (2014). 'Managerial Coaching: A Review of the Empirical Literature and Development of a Model to Guide Future Practice'. *Advances in Developing Human Resources*, 16/2, 184–201.

Beck, A. (1976). *Cognitive Therapy and the Emotional Disorders*. New York: International Universities Press.

——, and M. Wiersema (2013). 'Executive Decision Making: Linking Dynamic Managerial Capabilities to the Resource Portfolio and Strategic Outcomes'. *Journal of Leadership & Organizational Studies*, 20/4, 408–419.

Beheshtifar, M., H. Y. Nasab, and M. N. Moghadam (2012). 'Effective Talent Management: A Vital Strategy for Organisational Success'. *International Journal of Academic Research in Business and Social Sciences*, 2/12, 227–234.

Bond, C., and M. Seneque (2012). 'Conceptualizing Coaching as an Approach to Management and Organizational Development'. *Journal of Management Development*, 32/1, 57–72.

Bourdieu, P. (1990). *The Logic of Practice*. Stanford, California: Stanford University Press.

Boyatzis, R. E., D. Good, and R. Massa (2012). 'Emotional, Social, and Cognitive Intelligence and Personality as Predictors of Sales Leadership Performance'. *Journal of Leadership & Organizational Studies*, 19/2, 191–201.

——, K. Rochford, and S. N. Taylor (2015). 'The Role of the Positive Emotional Attractor in Vision and Shared Vision: Toward Effective Leadership, Relationships, and Engagement'. *Frontiers in Psychology*, 6, 670.

——, M. L. Smith, and A. J. Beveridge (2013). 'Coaching with Compassion: Inspiring Health, Well-Being, and Development in Organizations'. *The Journal of Applied Behavioral Science*, 49/2, 153–178.

Bozer, G., and J. C. Saros (2012). 'Examining the Effectiveness of Executive Coaching on Coachees' Performance in the Israeli Context'. *International Journal of Evidence Based Coaching and Mentoring*, 10, 14–32.

——, J. Sarros, and J. Santora (2014). 'Academic Background and Credibility in Executive Coaching Effectiveness'. *Personnel Review*, 43/6, 881 897.

Bright, D., and A. Crockett (2012). 'Training Combined with Coaching Can Make a Significant Difference in Job Performance and Satisfaction'. *Coaching: An International Journal of Theory, Research and Practice*, 5/1, 4–21.

Britton. J. (2008). 'Increasing Job Satisfaction: Coaching with Evidence-Based Interventions'. *Coaching: An International Journal of Theory, Research and Practice*, 1/2, 176–185.

——. (2015). 'Expanding the Coaching Conversation: Group and Team Coaching'. *Industrial and Commercial Training*, 47/3, 116–120.

Bruning, N. S., and R. L. Tung, (2013). 'Leadership Development and Global Talent Management in the Asian Context: An Introduction'. *Asian Business & Management*, 12/4, 381–386.

Caldwell, C. (2018). *Safety Culture and High-Risk Environments: A Leadership Perspective*. Boca Raton, Florida: CRC Press, Taylor; Francis Group.

Carey, W., D. J. Philippon, and G. G Cummings (2011). 'Coaching Models for Leadership Development: An Integrative Review'. *Journal of Leadership Studies*, 5/1, 51–69.

Cattell, R. (1947). 'Confirmation and Clarification of Primary Personality Factors'. *Psychometrika U6*, 12/3, 197–220.

Cerdin, J.-L., and C. Brewster (2014). 'Talent Management and Expatriation: Bridging Two Streams of Research and Practice'. *Journal of World Business*, 49/2, 245–252.

Charteris, J., C. Jennifer, and S. Dianne (2014). 'Dialogic Peer Coaching as Teacher Leadership for Professional Inquiry'. *International Journal of Mentoring and Coaching in Education*, 3/2, 108.

Church, A. H. (2014). 'Succession Planning 2.0: Building Bench through Better Execution'. *Strategic HR Review*, 13/6, 233–242.

Church, A. H., C. T. Rotolo, N. M. Ginther, and R. Levine (2015). 'How Are Top Companies Designing and Managing Their High-Potential Programs? A Follow-Up Talent Management Benchmark Study'. *Consulting Psychology Journal: Practice and Research*, 67/1, 17–47.

CIPD (2014). 'Learning and Development Survey'. *London, England: CIPD*.

Clarke, S. (1999). 'Perceptions of Organizational Safety: Implications for the Development of Safety Culture'. *Journal of Organizational Behavior*, 20/2, 185–198.

Clegg, S., C. Rhodes, and M. Kornberger (2003). 'An Overview of the Business Coaching Industry in Australia'. *Organization Studies*, 28/4: 495–513.

Clutterbuck, D. (2007). *Coaching the Team at Work*. London: Nicholas Brealey Publishing.

———. (2008). 'What's Happening in Coaching and Mentoring? And What Is the Difference between Them?'. *Development and Learning in Organisations*, 22/4, 8.

———. (2013). 'Time to Focus Coaching on the Team'. *Industrial and Commercial Training*, 45/1, 18–22.

Collings, D. G., and K. Mellahi (2009). 'Strategic Talent Management: A Review and Research Agenda'. *Human Resource Management Review*, 19/4, 304–313.

Cook, S., and S. Macaulay (2009). 'Talent Management'. *Training Journal*, 44–48.

Cooke, F. L., D. S. Saini, and J. Wang (2014). 'Talent Management in China and India: A Comparison of Management Perceptions and Human Resource Practices'. *Journal of World Business*, 49/2, 225–235.

Coulson-Thomas, C. (2012). 'Talent Management and Building High Performance Organisations'. *Industrial and Commercial Training*, 44/7, 429–436.

Cowan, K. (2013). 'What Are the Experiences of External Executive Coaches Working with Coaches' Assigned Goals? *International Journal of Evidence Based Coaching and Mentoring*, special issue no. 7 (June), 1–14.

Cox, E., T. Bachkirova, and D. Clutterbuck (2014). *The Complete Handbook of Coaching, second edition.* Los Angeles, California: SAGE.

Csikszentmihalyi, M. (1990). 'Flow: The Psychology of Optimal Experience'. New York: Harper & Row.

———, and I. Csikszentmihalyi (1988). 'Optimal Experience: Psychological Studies of Flow in Consciousness'. New York: Cambridge Press.

———, and I. Csikszentmihalyi (2006). *A Life Worth Living: Contributions to Positive Psychology.* New York: Oxford University Press.

Cummings, T. G., and C. G. Worley (2005). *Organization Development and Change* (8th ed.). Mason, Ohio: Thomson/South-Western.

Dana, H., B. Havens, C. Hochanadel, and J. Phillips (2010). 'An Innovative Approach to Faculty Coaching'. *Contemporary Issues in Education Research*, 3/11, 29–34.

Davis, G. F. (2005). *Social Movements and Organization Theory.* Cambridge, New York: Cambridge University Press.

Day, D. V., J. W. Fleenor, L. E. Atwater, R. E. Sturm, and R. A. McKee (2014). 'Advances in Leader and Leadership Development: A Review of 25 Years of Research and Theory'. *The Leadership Quarterly*, 25/1, 63–82.

De Meuse, K. P., G. Dai, and R. J. Lee (2009). 'Evaluating the Effectiveness of Executive Coaching: Beyond ROI?' *Coaching: An International Journal of Theory, Research and Practice*, 2/2, 117–134.

De Vos, A., and N. Dries (2013). 'Applying a Talent Management Lens to Career Management: The Role of Human Capital Composition and Continuity'. *International Journal of Human Resource Management*, 24/9, 1816–1831.

Devins, D., and J. Gold (2014). 'Re-conceptualising Talent Management and Development within the Context of the Low Paid'. *Human Resource Development International*, 17/5, 514–528.

Dewey, J. (1938). *Experience and Education*. New York U6: Macmillan.

Dutton, J. E., M. C. Worline, P. J. Frost, and J. Lilius (2006). 'Explaining Compassion Organizing'. *Administrative Science Quarterly*, 51/1, 59–96.

Dweck, C. (1990). 'Self-Theories and Goals: Their Role in Motivation, Personality, and Development'. *Nebraska Symposium on Motivation. Nebraska Symposium on Motivation*, 38, 199.

—— (2000). *Self-Theories: Their Role in Motivation, Personality, and Development*. Philadelphia, Pennsylvania: Psychology Press.

—— (2008). 'Can Personality Be Changed?: The Role of Beliefs in Personality and Change'. *Current Directions in Psychological Science*, 17/6, 391–394.

—— (2012). 'Mindsets and Human Nature: Promoting Change in the Middle East, the Schoolyard, the Racial Divide, and Willpower'. *American Psychologist*, 67/8, 614–622.

—— (2014). 'Teachers' Mindsets: "Every Student Has Something to Teach Me": Feeling Overwhelmed? Where Did Your Natural Teaching Talent Go? Try Pairing a Growth Mindset with Reasonable Goals, Patience, and Reflection Instead. It's Time to Get Gritty and Be a Better Teacher'. *Educational Horizons*, 93/2, 10–15.

—— (2015). 'Growth'. *British Journal of Educational Psychology*, 85/2, 242–245.

——, C. Chiu, and Y. Hong (1995). 'Implicit Theories: Elaboration and Extension of the Model'. *Psychological Inquiry*, 6/4, 322–333.

——, and E. Leggett (1988). 'A Social-Cognitive Approach to Motivation and Personality'. *Psychological Review*, 95/2, 256–273.

Edelman, A. J. (2011). 'Retain Talent with Positive Culture: Organizational Culture Can Fortify or Erode Staff Commitment'. *Health Care Registration: The Newsletter for Health Care Registration Professionals*, 21/3, 6–8.

Ellinger, A. (2013). 'Supportive Supervisors and Managerial Coaching: Exploring Their Intersections'. *Journal of Occupational and Organizational Psychology*, 86/3, 310.

——, and Bostrom, R. (1999). 'Managerial Coaching Behaviors in Learning Organizations'. *Journal of Management Development*, 18/9, 752–771.

——, A. Ellinger, D. Bachrach, Y. Wang, and A. Elmadagbas (2011). 'Organizational Investments in Social Capital, Managerial Coaching, and Employee Work-Related Performance'. *Management Learning*, 42/1, 67–85.

——, R. Hamlin, and R. Beattie (2008). 'Behavioural Indicators of Ineffective Managerial Coaching: A Cross-National Study'. *Journal of European Industrial Training*, 32/4, 240–257.

——, and S. Kim (2014). 'Coaching and Human Resource Development: Examining Relevant Theories, Coaching Genres, and Scales to Advance Research and Practice'. *Advances in Developing Human Resources*, 16/2, 127–138.

Ellis, A. (1995). 'Changing Rational-Emotive Therapy (RET) to Rational Emotive Behavior Therapy (REBT). *Journal of Rational-Emotive and Cognitive-Behavior Therapy*, 13/2, 85–89.

—— (1962). *Reason and Emotion in Psychotherapy.* New York: L. Stuart.

Erikson, E. (1959). *Identity and the Life Cycle: Selected Papers* (vol. 1). New York U6: International Universities Press.

Evered, R. D., and J. C. Selman (1989). 'Coaching and the Art of Management'. *Organizational Dynamics*, 18/2, 16.

Farry, M. (2014). 'PhotoBox Focuses on Employees' Strengths: Training Fosters a Positive and Energizing Culture'. *Human Resource Management International Digest*, 22/1, 15–17.

Feldman, and Lankau (2005). 'Executive Coaching: A Review and Agenda for Future Research'. *Journal of Management*, 31/6, 829–848.

Festinger, L. (1954). 'A Theory of Social Comparison Processes'. *Human Relations*, 7/2, 117–140.

—— (1957). *A Theory of Cognitive Dissonance*. Stanford, California: Stanford University Press.

—— (1964). *Conflict, Decision, and Dissonance*. Oxford, England: Stanford University Press.

Fillery-Travis, A., and D. Lane (2006). 'Does Coaching Work or Are We Asking the Wrong Questions?' *International Coaching Psychology Review*, 1/1, 23–36.

Flyvberg, B. (2006). 'Five Misunderstandings about Case-Study Research.' *Qualitative Inquiry*, 12/2, 219–245.

Fournies, F. F. (1987). *Coaching for Improved Work Performance*. Bridgewater, New Jersey: F. Fournies.

Garavan, T. N. (2012). 'Global Talent Management in Science-Based Firms: An Exploratory Investigation of the Pharmaceutical Industry during the Global Downturn. *The International Journal of Human Resource Management*, 23/12, 2428–2449.

Gettman, H. J. (2008). *Executive Coaching as a Developmental Experience: A Framework and Measure of Coaching Dimensions*. University of Maryland, College Park: Ann Arbor.

Gilley, A., J. W. Gilley, and E. Kouider (2010). 'Characteristics of Managerial Coaching'. *Performance Improvement Quarterly*, 23/1, 53–70.

Giorgi, S., C. Lockwood, and M. A. Glynn (2015). 'The Many Faces of Culture: Making Sense of 30 Years of Research on Culture in Organization Studies'. *The Academy of Management Annals*, 9/1, 1–54.

Gobalakrishnan, C. and D. Deepika (2013). 'A Study on Quality of Supervision among the Employees in the Public Sector Organization.

International Journal of Management Research and Reviews, 3/3, 2574–2578.

Goleman, D. (1995). *Emotional Intelligence: Why It Can Matter More Than IQ*. New York, New York: Bantam Books.

—— (2000). 'Leadership That Gets Results'. *Harvard Business Review*, 78/2, 78–90.

——, and C. Cherniss (2001). *The Emotionally Intelligent Workplace: How to Select For, Measure, and Improve Emotional Intelligence in Individuals, Groups, and Organizations*. Jossey-Bass.

Gormley, H., and C. van Nieuwerburgh (2014). 'Developing Coaching Cultures: A Review of the Literature'. *Coaching: An International Journal of Theory, Research and Practice*, 7/2, 90–101.

Grant. A. (2004). 'The Imperative of Ethical Justification in Psychotherapy: The Special Case of Client-Centered Therapy'. *Person-Centered and Experiential Psychotherapies*, 3/3, 152.

—— (2008). 'Coaching in Australia: A View from the Ivory Tower. *Coaching: An International Journal of Theory, Research and Practice*, 1/1, 54.

——, M. Cavanagh, S. Kleitman, G. Spence, M. Lakota, and N. Yu (2012). 'Development and Validation of the Solution-Focused Inventory'. *The Journal of Positive Psychology*, 7/4, 334–348.

——, and M. Hartley (2013). 'Developing the Leader-as-Coach: Insights, Strategies and Tips for Embedding Coaching Skills in the Workplace. *Coaching: An International Journal of Theory, Research and Practice*, 6/2, 1–14.

——, and S. O'Connor (2010). 'The Differential Effects of Solution-Focused and Problem-Focused Coaching Questions: A Pilot Study with Implications for Practice. *Industrial and Commercial Training*, 42/2, 102–111.

——, J. Passmore, D. Peterson, and T. Freire (2013). *Handbook of the Psychology of Coaching and Mentoring*. John Wiley & Sons.

Gray, D., Y. Gabriel, and H. Goregaokar (2015). 'Coaching Unemployed Managers and Professionals through the Trauma of Unemployment: Derailed or Undaunted?' *Management Learning*, 46/3, 299–316.

———, and H. Goregaokar (2010). Choosing an Executive Coach: The Influence of Gender on the Coach-Coachee Matching Process. *Management Learning*, 41/5, 525–544.

Guerci, M., and L. Solari (2012). 'Talent Management Practices in Italy—Implications for Human Resource Development. *Human Resource Development International*, 15/1, 25–41.

Hackman, J. R., and R. Wageman (2005). 'A Theory of Team Coaching'. *The Academy of Management Review*, 30/2, 269–287.

Hamlin, R., A. Ellinger, and R. Beattie (2008). 'The Emergent "Coaching Industry": A Wake-Up Call for HRD Professionals. *Human Resource Development International*, 11/3, 287–305.

Hannerz, U. (1969). *Soulside: Inquiries into Ghetto Culture and Community*. New York: Columbia University Press.

Hardingham, A., M. Brearley, A. Moorhouse, and B. Venter (2005). *The Coach's Coach: Personal Development for Personal Developers* (vol. 37). Emerald Group Publishing Limited.

Hart, W. (2005). 'Getting Culture: Imbuing Your Organization with Coaching Behavior'. *Leadership in Action*, 25/4, 7–10.

Hawkins, P. (2011). *Leadership Team Coaching*. London: Kogan Page.

——— (2012). *Creating a Coaching Culture* (1st ed.). Maidenhead: McGraw-Hill Education.

Herzberg, F., B. Mausner, and B. Snyderman (1959). *The Motivation to Work* (2nd vol). New York U6: Wiley.

Heslin, P. A., and D. VandeWalle (2011). 'Performance Appraisal Procedural Justice: The Role of a Manager's Implicit Person Theory'. *Journal of Management*, 37/6, 1694–1718.

Heslin, P. A., D. Vandewalle, and G. P. Latham (2006). 'Keen to Help? Managers' Implicit Person Theories and Their Subsequent Employee Coaching. *Personnel Psychology*, 59/4, 871–902.

Hicks, R., and J. McCracken (2010). 'Three Hats of a Leader: Coaching, Mentoring and Teaching'. *Physician Executive*, 36/6.

Horney, K. (1950). *Neurosis and Human Growth: The Struggle toward Self-Realization*. New York U6: Norton.

Howe-Walsh, L. (2015). 'Bank Stems the Loss of Employees Returning from Abroad: Talent-Management System Helps to Keep People

Loyal. *Human Resource Management International Digest*, 23/2, 25–27.

Hunt, J. M., and J. R. Weintraub (2007). *The Coaching Organization. A Strategy for Developing Leaders*. Thousand Oaks, California: SAGE Publications.

International Coach Federation (2014a). 'Building a Coaching Culture'. *http://www.coachfederation.org*.

—— (2014b). 'International Coach Federation Experiences Unprecedented Growth in March 2014'. *Investment Weekly News*, 342.

—— (2015a). 'Building a Coaching Culture for Increased Employee Engagement'. *Report of the Survey Conducted on Behalf of the International Coach Federation*.

—— (2015b). 'Definition of Coaching: International Coach Federation'. *http://www.coachfederation.org*.

Irby, B. J. (2012). 'Editor's Overview: Mentoring, Tutoring, and Coaching'. *Mentoring and Tutoring: Partnership in Learning*, 20/3, 297.

Ives, Y., and E. Cox (2012). *Goal-Focused Coaching: Theory and Practice*. New York: Routledge.

Jayakumar, G. S. D., and A. Sulthan (2014). 'Modelling: Employee Perception on Training and Development'. *SCMS Journal of Indian Management*, 11/2, 57–70.

Jayaweera, T. (2015). 'Impact of Work Environmental Factors on Job Performance, Mediating Role of Work Motivation: A Study of Hotel Sector in England'. *International Journal of Business and Management*, 10/3, 271–278.

Johan, S. (1997). 'How Institutions Learn: A Socio-Cognitive Perspective'. *Journal of Economic Issues*, 31/3, 729–740.

Joo, J. Sushko, and G. McLean. (2012). 'Multiple Faces of Coaching: Manager-as-Coach, Executive Coaching, and Formal Mentoring'. *Organization Development Journal*, 30/1, 19.

Jowett, S., K. Kanakoglou, and J. Passmore. (2012). 'The Application of the 3+1Cs Relationship Model in Executive Coaching'. *Consulting Psychology Journal: Practice and Research*, 64/3, 183–197.

Joyce, B., and B. Showers (1980). 'Improving Inservice Training: The Messages of Research'. *Educational Leadership* (February), 379–385.

Jung, C. (1917). *Collected Papers on Analytical Psychology* (vol. 2). London U6: Bailliere, Tindall and Cox.

—— (1921). *Personality Theory.* Zurich: Rascher.

Kam, C., S. D. Risavy, E. Perunovic, and L. Plant (2014). 'Do Subordinates Formulate an Impression of their Manager's Implicit Person Theory?' *Applied Psychology*, 63/2, 267–299.

Kampa, S., and R. P. White (2002). 'The Effectiveness of Executive Coaching: What We Know and What We Still Need to Know'. In Lowman, R. L. (ed.). *Handbook of Organizational Consulting Psychology: A Comprehensive Guide to Theory, Skills, and Techniques*, 139–158. San Francisco, California: Jossey-Bass.

Kaplan, D. M., V. M. Tarvydas, and S. T. Gladding (2014). '20/20: A Vision for the Future of Counseling: The New Consensus Definition of Counseling'. *Journal of Counseling & Development*, 92/3, 366–372.

Kegan, R., L. Lahey, A. Fleming, M. Miller, and I. Markus (2014). *The Deliberately Developmental Organisation.* Way to Grow Inc LLC.

Kennett, P., and T. Lomas (2015). 'Making Meaning through Mentoring: Mentors Finding Fulfilment at Work through Self-Determination and Self-Reflection'. *International Journal of Evidence Based Coaching and Mentoring*, 13/2, 29–44.

Kim, S. (2014). 'Assessing the Influence of Managerial Coaching on Employee Outcomes'. *Human Resource Development Quarterly*, 25/1, 59–85.

——, T. M. Egan, W. Kim, and J. Kim (2013). 'The Impact of Managerial Coaching Behavior on Employee Work-Related Reactions'. *Journal of Business and Psychology*, 28/3, 315–330.

——, T. M. Egan, and M. J. Moon (2014). 'Managerial Coaching Efficacy, Work-Related Attitudes, and Performance in Public Organizations: A Comparative International Study'. *Review of Public Personnel Administration*, 34/3, 237–262.

Knowles, M. (1980). *The Modern Practice of Adult Education: From Pedagogy to Andragogy.* New York: Cambridge Books.

———. (2004). *The Adult Learner: A Neglected Species* Houston, Texas: Gulf.

Knowles, S. (2018). *Positive Psychology Coaching.* Bloomington, Indiana: Xlibris.

Kolb, D. (1984). *Experiential Learning Experience as a Source of Learning and Development.* Englewood Cliffs, New Jersey: Prentice Hall.

Kolb, A., D. Kolb, A. Passarelli, and G. Sharma (2014). 'On Becoming an Experiential Educator: The Educator Role Profile'. *Simulation & Gaming*, 45/2, 204–234.

Komaki, J. (1986). 'Toward Effective Supervision: An Operant Analysis and Comparison of Managers at Work'. *Journal of Applied Psychology*, 71, 270–279.

———. (1998). *Leadership from an Operant Perspective.* New York: Routledge.

Kotter, J. P. (2001). 'What Leaders Really Do'. *Harvard Business Review*, 79/11, 85.

Kwon, W. J. (2014). 'Human Capital Risk and Talent Management Issues in the Insurance Market: Public Policy, Industry and Collegiate Education Perspectives'. *Geneva Papers on Risk & Insurance*, 39/1, 173–196.

Ladegard, G., and S. Gjerde (2014). 'Leadership Coaching, Leader Role-Efficacy, and Trust in Subordinates. A Mixed Methods Study Assessing Leadership Coaching as a Leadership Development Tool. *The Leadership Quarterly*, 25/4, 631–646.

Lamont, M. (2000). *The Rhetoric of Racism and Anti-Racism in France and the United States.* London: Cambridge University Press and Paris: Presses de la Maison des Sciences de l'Homme.

———, and L. Thévenot (2001). 'Rethinking Comparative Cultural Sociology: Repertoires of Evaluation in France and the United States'. *American Journal of Sociology*, 107/2, 529–531.

Latham, G. P. (2007). 'Theory and Research on Coaching Practices'. *Australian Psychologist*, 42/4, 268–270.

———, and C. C. Pinder (2005). 'Work Motivation Theory and Research at the Dawn of the Twenty-First Century'. *Annual Review of Psychology*, 56, 485–516.

Leonard-Cross, E. (2010). 'Development Coaching: Business Benefit— Fact or Fad? An Evaluative Study to Explore the Impact of Coaching in the Workplace'. *International Coaching Psychology Review*, 5/1, 36–47.

Lewin, K. (1935). *A Dynamic Theory of Personality: Selected Papers*. New York: McGraw-Hill.

—— (1943). 'Defining the "Field at a Given Time"'. *Psychological Review*, 50/3, 292–310.

—— (1944). 'Constructs in Psychology and Psychological Ecology'. *University of Iowa Studies in Child Welfare*, 20, 1–29.

Locke, E., and G. Latham (2002). 'Building a Practically Useful Theory of Goal Setting and Task Motivation: A 35-Year Odyssey'. *American Psychologist*, 57/9, 705–717.

—— (2006). 'New Directions in Goal-Setting Theory'. *Current Directions in Psychological Science*, 15/5, 265–268.

—— (2013). *Goal-Setting Theory*. Sage Publications.

Lopes, S. A., J. M. G. Sarraguça, J. A. Lopes, and M. E. Duarte (2015). 'A New Approach to Talent Management in Law Firms: Integrating Performance Appraisal and Assessment Center Data'. *International Journal of Productivity and Performance Management*, 64/4, 523–543.

Lounsbury, M., and M. A. Glynn (2001). 'Cultural Entrepreneurship: Stories, Legitimacy, and the Acquisition of Resources'. *Strategic Management Journal*, 22/6, 545.

MacKie, D. (2014). 'The Effectiveness of Strength-Based Executive Coaching in Enhancing Full Range Leadership Development: A Controlled Study'. *Consulting Psychology Journal: Practice and Research*, 66/2, 118.

—— (2015). 'The Effects of Coachee Readiness and Core Self-Evaluations on Leadership Coaching Outcomes: A Controlled Trial'. *Coaching: An International Journal of Theory, Research and Practice*, 8/2, 120–136.

Maltarich, M. A., J. Greenwald, and G. Reilly (2015). 'Team-Level Goal Orientation: An Emergent State and Its Relationships with

Team Inputs, Process, and Outcomes'. *European Journal of Work and Organizational Psychology*, 1–21.

Manion, J. (2015). 'The Leader-as-Coach'. *Journal of PeriAnesthesia Nursing*, 30/6, 548–552.

Maslow, A. H. (1943). 'A Theory of Human Motivation'. *Psychological Review*, 50/4, 370–396.

—— (1954). *Motivation and Personality*. New York: Harper & Row.

—— (1987). *Motivation and Personality* (3rd ed.). New York: Harper & Row.

Mason, C., M. Griffin, and S. Parker (2014). 'Transformational Leadership Development: Connecting Psychological and Behavioral Change. *Leadership & Organization Development Journal*, 35/3, 174–194.

Maurer, C., P. Bansal, and M. Crossan (2011). 'Creating Economic Value through Social Values: Introducing a Culturally Informed Resource-Based View'. *Organization Science*, 22/2, 432.

McClelland, D. (1951). 'The Effects of Motivation on Behavior'. *Personality* (pp. 478–525). New York, New York, USA: William Sloane Association.

—— (1967). *The Achieving Society*. New York: Free Press.

McGregor, D. (1960). *The Human Side of Enterprise*. New York U6: McGraw-Hill.

McLaughlin, M., and E. Cox (2015). *Leadership Coaching: Developing Braver Leaders*. Taylor and Francis.

McLean, G., B. Yang, M. Kuo, A. Tolbert, and C. Larkin (2005). 'Development and Initial Validation of an Instrument Measuring Managerial Coaching Skill'. *Human Resource Development Quarterly*, 16/2, 157–178.

McPherson, C. M., and M. Sauder (2013). 'Logics in Action: Managing Institutional Complexity in a Drug Court'. *Administrative Science Quarterly*, 58/2, 165–196.

McQuiston, L., and K. Hanna (2015). 'Peer Coaching'. *Nurse Educator*, 40/2, 105–108.

Megginson, D., and D. Clutterbuck (2006). 'Creating a Coaching Culture'. *Industrial and Commercial Training*, 38/5, 232–237.

Mensah, J. K. (2015). 'A "Coalesced Framework" of Talent Management and Employee Performance: For Further Research and Practice'. *International Journal of Productivity and Performance Management*, 64/4, 544–566.

Meyers, M. C., M. van Woerkom, and N. Dries (2013). 'Talent—Innate or Acquired? Theoretical Considerations and Their Implications for Talent Management'. *Human Resource Management Review*, 23/4, 305–321.

Mintzberg, H. (1987). 'The Strategy Concept I: Five Ps for Strategy'. *California Management Review*, 30/1, 11–24.

Mizokawa, A., and M. Koyasu (2015). 'Digging Deeper into the Link between Socio-Cognitive Ability and Social Relationships'. *British Journal of Developmental Psychology*, 33/1, 21–23.

Moen, F., and R. A. Federici (2012). 'The Effect of External Executive Coaching and Coaching-Based Leadership on Need Satisfaction'. *Organisation Development Journal*, 30/3, 63–74.

Molden, D. C., and C. S. Dweck (2006). 'Finding "Meaning" in Psychology: A Lay Theories Approach to Self-Regulation, Social Perception, and Social Development'. *American Psychologist*, 61/3, 192–203.

Molinsky, A. (2013). 'The Psychological Processes of Cultural Retooling'. *Academy of Management Journal*, 56/3, 683.

Morrill, C., M. N. Zald, and H. Rao (2003). 'Covert Political Conflict in Organizations: Challenges from Below'. *Annual Review of Sociology*, 29/1, 391.

Myers, I. B. (1980). *Gifts Differing*. Palo Alto, California: Consulting Psychologists Press.

Nagel, R. (2008). 'Coaching with a Solutions Focus—Focusing on the Solution Not the Problem'. *Development and Learning in Organizations: An International Journal*, 22/4, 11–14.

Neenan, M. (2008). 'From Cognitive Behaviour Therapy (CBT) to Cognitive Behaviour Coaching (CBC)'. *Journal of Rational-Emotive & Cognitive-Behavior Therapy*, 26/1, 3–15.

Noer, D. M., C. R. Leupold, and M. Valle (2007). 'An Analysis of Saudi Arabian and US Managerial Coaching Behaviours'. *Journal of Managerial Issues*, 19/2, 271–287.

O'Broin, A., and A. McDowall (2014). 'Coaching—Psychological Concepts and Coaching Cultures'. *Coaching: An International Journal of Theory, Research and Practice*, 7/2, 87–89.

O'Broin, A., and A. McDowall (2015). 'Specificity Is the Key, if We Really Want to Understand Coaching!' *Coaching: An International Journal of Theory, Research and Practice*, 8/2, 69–72.

O'Connell, B., S. Palmer, and H. Williams (2013). *Solution Focused Coaching in Practice*. Florence: Taylor and Francis.

Ohlrich, K. (2015). 'Exploring the Impact of CSR on Talent Management with Generation Y'. *South Asian Journal of Business and Management Cases*, 4/1, 111–121.

Opengart, R., and L. Bierema (2015). 'Emotionally Intelligent Mentoring: Reconceptualizing Effective Mentoring Relationships'. *Human Resource Development Review*, 14/3, 234–258.

Parker, P., K. Kram, and D. Hall (2014). 'Peer Coaching: An Untapped Resource for Development'. *Organizational Dynamics*, 43/2, 122–129.

——, M. Lawrie, and P. Hudson (2006). 'A Framework for Understanding the Development of Organisational Safety Culture'. *Safety Science*, 44/6, 551–562.

——, I. Wasserman, K. Kram, and D. Hall (2015). 'A Relational Communication Approach to Peer Coaching'. *The Journal of Applied Behavioral Science*, 51/2, 231–252.

Passmore, J. (2009). *Diversity in Coaching: Working with Gender, Culture, Race and Age*. London; Philadelphia: Kogan Page.

Pavlov, I. P. (1927). *Conditioned Reflexes: An Investigation of the Physiological Activity of the Cerebral Cortex*. Oxford U6: Oxford University Press.

Piaget, J. (1950). *The Psychology of Intelligence*. London U6: Routledge and Paul.

Pousa, C., and A. Mathieu (2015). 'Is Managerial Coaching a Source of Competitive Advantage? Promoting Employee Self-Regulation through Coaching'. *Coaching: An International Journal of Theory, Research and Practice*, 8/1, 20–35.

Rahim, N. S., N. N. A. Mansor, and R. Anvari (2014). 'Driving the Involvement of Line Managers' Role in Creating Coaching Culture in Malaysia'. *Procedia—Social and Behavioral Sciences*, 129/0, 221–226.

Roberts, C. (2013). 'Building Social Capital through Leadership Development'. *Journal of Leadership Education*, 12/1, 54–73.

Roeden, J. M., M. A. Maaskant, and L. M. G. Curfs (2012). 'The Nominal Group Technique as an Evaluation Tool for Solution-Focused Coaching'. *Journal of Applied Research in Intellectual Disabilities*, 25/6, 588–593.

Rogers, C. (1951). *Client-Centred Therapy: Its Current Practice, Implications and Theory*. Boston: Houghton Mifflin.

—— (1961). *On Becoming a Person*. Oxford, England: Houghton Mifflin.

—— (1959). 'A Theory of Therapy, Personality, and Interpersonal Relationships, as Developed in the Client-Centered Framework'. In S. Koch (ed.). *Psychology: A Study of a Science—Vol. 3: Formulations of the Person and the Social Context*, 184–256. New York: McGraw Hill,.

Ryan, J. C. (2014). The Work Motivation of Research Scientists and Its Effect on Research Performance. *R&D Management*, 44/4, 355–369.

Salih, A. A., and L. Alnaji (2014). 'The Impact of Talent Management in Enhancing Organizational Reputation: An Empirical Study on the Jordanian Telecommunications Companies'. *Journal of Applied Business Research*, 30/2, 409.

Schein, E. (1985). *Organizational Culture and Leadership: A Dynamic View*. San Francisco, California: Jossey-Bass.

—— (1990). 'Organizational Culture'. *American Psychologist*, 45/2, 109–119.

Schwieterman, B. (2009). 'Leaders as Coaches'. *Leadership Excellence*, 26/4, 4.

Scully, M., and A. Segal (2002). 'Passion with an umbrella: Grassroots Activists in the Workplace'. *Research in the Sociology of Organizations*, 19, 125.

Seah, M., M.-H. Hsieh, and H.-Y. Huang (2014). 'Leader Driven Organizational Adaptation'. *Management Decision*, 52/8, 1410–1432.

Segers, J., D. Vloeberghs, E. Henderickx, and I. Inceoglu (2011). 'Structuring and Understanding the Coaching Industry: The Coaching Cube'. *Academy of Management, Learning & Education*, 10/2, 204–221.

Seidel, V. P., and S. O'Mahony (2014). *Organization Science*, 25/3, 691.

Seligman, M. (1972). 'Learned Helplessness'. *Annual Review of Medicine*, 23/1, 407–412.

—— (2007). 'Coaching and Positive Psychology'. *Australian Psychologist*, 42/4, 266–267.

—— (2008). 'Positive Health'. *Applied Psychology*, 57, 3–18.

—— (2011). *Authentic Happiness: Using the New Positive Psychology to Realise Your Potential for Lasting Fulfilment.* London: Nicholas Brealey Publishing.

——, and A. Altenor (1980). 'Part II: Learned Helplessness'. *Behaviour Research and Therapy*, 18/5, 462–473.

——, and M. Csikszentmihalyi (2000). 'Positive Psychology: An Introduction'. *American Psychologist*, 55/1, 5–14.

——, R. Ernst, J. Gillham, K. Reivich, and M. Linkins (2009). 'Positive Education: Positive Psychology and Classroom Interventions'. *Oxford Review of Education*, 35/3, 293–311.

——, T. Steen, N. Park, and C. Peterson (2005). 'Positive Psychology Progress: Empirical Validation of Interventions'. *American Psychologist*, 60/5, 410–421.

Shaneberger, K. (2008). 'When a Staff Member Needs to Improve'. *OR Manager*, 24/11, 19.

Shi, Y., and R. Handfield (2012). 'Talent Management Issues for Multinational Logistics Companies in China: Observations from the Field'. *International Journal of Logistics Research and Applications*, 15/3, 163–179.

Sidani, Y., and A. Al Ariss (2014). 'Institutional and Corporate Drivers of Global Talent Management: Evidence from the Arab Gulf Region'. *Journal of World Business*, 49/2, 215–224.

Singh, A., and J. Sharma (2015). 'Strategies for Talent Management: A Study of Select Organizations in the UAE'. *International Journal of Organizational Analysis*, 23/3, 337–347.

Sisson, M. (2014). 'How Do We Begin to Embed a Coaching Culture in Our Organizations?' *Strategic HR Review*, 13/3.

Sita, V., and A. Pinapati (2013). 'Competency Management as a Tool of Talent Management: A Study in Indian IT Organizations'. *Journal of Economic Development, Management, IT, Finance, and Marketing*, 5/1, 44–56.

Skinner, B. F. (1938). *The Behaviour of Organisms: An Experimental Analysis*. New York: Apple-Century-Crofts.

Small, M. L., D. Harding, and M. Lamont (2010). 'Reconsidering Culture and Poverty'. *Annals of the American Academy of Political and Social Science*, 629/6, 27.

Sparrow, P. R., and H. Makram (2015). 'What Is the Value of Talent Management? Building Value-Driven Processes within a Talent Management Architecture'. *Human Resource Management Review*, 25/3, 249–263.

Stober, D., and A. Grant (2006). *Evidence Based Coaching Handbook: Putting Best Practices to Work for Your Clients*. Hoboken, New Jersey: John Wiley & Sons.

Sue-Chan, C., R. E. Wood, and G. P. Latham (2012). 'Effect of a Coach's Regulatory Focus and an Individual's Implicit Person Theory on Individual Performance'. *Journal of Management*, 38/3, 809–835.

Swailes, S., Y. Downs, and K. Orr (2014). 'Conceptualising Inclusive Talent Management: Potential, Possibilities and Practicalities'. *Human Resource Development International*, 17/5, 529–544.

Swidler, A. (1986). 'Culture in Action: Symbols and Strategies'. *American Sociological Review*, 51/2, 273–286.

—— (2001). *Talk of Love: How Culture Matters*. Chicago, Illinois: University of Chicago Press.

——, K. Knorr-Cetina, T. R. Schatzki, and E. von Savigny (2001). *The Practice Turn in Contemporary Theory*. London: Routledge.

Theeboom, T., B. Beersma, and A. E. M. van Vianen (2014). 'Does Coaching Work? A Meta-Analysis on the Effects of Coaching on Individual Level Outcomes in an Organizational Context. *The Journal of Positive Psychology*, 9/1, 1–18.

Thompson, R., D. M. Wolf, and J. M. Sabatine (2012). 'Mentoring and Coaching: A Model Guiding Professional Nurses to Executive Success'. *Journal of Nursing Administration*, 42/11, 536.

Thorndike, E. L. (1911). *Animal Intelligence: Experimental Studies*. New York U6: Macmillan.

Thornton, C. (2010). *Group and Team Coaching*. London: Routledge.

Tolhurst, J. (2010). *Coaching and Mentoring*. Harlow: Pearson Education Ltd.

Trathen, S. (2011). 'Executive Coaching: Implications for Developing Leaders in the Middle East and Africa'. *Career Planning and Adult Development Journal*, 27/1, 138–154.

Tse, H. H. M., and M. T. Dasborough (2008). 'A Study of Exchange and Emotions in Team Member Relationships'. *Group & Organization Management*, 33/2, 194–215.

Van Nieuwerburgh, C. (2012). *Coaching in Education: Getting Better Results for Students, Educators, and Parents*. London: Karnac.

Vernon-Feagans, L., K. Kainz, S. Amendum, M. Ginsberg, T. Wood, and A. Bock (2012). 'Targeted Reading Intervention: A Coaching Model to Help Classroom Teachers with Struggling Readers'. *Learning Disability Quarterly*, 35/2, 102–114.

Vroom, V. (1964). *Work and Motivation*. New York U6: Wiley.

Vygotskiĭ, L., and M. Cole (1978). *Mind in Society: The Development of Higher Psychological Processes*. Cambridge: Harvard University Press.

Vygotsky, L. (1934). 'Thinking and Speech'. In R. W. Rieber and A. S. Carton (eds.). *The Collected Works of L. S. Vygotsky, vol. 1: Problems of General Psychology*, 39–288. New York: Plenum Press.

Wakefield, M. (2006). 'New Views on Leadership Coaching'. *The Journal for Quality and Participation*, 29/2, 9–12, 43.

Walker-Fraser, A. (2011). 'Coaching and the Link to Organizational Performance: An HR Perspective on How to Demonstrate Return on Investment'. *Development and Learning in Organizations: An International Journal*, 25/4, 8–10.

Watson, J. B. (1931). *Behaviorism* (vol. 2). London U6: Kegan Paul, Trench, Trubner.

Weber, K. (2005). 'A Toolkit for Analyzing Corporate Cultural Toolkits. *Poetics*, 33/3, 227–252.

White, M. K., and P. Barnett (2014). *A Five Step Model of Appreciative Coaching: A Positive Process for Remediation*. New York: Springer.

Whitmore, J. (2002). *Coaching for Performance: Growing People, Performance and Purpose*. London; Naperville, USA.

Wilson, C. (2004). 'Coaching and Coach Training in the Workplace'. *Industrial and Commercial Training*, 36/3, 96–98.

Woerkom, M. V., and M. Croon (2009). 'The Relationships between Team Learning Activities and Team Performance'. *Personnel Review*, 38/5, 560–577.

Yates, J. (2013). *The Career Coaching Handbook*. Hoboken: Taylor and Francis.

Zald, M. N., C. Morrill, H. Rao, G. F. Davis, D. McAdam, W. R. Scott, and M. N. Zald (2005). *Social Movements and Organization Theory*. Cambridge: Cambridge University Press.

Zeus, P., and S. Skiffington (2002). *The Coaching at Work Toolkit : A Complete Guide to Techniques and Practices*. Sydney: McGraw-Hill.

Zimbardo, P., L. Goldstein, and G. Utley (1971). 'The Stanford Prison Experiment'. *Chronology*. New York, New York (NBC-TV).

INDEX

A

accredited coach networks   75, 83, 170, 172, 176, 211
Adams, John Stacey   216
Alderfer, Clayton   215
Allport, Floyd   217
American Society for Training and Development (ASTD)   16
Asch, Solomon   218

B

Bandura, Albert   219
behaviourism   213
business case   126-7, 185, 195
business units   61, 87, 93, 105, 114, 135, 140, 167, 201
  coaching within   94, 103, 105-6, 134, 144, 148, 180, 212
    leaders of   13, 89, 105, 107, 115, 179, 199
  productivity of   134

C

capability development framework   91, 98
Cattell, Raymond   217
Chartered Institute of Personnel and Development (CIPD)   2, 16

coach training
  external   166, 206-7
  in-house   79-80, 92-3, 169
  programs for   78, 115
coachees   2-3, 16, 18, 23, 35, 44, 86
coaches   2, 4-5, 9, 18, 35, 37, 44-5, 53, 60, 70, 90, 196, 201
  call centre   83-4
  duty of   39, 83, 112
  executive   8, 13, 19, 40, 68, 71, 80, 126, 138, 141, 154, 172, 175, 183, 190
  external   4, 16, 25, 37, 39, 42-4, 48, 80, 83, 100-1, 107, 171-2, 176
  HR professionals as   170
  internal   101, 113, 115, 182-4, 207, 212
  leaders as   114, 124, 130, 133, 169, 171, 179, 191, 205
  senior executives as   187
  specialist   112, 181-2, 212
  volunteer   75, 139, 170, 172, 211
coaching   1-9, 12-13, 15-20, 25-7, 36-8, 56-8, 65-7, 87-9, 109-11, 121-5, 127-9, 132-4, 146-8, 193-4, 199
  application of   131
  behavioural   63, 105

benefits of 5-8, 12, 17, 136, 138, 142, 167, 175, 189, 195, 197-8, 208, 210, 212
capability for 92, 174
champion for 141-2
cost of 45
developmental motivation for 63, 67, 69
executive 19
foundations of 160
global revenues from 15
growth of 16
individual 19, 44, 78, 80, 111
instrumental motivation for 40-1
leader-led 115, 154, 180
leadership 20
managerial 20
misconceptions of 5
one-on-one 108, 167, 179
peer 19, 21-2, 147-8, 202, 208, 212
performance 3, 95, 106, 206
pure 2-3, 84, 113, 183, 206
return on investment from 196
role 74
role-modelling 138, 149, 153, 201
solution-focused 23
team 5, 21, 110, 179
theoretical basis for 22
transformational motivation for 129-31, 134
types of 19
value of 17, 88, 134, 189
Coaching-as-Culture 121, 126
Coaching-as-HR-Function 57, 125, 209
Coaching-as-Intervention 14, 34, 125, 209
coaching-as-leader-capability 14
Coaching Circles 75, 82, 171, 211
Coaching Communities 75-6, 164, 171

coaching culture 13, 31, 40, 43, 57, 73, 87, 106, 121, 127, 138, 145-6, 149, 176, 201
definition of a 30
transformational 128
coaching leadership style 20-1, 64, 74, 90, 98, 111
coaching philosophy 3, 90
cognitive-based therapy 24, 214
cognitive development theory 216
command-and-control ix, 7, 64, 79, 90, 159, 176, 189
Csikszentmihalyi, Mihali 219
cultural change 13, 55, 126-7

D

deliberately developmental organisation (DDO) 31, 209, 233

E

Enterprise Agreement (EA) 156
equity theory 216
ERG need theory 215
Erikson, Erik 216
European Mentoring and Coaching Council (EMCC) 2, 15
expectancy theory 215

F

Festinger, Leon 218
flow theory 219
front-line staff 84, 104, 179

G

GenAdvance 116-17
Global Services Division (GSD) 117-18
GlobalNetworks 155-7
goal-setting theory 214
growth mindset 129, 140, 189-90, 212

H

Horney, Karen 217
Human motivation theory 215
human resource (HR) 72, 76-7, 79, 108, 170-1, 188

I

implicit person theory 22
individual career coaching 100, 111
International Coach Federation (ICF) 15, 59, 80, 166, 168, 206-7

J

Jung, Carl 216-17

K

key performance indicator (KPI) 66, 76, 95

L

leader-as-coach 114
  role of 79
  training program for 100
leadership 27, 30, 56, 168
leadership framework 116
Lewin, Kurt 218
line managers 8, 25, 34, 40, 42-3, 90, 168, 174, 177

M

managers 6, 20-1, 25, 36-8, 41, 43-4, 64, 173-4, 177, 190
  coaching account 148
Maslow, Abraham 214
McClelland, David 215
McGregor, Douglas 215
mentoring 9, 18

N

need hierarchy theory 214

O

organisational development (OD) 16

P

Pavlov, Ivan 213
performance management 74, 97, 138-9, 207
performance motivation 95, 97-8, 107
  elements of 95, 98, 100
person-centred theory 217
personality factors 217, 225
personality theory 216
Piaget, Jean 216
position description 73, 76, 184
psychology
  positive 23
  social 23
psychosocial development 216

R

rational emotive therapy 214
Rogers, Carl 217

S

SecureWealth 152-4
self-efficacy 214
Seligman, Martin 220
senior executives 56, 63, 75, 121, 134, 136, 139-40, 144, 170, 187-90, 194, 210
Skinner, B. F. 214
Social cognitive theory 219
social comparison theory 218
social pressure 218
sociocultural theory 218
solution-based therapy 214
strategic planning 161

T

talent management 26, 102
 cycle of 101
theory X and Y 215
Thorndike, Edward 213
TotalCare 48

transformational motivation 121, 128-9, 149
two-factor theory 215

V

Vygotsky, Lev 218

ABOUT THE AUTHOR

Susanne is an educational, counselling, and organisational psychologist and the Chair of the *Australian Institute of Professional Coaches*. With three Masters degrees in Education, Psychology and Business Administration, she is focused on assisting individuals in achieving their personal and professional goals, motivating teams to peak performance, and supporting organisations to increase employee engagement, retain talent, and improve profitability. She has held senior executive positions in government and private sector organisations and served as a Board member on several government, not-for-profit, and professional services firms. Her executive coaching experience has been gained from twenty years as a consultant to national and international organisations, focused on facilitating the strategic direction of these firms. Susanne's PhD at the University of Queensland investigated how organisations develop a coaching culture.

TAKING ACTION

If you are interested in learning more about how your organisation can develop a coaching culture, contact the Australian Institute of Professional Coaches at (+61)1300 309 360 or email careers@professionalcoachtraining.com.au.

Bachkirova, T., & Kauffman, C. (2009). The blind men and the elephant: Using criteria of universality and uniqueness in evaluating our attempts to define coaching. *Coaching: An International Journal of Theory, Research and Practice, 2*(2), 95-105.

Brant, J., Dooley, R., & Iman, S. (2008). Leadership succession: an approach to filling the pipeline. *Strategic HR Review, 7*(4), 17-24.

Hamlin, R., Ellinger, A. D., & Beattie, R. (2008). The emergent 'coaching industry': A wake-up call for HRD professionals. *Human Resource Development International, 11*(3), 287-305.

Kim, S., & McLean, G. (2012). Global talent management: Necessity, challenges, and the roles of HRD. *Advances in Developing Human Resources, 14*(4), 566-585.

www.ingramcontent.com/pod-product-compliance
Lightning Source LLC
Chambersburg PA
CBHW021353210526
45463CB00001B/87